A Companion to Muslim Cultures

The Institute of Ismaili Studies

MUSLIM HERITAGE SERIES, 3

General Editor: Amyn B. Sajoo

This series will explore vital themes in the civilisations of Islam – including the nature of religious authority, ethics and law, social justice and civil society, the arts and sciences, and the interplay of spiritual and secular lifeworlds. In keeping with the Institute's mandate, the series will be informed by the plurality of communities and interpretations of Islam, as well as their locus in modernity and tradition.

A Companion to Muslim Cultures

Edited by
AMYN B. SAJOO

I.B.Tauris *Publishers*
LONDON • NEW YORK
in association with
The Institute of Ismaili Studies
LONDON

Published in 2012 by I.B.Tauris & Co. Ltd
6 Salem Road, London W2 4BU
175 Fifth Avenue, New York, NY 10010
www.ibtauris.com

in association with The Institute of Ismaili Studies
210 Euston Road, London NW1 2DA
www.iis.ac.uk

Distributed in the United States and Canada Exclusively by Palgrave Macmillan,
175 Fifth Avenue, New York, NY 10010

Copyright © Islamic Publications Ltd, 2012

All rights reserved. Except for brief quotations in a review, this book, or any part thereof, may not be reproduced, stored in or introduced into a retrieval system, or transmitted, in any form or by any means, electronic, mechanical, photocopying, recording or otherwise, without the prior written permission of the publisher.

ISBN: 978 1 78076 127 5

A full CIP record for this book is available from the British Library
A full CIP record for this book is available from the Library of Congress

Library of Congress catalog card: available

Typeset in Minion Tra for The Institute of Ismaili Studies
Printed and bound in Great Britain by TJ International Ltd, Padstow, Cornwall

The Institute of Ismaili Studies

The Institute of Ismaili Studies was established in 1977 with the object of promoting scholarship and learning on Islam, in the historical as well as contemporary contexts, and a better understanding of its relationship with other societies and faiths.

The Institute's programmes encourage a perspective which is not confined to the theological and religious heritage of Islam, but seeks to explore the relationship of religious ideas to broader dimensions of society and culture. The programmes thus encourage an interdisciplinary approach to the materials of Islamic history and thought. Particular attention is also given to issues of modernity that arise as Muslims seek to relate their heritage to the contemporary situation.

Within the Islamic tradition, the Institute's programmes promote research on those areas which have, to date, received relatively little attention from scholars. These include the intellectual and literary expressions of Shi'ism in general, and Ismailism in particular.

In the context of Islamic societies, the Institute's programmes are informed by the full range and diversity of cultures in which Islam is practised today, from the Middle East, South and Central Asia, and Africa to the industrialized societies of the West, thus taking into consideration the variety of contexts which shape the ideals, beliefs and practices of the faith.

These objectives are realised through concrete programmes and activities organized and implemented by various departments of the Institute. The Institute also collaborates periodically, on a programme-specific basis, with other institutions of learning in the United Kingdom and abroad.

The Institute's academic publications fall into a number of inter-related categories:

1. Occasional papers or essays addressing broad themes of the relationship between religion and society, with special reference to Islam.
2. Monographs exploring specific aspects of Islamic faith and culture, or the contributions of individual Muslim thinkers or writers.
3. Editions or translations of significant primary or secondary texts.
4. Translations of poetic or literary texts which illustrate the rich heritage of spiritual, devotional and symbolic expressions in Muslim history.
5. Works on Ismaili history and thought, and the relationship of the Ismailis to other traditions, communities and schools of thought in Islam.
6. Proceedings of conferences and seminars sponsored by the Institute.
7. Bibliographical works and catalogues which document manuscripts, printed texts and other source materials.

This book falls into category two listed above.

In facilitating these and other publications, the Institute's sole aim is to encourage original research and analysis of relevant issues. While every effort is made to ensure that the publications are of a high academic standard, there is naturally bound to be a diversity of views, ideas and interpretations. As such, the opinions expressed in these publications must be understood as belonging to their authors alone.

Contents

About the Contributors	xi
List of Illustrations	xvii

1. Introduction: Faith and Culture
   AMYN B. SAJOO — 1

2. Everyday Tradition
   EARLE WAUGH — 21

3. Modernity: Secular and Sacred
   ABDULLAHI AN-NAIM — 37

4. Spiritual Life
   CARL W. ERNST — 57

5. Gender and Identity
   ELENA CAPRIONI AND EVA SAJOO — 77

6. Science and Social Change
   MORGAN CLARKE — 103

7. Architecture and Community
   HUSSEIN KESHANI — 117

8. Moving Words
   JONATHAN M. BLOOM — 137

9. Moving Sounds JONATHAN SHANNON	165
10. A Taste of Mecca MAI YAMANI	185
11. Cosmopolitanism: Ways of Being Muslim KARIM H. KARIM	201
Index	221

'[W]henever a masterpiece is made, whenever a splendid picture makes my eyes water out of joy and causes a chill to run down my spine, I can be certain of the following: Two styles heretofore never brought together have come together to create something new and wondrous. We owe Bihzad and the splendor of Persian painting to the meeting of an Arab illustrating sensibility and Mongol-Chinese painting. Shah Tahmasp's best paintings marry Persian style with Turkish subtleties. Today, if men cannot adequately praise the book-arts workshops of Akbar Khan in Hindustan, it's because he urged his miniaturists to adopt the styles of the Frankish masters. To God belongs the East and the West. May He protect us from the pure and the unadulterated.'*

Enishte Effendi, in Orhan Pamuk's
My Name is Red (2001), p. 194.

About the Contributors

Abdullahi An-Naim is the Charles Howard Candler Professor of Law at Emory Law School in the United States. A widely recognised authority on Islam and cross-cultural perspectives on human rights, he served as executive director of the Africa division of Human Rights Watch (New York) from 1993 to 1995. An-Naim was part of a movement for political reform in Sudan, where he taught at the University of Khartoum until his departure in 1985. He currently directs several projects that focus on advocacy strategies for reform through internal cultural transformation, including on issues of gender, minority rights and religious freedom. His books include *Toward an Islamic Reformation* (Syracuse, NY, 1990), *Human Rights in Cross-Cultural Perspectives: Quest for Consensus* (Philadelphia, 1992) and *Islam and the Secular State: Negotiating the Future of Shari'a* (Cambridge, MA, 2009), where an earlier version of his chapter here appeared.

Jonathan M. Bloom shares the Norma Jean Calderwood Professorship of Islamic and Asian Art at Boston College, and the Hamad bin Khalifa Endowed Chair of Islamic Art at Virginia Commonwealth University, with his wife and colleague Sheila Blair. His interests span all aspects of Islamic art from the seventh century to modern times, with a focus on the Islamic Mediterranean in the medieval period. Bloom's publications include *Arts of the City Victorious: Islamic Art and Architecture in Fatimid North Africa and Egypt* (New Haven, 2007), the three-volume *Grove Encyclopedia of Islamic Art and Architecture* (Oxford, 2009, co-edited with Sheila Blair), and *Paper before Print: The History and Impact of Paper in the Islamic World* (New Haven, 2001), from

xii   *A Companion to Muslim Cultures*

which his chapter here is adapted. Bloom's works have been translated into Arabic, French, Greek, Japanese, Korean, Persian, Spanish, Russian and Turkish.

Elena Caprioni is a fellow at the Institute of Asian Research at the University of British Columbia in Vancouver, working on themes of nationalism and gender in Uyghur society in Xinjiang. She is also affiliated with Beijing's Renmin University of China, where she is involved in a research project on the 'Western Development Program' directed at China's periphery. Caprioni's writings on various facets of cultural life in Xinjiang have appeared in several international journals.

Morgan Clarke is a Simon Research Fellow in Middle Eastern studies at the University of Manchester, having previously been affiliated with the University of Cambridge as a British Academy Fellow. As a social anthropologist with a special interest in the interface of law, ethics and the civil state, he has conducted extensive field research in Lebanon, notably on Islamic biomedical ethics and on the workings of sharia courts. Clarke is the author of *Islam and New Kinship: Reproductive Technology and the Shariah in Lebanon* (New York, 2009), as well as numerous scholarly articles on themes relating to biomedical technologies in Muslim settings.

Carl W. Ernst is the William R. Kenan, Jr., Distinguished Professor in religious studies at the University of North Carolina at Chapel Hill, and director of the Carolina Center for the Study of the Middle East and Muslim Civilizations. His book, *Following Muhammad: Rethinking Islam in the Contemporary World* (Chapel Hill, 2003), has received several international awards, and is the basis of his chapter here. Ernst's other recent works include *Rethinking Islamic Studies: From Orientalism to Cosmopolitanism* (Columbia, SC, 2010, co-edited with Richard Martin), and *Sufi Martyrs of Love: Chishti Sufism in South Asia and Beyond* (New York, 2002, co-authored with Bruce Lawrence). His current research focuses on the Quran as literature, Muslim interpreters of Indian religions, and a translation of the Arabic poetry of al-Hallaj. Ernst is a Fellow of the American Academy of Arts and Sciences.

About the Contributors

Karim H. Karim is a professor of communication studies at Carleton University in Ottawa, where he was previously director of the School of Journalism and Communication. He has also served as a co-director of The Institute of Ismaili Studies, and was a visiting scholar at Harvard University's Department of Near Eastern Languages and Civilizations. Karim's books include *Islamic Peril: Media and Global Violence* (Montreal, 2000), which received the 2001 Robinson Prize for Canadian studies in communications, and *The Media of Diaspora* (London, 2003). He has contributed widely to scholarly journals on themes relating to the cultural contexts of religion, transnationalism and technology.

Hussein Keshani is a professor of art history at the University of British Columbia, having previously taught at the University of Victoria (Canada) and Stanford University. His research interests include the architecture of Muslim India, and the applications of gender theories and digital technologies to the study of Islamic art. Keshani's scholarly contributions include chapters on the court culture of Awadh and on Lucknow's Great Imambara complex, both in India; his survey of Muslim architecture at large appeared in *The Islamic World* (New York, 2008, ed. A. Rippin), and serves as the basis of his chapter here. Keshani is currently working on a book on the intertwining of image, space and gender in Awadh.

Amyn B. Sajoo is Scholar-in-Residence at Simon Fraser University's Centre for the Comparative Study of Muslim Societies and Cultures (Vancouver). He has held visiting appointments at Cambridge and McGill universities, the Institute of Southeast Asian Studies in Singapore, and The Institute of Ismaili Studies in London. Sajoo has also served as an advisor on human rights policy with the Canadian Department of Justice. His books include *Pluralism in Old Societies and New States* (1994), *Muslim Ethics* (2004), and the edited volumes *Civil Society in the Muslim World* (2002) and *Muslim Modernities* (2008). He is the general editor of the Muslim Heritage Series, and a frequent contributor to the news media on both sides of the Atlantic. Sajoo was the 2010 recipient of the Middle East visiting academic award of the Canadian Department of Foreign Affairs, and delivered the 2011 Distinguished Lecture in Islam at the University of Victoria (Canada).

xiv *A Companion to Muslim Cultures*

Eva Sajoo is a research associate at Simon Fraser University's Centre for the Comparative Study of Muslim Societies and Cultures in Vancouver. She has taught at the University of Science and Technology in Beijing as well as the University of British Columbia, and currently lectures at Simon Fraser University. Sajoo has published widely on gender, development and education in Muslim societies, and is a regular contributor to the news media, notably on Afghanistan. Her research on women's education in Afghanistan won first place in a 2010 competition sponsored by the Inter-agency Network for Education in Emergencies (Geneva).

Jonathan Shannon is a professor of cultural anthropology at the City University of New York's Hunter College. His research looks at the aesthetics and music performance in the Mediterranean and Arab world, with special regard to Syria and Morocco. As a 2009 Guggenheim Foundation Fellow, Shannon began work on projects relating to cultural memory and Andalusian music in Syria, Morocco and Spain, and on cultural itineraries of sounds and spices around the Mediterranean. He is the author of numerous scholarly articles and the book *Among the Jasmine Trees: Music and Modernity in Contemporary Syria* (Middletown, CT, 2006), from which his chapter here is adapted. He is also a performer of the *oud* and a jazz saxophonist.

Earle Waugh is an emeritus professor of religious studies at the University of Alberta, and director of the university's Centre for the Cross-Cultural Study of Health and Healing in Family Medicine. He has authored/edited over a dozen books, dictionaries and studies, which have won several awards. His most recent book in Islamic studies is *Visionaries of Silence* (Cairo, 2008), and his contribution on 'popular piety and cultural practices' in *The Islamic World* (New York, 2008, ed. A. Rippin) is the basis of his chapter here. Waugh's present work is focused on the interface of culture and medicine in Muslim and indigenous settings, including issues of biotechnology and end-of-life choices. He received the 2005 Salvos Award for Peace Education from Canada's Project Ploughshares.

Mai Yamani has been affiliated with several major academic institutions, including the Royal Institute of International Affairs in London, the

About the Contributors

Carnegie Middle East Centre in Beirut, and the Brookings Institute in Washington, DC. She lectured in anthropology and sociology at the King Abdul Aziz University, Jeddah, from 1981 to 1984. Yamani's many books include *Cradle of Islam: The Hijaz and the Quest for an Arabian Identity* (London, 2004), and *Feminism and Islam: Legal and Literary Perspectives* (New York, 1996). She has also published widely on the culture of her native Mecca; an earlier version of her chapter here appeared in *A Taste of Thyme* (London, 2010, ed. S. Zubaida and R. Tapper).Yamani is an established commentator on Middle East affairs, and her columns have appeared in major newspapers around the world.

List of Illustrations

PL. 1: Prince Farrukh-Nizhad lifts an elephant, *Hamzanama*, c. 1570.
© MAK (Vienna)/Georg Mayer.

PL. 2: 'Pleasure Pillars', by Shahzia Sikander, 2001.
Courtesy of Sikkema Jenkins & Co., New York.

PL. 3: Kashgar Market, Xinjiang, China.
© Photo Elena Caprioni, 2007.

PL. 4: Afghan *attan* dance.
Photo by Marty Sohl; courtesy of Ballet Afsaneh © 2002.

PL. 5: Registan Square, Samarkand, 15th-17th centuries.
© Süha Özkan/Aga Khan Trust for Culture, 1991.

PL. 6: Yalbugha *hammam*, Aleppo, 15th century.
© Nabil Kassabji/Aga Khan Trust for Culture, 1989.

PL. 7: Khwaju bridge and weir, Isfahan, 18th century.
© Justin Fitzhugh/Aga Khan Trust for Culture, 1996.

PL. 8: Istiqlal Mosque, Jakarta, 1984.
© F. Silaban/Aga Khan Trust for Culture, 1988.

PL. 9: Al-Azhar Park, Cairo, 2005.
© Gary Otte/Aga Khan Trust for Culture, 2006.

PL. 10: Quran manuscript on parchment, c. 9th century.
Courtesy of Freer Gallery of Art, Smithsonian, Washington, DC.

xviii   *A Companion to Muslim Cultures*

PL. 11: Papyrus receipt of payment, Egypt, 723 CE.
Courtesy of The Nasser D. Khalili Collection of Islamic Art, London.

PL. 12: Quran manuscript on paper, Ali b. Shadan al-Razi, 971–972 CE.
Courtesy of the Trustees of the Chester Beatty Library, Dublin.

PL. 13: Two Quran pages on parchment, Palermo, 982–983 CE.
Courtesy of The Nasser D. Khalili Collection of Islamic Art, London.

PL. 14: Colophon page of Quran, Ahmed b. al-Suhrawardi, Baghdad, 1307.
Courtesy of the Metropolitan Museum of Art, New York, Rogers Fund, 1955.

PL. 15: Frontispiece, *Epistles of the Brethren of Purity*, Iraq, 1287.
Courtesy of the Sülemaniye Library, Istanbul.

PL. 16: Frontispiece, Arabic translation of Dioscorides' *De materia medica*, Iraq or Syria, 1229.
Courtesy of the Topkapi Palace Library, Istanbul.

PL. 17: Arabic library from al-Hariri's *Assemblies*, illustrated by al-Wasiti, Baghdad, 1237.
Courtesy of Bibliotheque Nationale de France, Paris.

PL. 18: Blue Chinese paper with gold decoration, inscribed by Sultan-Ali Qaini, Tabriz, 1478.
Courtesy of Spencer Collection, The New York Public Library, Astor, Lenox and Tilden Foundation.

1

Introduction: Faith and Culture

Amyn B. Sajoo

'Have they not travelled through the land?
Have they no hearts (or minds) to learn wisdom,
or ears to hear the Truth?'
Quran, 22: 46

'The arts (al-adab) belonging to fine culture are ten: Three
Shahradjanic (playing lute, chess, and with the javelin),
three Nushirwanic (medicine, mathematics and equestrian
art), three Arabic (poetry, genealogy and knowledge of
history); but the tenth excels all: the knowledge of the stories
which people put forward in their friendly gatherings.'
Wazir al-Hasan b. Sahl, 9th-century Baghdad[1]

In a post-September 11 world where a prime image of the Muslim appears to be that of the *jihadi*, the warrior in the path of God, it is well to remember that the *hakawati*, the storyteller, looms far larger in the making of Islam's many civilisations. True, no tradition – whether secular or sacred – can exist without its narratives. How else are the aspirations, laments and identities that make (and remake) a tradition to be captured? In Muslim societies and communities, however, the place reserved for the narrator has been a very special one. The fables and sketches of wandering

---

[1] Quoted in J.D. Dodds, et al, *The Arts of Intimacy: Christians, Jews, and Muslims in the Making of Castilian Culture* (New Haven and London, 2008), p. 229.

2   *A Companion to Muslim Cultures*

dervishes, seasoned sailors and coffeehouse entertainers vie for attention with the colourful accounts of court chroniclers and the parables of jurists and preachers. Even the trickster has his space, peddling yarns at the expense of inept officials and nobles of excessive wealth.

'Listen. Allow me to be your god. Let me take you on a journey beyond imagining. Let me tell you a story.' Thus begins Rabih Alameddine's *The Hakawati*, a celebration of a cultural institution that includes memories such as this:

> It is said that in the eighteenth century, in a café in Aleppo, the great one, Ahmad al-Saidawi, once told the story of King Baybars for three hundred and seventy-two evenings, which may or may not have been a record. It is also said that al-Saidawi cut the story short because the Ottoman governor begged him to finish it . . .'[2]

The *jihadi*, too, needs a narrative. But an exclusivist and puritanical tenor must compete with a lively mistrust that runs through Muslim cultural narratives when it comes to figures that flaunt their piety and loudly proclaim to know the will of God. There is also a stubborn cosmopolitanism that takes delight in the narratives of others, beginning with the Quran itself in its affirmation of Jewish and Christian stories as part of the foundational teaching of the Prophet Muhammad. The 'Abrahamic' tradition common to Christians, Jews and Muslims stands in the way of a zealous insistence on a God who plays favourites. Not surprisingly, that spirit is caught in Muslim narratives that range freely across Hindu, Buddhist, Confucian and African traditions, among others, in the unfolding of values in the real world. The *hakawati* is not about to let a fine tale go to waste merely because its earliest sources are Indian or Chinese.

Shehrazade makes this inclusive generosity familiar in the

---

[2] *The Hakawati* (New York, 2008), p. 36. On the vital role of stories in Muslim culture and teaching, see Eric Ormsby's chapter, 'Literature', in Amyn B. Sajoo, ed., *A Companion to Muslim Ethics* (London, 2010), and John Renard, 'Heroic Themes', in Amyn B. Sajoo, ed., *Muslim Modernities: Expressions of the Civil Imagination* (London, 2008), pp. 51-72.

Thousand and One Nights, where she expertly spins her nightly tales from a stock of Perso-Indian fables to ward off the king's executioner. Still more universal in borrowing from an array of indigenous cultures are the stories of the *Hamzanama*, told not only in Arabic and Persian but also in Turkish, Urdu, Georgian and Malay. At the heart of the tales is Amir Hamza, named after the Prophet's uncle who, after his conversion around 615 CE, became a gallant supporter of Muhammad; but there are local 'Hamza' figures too, like the sixth-century Persian king Anushirwan, and Hamza b. Abdullah who fought the Abbasid ruler Harun al-Rashid (r. 786–809). The *Hamzanama* has an exuberant energy: good and evil clash with relentless wit and humour on a cosmic plane that knows no bounds of gravity or time. Unlike the *Thousand and One Nights*, the *Hamzanama* was purely oral – until the commissioning of manuscripts in India, first in the mid-15th century, then in its grandest form by the Mughal emperor Akbar between 1557 and 1573.[3]

It may well have been the oral nature of the *Hamzanama* which gave it the fluid and ultra-cosmopolitan flavour that appealed to Akbar's famously pluralist sensibility. The *dastango*, as the storyteller was known in South Asian settings, could embellish each tale with local twists and turns: sorcerers travelled on flying urns rather than carpets, for example.[4]

But what distinguishes the Mughal court's contribution to the tales was a trove of paintings to accompany the stories, done in Central Asian, Persian, regional Indian and European styles. In fact, the actual texts are rather terse; the paintings, on the other hand, are graphic and far exceed the traditional Persian-miniature scale. This suggests that court narrators delivered the stories each time with fresh colour, unconfined by a tight script, while the paintings were displayed for the visual pleasure of the audience.

---

[3] See John Seyller, *The Adventures of Hamza: Painting and Storytelling in Mughal India* (Washington, DC, 2002), the most detailed account of the surviving manuscripts and accompanying depictions.

[4] William Dalrymple, 'Eat Your Heart Out, Homer', *New York Times*, January 6 (2008), on the new translation by M.A. Farooqi of Ghalib Lakhnavi and Abdullah Bilgrami, *The Adventures of Amir Hamza* (New York, 2008).

4 *A Companion to Muslim Cultures*

After all, the point of such an orchestration was to entertain and edify much like a modern cinematic or stage performance.

Two examples of the pictorial *Hamzanama* appear in this volume, on the cover and in Plate 1. The former depicts an episode in which the wily Mahiya, disguised as a fruit vendor, is accompanied by the spy Zambur as they search for Prince Ibrahim's kidnapped spouse, Khwarmah. Along the way, they encounter an unhappy medicine woman, Ustad Khatun, whom Mahiya promptly befriends, seeing her as a cover as well as a possible lead in her search. Although the painting is filled with architectural and street detail, it is the action that matters: the women occupy centre stage, with their expressive motions and gestures. The same is true of the episode in Plate 1, where Prince Farrukh-Nizhad responds to a pair of villainous brothers who had just taken hold of the front and back legs of an elephant, defying the 'God-worshippers' to match such strength. In response, Prince Farrukh-Nizhad comes forward with the retort, 'Two people, one elephant . . .?', and seizes the beast all by himself. The brothers are suitably chastened by this display and promptly submit to the Prince's faith, Islam. A cartoon-like thrust marks the paintings, consistent with their function; yet there is a delicacy to the keen appreciation of nature in the plentiful trees and grasses as well as the vivid animals.[5]

This relishing of graphic humour and ridicule in such full measure surely has a message for our times. Orthodoxies that imagine an austere and unitary Islam are reminded of the manifold cultural expressions that have always shaped its lived experience and meaning. Nor will it do to reduce the complexity of *political* conflicts to 'Islam' as a faith, or as a single civilisation. A case in point is the controversy over the Danish media cartoons of the Prophet Muhammad in 2005. The vocal distress of Muslims had much to do with the bigotry directed at their faith in the guise of free expression,[6] rather than a supposed cultural inability to grasp the nature of satire.

---

[5] Seyller, *Adventures of Hamza*, pp. 165, 186.

[6] John L. Esposito and Delia Mogahed, ed., *Who Speaks for Islam?* (New York, 2007), pp. 142-144, drawing on a worldwide Gallup sampling of opinion among Muslims as well as non-Muslims.

Introduction   5

Failing to understand this merely feeds the myth of a 'clash of civilisations', in which the cultural distance between Islam and the West is thought to provide a decisive explanation of all manner of ideological differences. Even before our age of globalisation and mass migration, it is the *overlapping* nature of cultural traditions that marks the history of civilisations. Narratives of denial in this regard must contend with the evidence presented in this volume from the far-flung domains of the Muslim world.

'If God had willed, He would have made you a single community'

As Islam's founding figure, the Prophet Muhammad (570–632 CE) was tasked not only with conveying the Revelation but also with putting into place its ethical framework. This was as true in the realm of duties toward God (*ibadat*) as it was in the details of social relations among the faithful (*muamalat*). Muhammad's dual role is fully evident in the 'Constitution of Medina' (c. 622 CE), the concluding part of which affirms him both as a 'messenger' and as 'protector' of the faithful covenanters.[7] A defining aspect of the ethical framework at large were the 'pillars' of the faith: bearing witness to God and his prophet, ritual prayer, alms-giving, fasting and pilgrimage. The body of normative guidance that grew out of the original framework, during and after the time of Muhammad, came to be called the sharia (from *shar*, 'the way').

A commonly-heard narrative about the sharia is that it stands for the 'divine law', and hence binds Muslims everywhere for all time. In support of this universalist view is invoked the Quranic verse, 'Now we have set you on a clear religious path, so follow it' (45:18). Yet the 'path' here, or 'the way' of the sharia, is clearly an ethical compass – which came to give birth over time to the Muslim legal tradition or *fiqh*. Precisely because the Quran is *not* a book

---

[7] See Said Amir Arjomand, 'The Constitution of Medina: A Sociolegal Interpretation of Muhammad's Acts of Foundation of the *Umma*', *International Journal of Middle East Studies,* 41 (2009), pp. 555-575, notably at p. 570.

6   *A Companion to Muslim Cultures*

of laws; human endeavour has been required to construct the *fiqh*. The stock of Quranic commandments that the legal tradition could build on was actually fairly small. 'If divine guidance is needed, it is for the purpose of setting human life in good order', notes the eminent sharia scholar Wael Hallaq, 'not to control or discipline, the two most salient missions of modern law and the modern state that commands it.'[8] Indeed, there is continuity from pre-Islamic practice in many of the Quran's norms on a whole range of matters, both sacred and secular; it is the moral content of the Revelation that injects fresh meaning into the practices. The pilgrimage to the Kaaba, for example, took an established pagan practice – which gave Mecca its particular significance as an urban hub – and transformed it into one of Islam's pillars.

What was distinctive about these transformations was the community or umma as the ethical and social context in which they were located. Time and again, the Quran invokes this collective ideal (e.g. 3:104), one of both solidarity and a common under-standing with regard to what is entailed for the individual Muslim. Just as the cultural practices of pre-Islamic Arabia and beyond were appropriated into 'Islam', so, inevitably, were the cultural realities of the growing Muslim world becoming part of how the umma experienced solidarity and shared its understanding. Quranic values, in all their universality, had to find practical expression in the particulars of various cultures. Modesty as a teaching might fit into a local practice of veiling, or more radically into a full face covering or *niqab*, or simply an avoidance of ostentatious display. The *masjid* as a space for prayer could be encased within minarets and domes in the Middle East, pagoda-like structures in East Asia, and turreted earthen buildings in West Africa. Charity as a core scriptural value found expression in many societies through the *waqf* or endowment for public benefit, to which there is no reference at all in the Quran.

What are often thought of in the West as peculiarly 'Islamic' features of the faith are no more than local cultural choices that

---

[8] Wael Hallaq, *The Shari'a: Theory, Practice, Transformations* (Cambridge, 2009), p. 84.

Introduction 7

have been adopted far and wide. Muslim names, for instance, are almost always derived from Arabic and Persian roots; no theology requires this, any more than it requires breaking the Ramadan fast with dates, in affectionate memory of the Prophet's practice. Or consider the punishments attached to 'sharia offences' like murder, theft and adultery; lashings, amputations and stoning are said to be proper responses in keeping with what is required by the Quran or foundational Islamic practice. Yet these *hudud* punishments are part of the cultural milieu of antiquity in which Muhammad's Arabia was situated, with its patriarchy and codes of justice.[9] One may sacralise either the punishments, insisting that cultural practices are fixed for all time, or the teaching that says the offences are serious violations of one's covenant with the divine. The idea that specific practices are the *only* way to express the underlying ethics is belied by the fact that societies habitually leave behind practices that are now deemed to violate the cherished values that they were once felt to uphold. Examples include public executions, castrations, and incarcerating people with mental disabilities; more broadly, all societies undergo shifts in expectations with regard to modes of governance, communication and social etiquette.

Diversity and change rather than a rigid uniformity is the norm within the Quran itself and in the outlook of Islam's foundational phase, including the nascent legal tradition. After all, the new Revelation was presumed to renew and refresh the traditions of the 'People of the Book' (Jews and Christians). Lest Muslims take this to mean a license to impose their understanding of the faith upon others, the Quran warns, 'If God had so willed, He would have made you one community, but He wanted to test you through that which He has given you' (5:48). Constancy may be a mark of one's faith; but fixity, in human interpretation of divine guidance, was not the natural order of things. Salvation is not the exclusive preserve of Muslims, according to the Quran: 'All those who believe – the Jews, the Sabians, the Christians – anyone who believes in

---

[9] See the chapters by Reza Aslan and Azizah al-Hibri in Amyn B. Sajoo, ed., *A Companion to the Muslim World* (London, 2009).

8   *A Companion to Muslim Cultures*

God and the Last Days, and who does good deeds, will have nothing to fear or regret' (5:69).

Numerous instances from Muhammad's life and that of his earliest successors speak to an acute sensitivity to cultural diversity and change in the practice of the faith. The Constitution of Medina required only that the city's various religious and tribal communities pledge loyalty to shared civic principles and to Muhammad's authority as the overseer, with no 'Islamic' test for membership in an inclusive umma. On the contrary, a host of non-Muslim practices in matters such as the direction of prayer, dietary constraints and taxation were adopted by the Prophet; he also encouraged Muslims to marry Jews, and did so himself. In a fine appreciation of the difference between values and forms, the caliph Umar (r.634–644) agreed to a request from Christian communities to have their poll tax (*jizya*) referred to as the Muslim *zakat* (alms-giving) on grounds of dignity; earlier, Muhammad waived the *jizya* altogether for non-Muslims who were felt not to merit the burden.[10] For the caliph Ali (r.656–661), a primary truth to be faced by all governors was the need for familiarity with the actual ways of the governed, each of whom was 'either your brother in religion or your like in creation'.[11]

That such a pluralist spirit is in tension with the preference for the particulars of one's own cultural ways is evident in the histories of all faith traditions. For Muslims, whose heritage is born of civilisations that have spanned Asian, Afro-Arab and European domains, the tension is undeniable. The cosmopolitanism that runs through the articulation and expressive practice of the faith immediately raises for some the need for separateness. Indeed, Muhammad's openness to the ways of Christians, Jews and others has sometimes been taken as evidence of a lack of originality, and worse, as leading to the triumph of ideology over a lean theology.

---

[10] Khaled Abu El Fadl, *The Place of Tolerance in Islam* (Boston, 2002), p. 22, noting that the tax was clearly not a theological matter but a rather a pragmatic one, 'in response to a specific set of historical circumstances'.
[11] Ali's Instruction to Malik al-Ashtar: Letter 33, *Nahj al-balagha*, tr. Sayid Ali Reza as *Peak of Eloquence* (New York, 1996), pp. 535, 544.

Introduction 9

It is true that there have been phases in Muslim history when narrow cultural preferences in law and theology have stifled rich discourses in ethics and philosophy. A prime example is the traditionalism of the Asharites, on whose behalf al-Ghazali (1058–111) wielded potent influence against the liberal rationalism of the Mutazilites.[12]

Some might see echoes of that tide in our own time, especially in the rise of absolutist tendencies in the name of a unitary Islam. But these conservative assaults are sparked by the firm embedding of the theological and ethical traditions in diverse cultural realities – wherein is their enduring strength.

'That you may know one another'

The attachment to particular forms of religious expression as 'distinctive' points to a key aspect of the relationship between faith and culture: the demands of identity. Religions, after all, seek to offer responses to questions such as 'Who are we?' and 'What gives meaning to our lives?' Answers that categorically embrace a single, exclusive view of the world have an instant attraction, just as they do in a secular context such as nationalism. Defining oneself or one's outlook *against* those of others has the appeal not only of clarity, but also of allowing the opportunity to cast one's own side as superior in merit even as a victim more deserving of justice. In this vein, cultural forms that lend themselves to supporting a well-defined and exclusive religious identity will trump less distinctive forms. The symbolic value of a minaret or *hijab*, like that of a cross or *yarmulke*, is as obvious as that of a national flag. All serve as markers of identity, staking out their particular ways of being in and seeing the world.

These symbols are important in fostering solidarity, a prized ethical value in faith traditions such as Islam. As the work of Bryan S. Turner and Robert Putnam on religion and civil society has shown, such solidarity has been a strong source of social capital

---

[12] George F. Hourani, *Reason and Tradition in Islamic Ethics* (Cambridge, 1985), notably pp. 98-166.

10   *A Companion to Muslim Cultures*

with which to develop empathy and a civic sensibility. Yet this binding can also spur social polarisation and 'enclave' communities with inward-looking 'rituals of intimacy', especially in migrant communities.[13] Like secular nationalism, faith traditions may appeal to the best and the worst in the human quest for identity, with cultural symbols serving as handy tools of mobilisation. Much has been written about the waves of globalisation that wash over local traditions, both secular and sacred, in matters ranging from commerce and social taste to political preferences. The ensuing revolt of the local against the global, or 'localism', has also been noted the world over, whether in politics or cultural life; it is a reminder of the human attachment to indigenous particulars.

Far from being a modern sentiment, the stubborn preference for what is regarded as 'one's own' is, of course, a deeply rooted impulse. The very term 'rootedness' speaks to the positioning of individuals and communities in their native soil. A poignant reminder of this sentiment comes from a 12th-century observation by Hugo of St. Victor, a monk from Saxony:

> The person who finds his homeland sweet is still a tender beginner; he to whom every soil is as his native one is already strong; but he is perfect to whom the entire world is a foreign place. The tender soul has fixed his love on one spot in the world; the strong person has extended his love to all places; the perfect man has extinguished his.[14]

By the same token, finding the homeland of others as sweet as if it were one's own patch also draws an admonition. When the all-conquering Alexander inquires as to why his territorial gains in fourth-century India fail to impress the local philosophers, Jain thinkers tell him: 'King Alexander, every man can possess only so

---

[13] See especially Bryan S, Turner, ed., *Religious Diversity and Civil Society* (Oxford, 2008), notably at pp. 49-71; Robert Putnam (with David Campbell), *American Grace: How Religion Divides and Unites Us* (New York, 2010).
[14] Quoted in Edward Said, *Culture and Imperialism* (New York, 1993), p. 335.

Introduction

much of the earth's surface as this we are standing on . . . You will soon be dead, and then you will own just as much of the earth as will suffice to bury you.'[15]

The twin perils of parochialism, a smallness of self in the world, and of triumphalism, an undue enlargement of the self in relation to others, are opposite sides of the same coin. For the medieval historian Ibn Khaldun, the power of communal attachments or *asabiyya* – was best on display in small kinship groups and tribes – in the absence of which civilisations lost their cohesion and underwent decline. Only religion could trump *asabiyya*, though without denying it; rather, it did so by reconfiguring it in the shape of the umma, whose bonds are not defined by kinship but by ethical commitments. Telling Muslims that solidarity was a favoured value in the eyes of God, as the Quran repeatedly urged, clearly required navigating between parochialism and triumphalism. This was all the more critical with the swift and extraordinary growth of Islam as faith and empire. And the moral balance is signalled in the Quran itself, in proclaiming diversity as part of the divine plan:

> O mankind! We created you from a single man and a single woman, and made you into nations and tribes, that you may know each other (not that you may despise each other). (49:13)

Pluralism in culture and identity is cast here not as a passive reality, but as a project: human communities are expected to 'know each other' as a fulfilment of the covenant with God. The expectation is explicitly aimed at all of mankind, not a particular community. *Asabiyya* is recognised as part of the warp and woof of human society – then treated as an opportunity and a duty to widen horizons. In keeping with the sense of a project, this vision fits into the constant Quranic urging to pursue knowledge; there is even gentle mocking of those who fail to get around and use their eyes and ears in understanding their world (22:46, quoted in the epigraph to this chapter). Cultural pluralism, in other

---

[15] Peter Green, *Alexander of Macedon, 356-323 B.C.: A Historical Biography* (Berkeley, CA, 1992), p. 428.

12 *A Companion to Muslim Cultures*

words, does not just happen; it is an outlook that requires cultivation. The challenge begins with the very first revelation, where Muhammad is told to 'Read in the name of thy Lord ... Who taught by the pen ... Taught man that which he knew not' (96:1–5). He soon launches into a long and intense dialogue with Christians and Jews as to the implications of this and what is to follow, since the teaching is but the latest phase in a long history.

This embrace of a Muslim identity that was pluralist in the making laid the foundations for a complex narrative. How could it be otherwise in the unfolding of an umma whose member-groups spanned all of the Middle East and Mediterranean, the Balkans, vast tracts of Asia and much of sub-Saharan Africa? Arabic, the language of the Quran, is spoken by less than a quarter of the world's Muslims. Local custom or *adat* has deeply influenced how a Muslim, whether Shia or Sunni, actually puts into practice the norms of theology, ethics and law, including the very 'pillars' of the faith. Spiritual orders, to which millions of Muslims belong, mostly have a regional identity, from West Africa to Central Asia. Western China and Indonesia have been radically different environments for centuries-old Muslim communities – no less than contemporary France or the United States. 'Diaspora identity' is hardly a modern idea; its novelty can only be asserted in a narrative which ignores Islam's pluralist reality from the outset. In each locale, the social relationship between Muslims and other communities has had a formative role in how identity is constructed.

Modernity has made identity more sensitive than ever to competing claims, because the globalised world we inhabit makes us more aware of the multitudes in our midst; and the demands of civic membership today (from citizenship to civil society) require us to 'belong' in more places than one. In principle, this pluralist narrative of identity is at one with the outlook professed by the earliest umma: the inclusive thrust of the Constitution of Medina was premised on civic as well as religious membership, not to mention clan affinities. Yet the challenge of accommodating the multiple identities that stem from today's national and global landscapes is acute, and not for Muslim societies alone. A useful point of departure might be to acknowledge that modernity itself

Introduction 13

is the outcome of varied journeys. The western tussle of Church and State in the Enlightenment that began in the 17th century is one narrative that looms large, but there are others.

Muslim journeys to modernity share similarities and differences with the western one. The place of religion in public life, for example, fits into an enduring Islamic narrative of balance between the secular and sacred for individuals and communities. This frames how modern technology is perceived and applied, with its ethical implications; it is also true of cultural products such as art and, in varying degrees, music. Individual human rights, the rule of law and accountable governance are a vital part of this picture – as the world witnessed in the 'Arab Spring' of 2011, which will doubtless run its course for some time to come. Seeing Muslim identities as traditionalist and closed to the modern world finds little resonance; on other hand, both Muslims and non-Muslims hold strong negative stereotypes about one another, especially with regard to attributes of violence, arrogance and selfishness.[16] The social intimacies of modernity alone can offer no assurance that pluralist attitudes will readily prevail; there are yet more stories to be told in the unending quest to 'know one another'.

This *Companion*

Ancient deserts and today's urban landscapes may echo with the same call for upliftment, but in voices that come from very different everyday realities. Culture shapes every aspect of the relationship

---

[16] See respectively the Pew Research Centre reports in the 'Global Attitudes Project' on opinions about democratic life and aspirations in Muslim-majority countries (Washington, DC, May 2011; accessible at http://pewresearch.org/pubs/1997/international-poll-arab-spring-us-obama-image-muslim-publics); and in the 'Pew Forum on Religion in Public Life' (Washington, DC, October 2007; accessible at http://pewforum.org/Politics-and-Elections/Widespread-Negativity-Muslims-Distrust-Westerners-More-than-Vice-Versa.aspx). See also Pankaj Mishra's review of a spate of 'mainstream' literature that feeds into the post-September 11 paranoia, notably in Europe: 'A culture of fear', *The Guardian*, 15 August 2009 (accessible at http://www.guardian.co.uk/books/2009/aug/15/eurabia-islamophobia-europe-colonised-muslims).

14 *A Companion to Muslim Cultures*

between God and the believer – as well as among believers, and with those beyond the fold. Fasts, prayers and pilgrimages are attuned to social rhythms old and new, no less than the designs of mosques and public gardens, the making of 'religious' art and music, and ways of thinking about physical wellbeing. Scripture itself, as Muhammad knew, is ever seen through a cultural lens; language and what it says are intimately tied to the context. The cosmopolitanism that runs through Muslim history from the beginning recalls T.S. Eliot's remark that culture is 'that which makes life worth living', a space where human flourishing occurs in all its intricacy.[17] It is where the deepest religious values are understood and practised: Muslims have never been content with an easy separation of faith from daily life, public or private.

What are the implications of this holistic view in a diverse world of Muslims and non-Muslims? How do core ethical values interface with the dense particulars of local cultures, especially when gender and the social order are affected? The answers, at a time when secular and Muslim identities often seem to be locked in conflict, are explored in the chapters that follow. They treat neither culture nor the identities that emerge from it as fixed – mindful too that the world's 1.6 billion Muslims belong to a myriad of cultures. Earle Waugh brings this home in his colourful survey of 'everyday piety' not only around the Quran but also Muhammad, the Shia Imams and saintly figures whose tombs can be places of uniquely evocative practises. Secular culture may also serve religious ends in highly non-traditional ways, such as when 'Muslim rap' makes the music charts. Objects like rosaries or, in Egypt, the eye of Horus, can acquire a sacred quality through use in rituals. Waugh regards popular piety as engaging key aspects of how we see ourselves and our solidarities; as such, it becomes 'an essential part of the journey of modernity'.

But if religious expression is to extend into the public domain where it must coexist with secular (and other religious) identities,

---

[17] T.S. Eliot, *Notes Towards the Definition of Culture* (London, 1948), p. 27; T. Bennett, 'Culture', in T. Bennett, et al, ed., *New Keywords: A Revised Vocabulary of Culture and Society* (Oxford, 2005), pp. 63-69.

PL. 1: Prince Farrukh-Nizhad lifts an elephant, convincing two brothers from a warring army to convert to Islam. Illustration from the *Hamzanama*, Mughal India, attributed to Mahesa and Kesava Dasa, c. 1570.

PL. 2: Shahzia Sikander's 'Pleasure Pillars' (2001), a layered adaptation of the Persian miniature style of painting, done on Wasli paper with vegetable colour, dry pigment, watercolour, ink and tea.

PL. 3: A market in the ancient city of Kashgar, an administrative and social hub at the western end of the Xinjiang Autonomous Region in China.

PL. 4: A performance of the *attan*, of Pashtun origin but now considered the national dance of Afghanistan. The *kuchi*-style dress is most often worn in the countryside.

PL. 6: A medieval spa: Aleppo's restored Yalbugha public bath or *hammam*, built in the 15th century.

PL. 5: Registan Square in Samarkand, Uzbekistan, where religious colleges or *madrassa*s helped shape the urban community.

PL. 7: Practical beauty: the 18th-century Khwaju bridge and weir of Isfahan, which crosses the Zayandeh River and regulates its flow, while also creating a place for social gathering.

PL. 8: International modernism overshadows Javanese building traditions in Jakarta's Istiqlal Mosque, completed in 1984.

PL. 9: New heritage: Al-Azhar Park, completed in 2005, serves as an oasis amid the din of Cairo, against a backdrop of modern high-rises as well as mosques and fortifications from the Fatimid, Ayubbid, Mamluk and Ottoman periods.

Introduction 15

what is the proper role of the state? Abdullahi An-Naim's chapter revisits the common understanding of the sharia as an institution embedded in the cultural evolution of Muslim societies, and its relationship with modern constitutions as the framework of the state. While the ethical tenets of the sharia make it the 'passageway' into the faith, he distinguishes sharply its interpretive heritage, of which the legal tradition (*fiqh*) is a part. There is 'certainly more to Islam than the sharia, which is only part of the rich experience of being a Muslim', notes An-Naim. The individual's *voluntary* submission is of the essence in the theology of the sharia itself, and it is impaired by any coercion. Claims by the state to be its enforcer are exercises in secular politics, and violate the civic pluralism to which both Islamic and contemporary human rights principles hold the state accountable. An-Naim recognises that this outlook requires a struggle for 'cultural legitimacy' in each society; the prize is genuinely equal citizenship as the basis for religious freedom.

That freedom is vital not merely in public expressions of faith but in spiritual life as well. And it is about more than political freedom alone, as Carl Ernst shows in his chapter on the extraordinarily varied expressions of spirituality in Islam's past and present. Sufi traditions that celebrate the inner experience of faith are found everywhere in the Muslim world, but though rooted in the Quran (and Muhammad's own practice), they have run afoul of orthodoxies that seek to regulate worship, sometimes forcibly. Ironically, it is modernity that has generated some of the fiercest puritanism, including Protestant forms in the West, in the name of an egalitarian ethic that opposes the saintly hierarchies and veneration of Sufi orders. Yet there has always been a place in religiosity for what Ernst calls 'spiritual athletes, who through a combination of effort and divine grace have achieved special status' as 'keepers of the gate on the path to the inner sanctum'. This extends to cultural expressions such as art and even cinema, where the appreciation of beauty is cast as an integral aspect of the spiritual unity of creation. An-Naim would argue that the safeguarding of all these forms of religiosity is what modern constitutionalism is about, in keeping here with Islam's inclusive ethos.

16 *A Companion to Muslim Cultures*

Perhaps nowhere is the influence of culture on 'religious' identities as robust as when the status of women is concerned. From the earliest days, as Elena Caprioni and Eva Sajoo note in their chapter, the tension between the ethical and social voices in Muslim society has gendered faith and its practice – part of a global reality in which women have been 'used as ideological markers by political and religious groups, from Soviet Communists to Christian fundamentalists'. Caprioni and Sajoo find that women in Afghanistan and China's Xinjiang region often apply those markers to themselves, affirming social stereotypes believed to have the support of the Quran (despite its assertion of the moral equality of the sexes). 'Firewood serves for winter, a wife serves for her husband's pleasure', and 'Allah is God for a woman, the husband is half God' are proverbs heard among Uyghur women in Xinjiang. Similar sentiments prevail under the *pashtunwali*, a patriarchal code that binds Afghanistan's largest ethnic group, the Pashtun. While communist and western ideologies may seem to offer the best prospect of equality, many have looked to the emancipatory 'models of womanhood' within Islam. The interplay of faith and culture, it turns out, 'cannot be reduced to a simple choice between identity and freedom'.

The choices can be at least as difficult for women and men alike in the face of new reproductive technologies, with their promise of fertility treatments in settings which also cherish traditional forms of kinship. Morgan Clarke finds that the availability of in-vitro fertilisation (IVF) in the Middle East since the 1980s has enjoyed the blessing of the religious and political establishment, sympathetic to the needs of infertile couples. But what of the public at large where legitimacy for such choices, including with regard to donor eggs and sperm, is ultimately determined? With its array of faith traditions, Lebanon is an especially rewarding testing ground: distinctive stances are taken even within Christian, Jewish, Shia and Sunni communities. As the technologies and their social implications have shown themselves to be increasingly complex, Clarke traces the shifts in official and public responses – and reveals how innovative religious perspectives can be, notably among Shia clerics who have generally

Introduction 17

been the most permissive in their rulings. That 'Islam is not opposed to science and biomedicine as the secularist stereotype would have one believe' is a commonly held view among scholars, Clarke reports, harkening back to an age of outstanding scientific achievement in the medieval Middle East.

Heritage and modernity make similar claims in the built environment of Muslim cities, old and new, where civic and religious identities are tightly interlocked. Hussein Keshani's exploration of the role of architecture in shaping the everyday life of communities draws out an ethos at play from Samarkand and Isfahan to Fez and Zanzibar; here, stylistic grace and functionality know no easy barriers of secular and sacred. While the focus is on the civic environment – palace communities, urban fortifications, bathhouses, bazaars, public squares, gardens – there are recurrent themes that overlap with religious architecture. Wide reliance on arches, courtyards, pillared halls and elaborate screens (*mashrebiyyas*), for example, creates an 'ever-evolving group of aesthetic identities' around shared tastes. But as such local preferences are displaced by western tastes brought in by globalisation, is there a future for a 'Muslim' architecture? Keshani finds inspiration in the Historic Cities initiative of the Aga Khan Trust for Culture, which since 1988 has evolved an approach to heritage that eschews both traditionalism and western imitation. Among its finest accomplishments is Cairo's Al-Azhar Park (Plate 9), now a model for civic projects in Asia and Africa. Meanwhile, the Trust's Award for Architecture is an ambitious bid to revive the creativity of modern building in the Muslim world.

A civic building that could be found in historic towns and cities from Mali to the Malay peninsula was the library (*maktaba*), whose prestige as an institution speaks to the status of the written word in Islam. In Jonathan Bloom's account of how paper thrived as a medium before the advent of print, libraries such as those of Umayyad Cordoba, Abbasid Baghdad, Buyid Shiraz and Fatimid Cairo are heroic measures of just how sophisticated the culture of writing was in Muslim lands. Even private collections could outstrip anything that a European library could muster, including Paris's mighty Sorbonne with its meagre 2000 books in the 14th

18 *A Companion to Muslim Cultures*

century. It was Chinese paper, made efficiently and cheaply in the Middle East, which made all this possible; suddenly everyone from artisans and astronomers to calligraphers, map-makers, poets and preachers used paper. Bloom regards the shift from 'oral to scribal culture' as so effective that it stalled interest in printing, which Europe mastered in the 15th century after learning from the Middle East how to make paper. Although the resistance to printing doubtless had a negative impact on economic and scientific development in the Muslim world, the aesthetics of a culture of the pen that included calligraphy and Persian miniatures thrived long and splendidly (Plates 10–18).

Among the glories of a 'paper culture' was the rising popularity in the ninth century of cookbooks in Muslim lands; a surviving one by al-Baghdadi classed food as the noblest of all the forms of pleasure, ahead of clothes, music, perfume and sex. One suspects that this had as much to do with the subtle delights of how and where the food was served as with what was on the plate, judging by Mai Yamani's chapter on culinary culture. That food is a central aspect of the ritual and social life of Muslims is no surprise; but locating her appraisal in Mecca, Yamani links the city's special status in Islam to the meeting of global traditions of cooking and serving. Such is the emphasis on hospitality that even in households with large domestic staffs, the 'people of the house' (*ahl al-bayt*) personally serve their guests – plying them with more food long after their appetites are sated, as required by the rules of etiquette. Still, al-Baghdadi's insistence that food is the greatest of pleasures is challenged by the sensory joys of music and its setting, in Jonathan Shannon's recollection of a concert in the Syrian city of Aleppo. Master vocalist Sabah Fakhri entertains his audience in a *nadi* (clubhouse) evening that stretches over more than five hours, where folk, classical-religious and contemporary songs culminate in an ecstatic dance (*saltana*) that has everyone in thrall. In Fakhri's popularity among the youth, despite his old-style rendition, Shannon sees a hunger for 'authenticity' in the profusion of synthetic sounds in techno-pop music.

Authenticity comes in many guises, of course. Shannon tells us of the longing for integrity in vocal performance, the emotional

Introduction 19

honesty that characterises the *saltana*. Fakhri's concert brings this integrity to borrowings from an array of regional musical styles, with the backing of instruments that span even more cultural traditions. Like the many national cuisines that have contributed to 'Meccan food', or the diverse styles of building that have melded into what are considered Islamic forms of architecture or art, or the pluralist customary and legal contributions to the sharia itself, there is no escaping the sheer variety of ways in which Muslim lives are experienced. Yet this reality impels some to look for authenticity in a return to historical or cultural particulars that are thought of as inherently Islamic. Karim H. Karim calls attention to this 'anti-cosmopolitanism' (and not only among Muslims), of which al-Qaeda and the Taliban are obvious exemplars with their version of cultural and religious integrity. These impulses, Karim observes, are at odds with the 'everyday cosmopolitanism' so typical of the lived reality of Muslims, and rooted in the 'fundamental openness of *din* [faith] toward *dunya* [the world]' which is Islam's heritage.

Shahzia Sikander is a *hakawati* of sorts, a Pakistani-American Muslim who tells her stories of modernity through paintings which adapt the Persian miniature in utterly contemporary ways. In 'Pleasure Pillars' (Plate 2), done after the events of September 11, 2001, she gathers symbols of technology, mythology and tradition in lush and painstakingly fine detail. The narratives that tie them together are neither singular nor straightforward, but layered and overlapping. Familiar images and tales are made the subject of Sikander's 'personal meditations on the larger issues of culture and identity, tradition and modernity, Islam and the West'.[18] It comes as no surprise that she has won acclaim as among the most gifted young Muslim artists. Hindu and western cultural borrowings are integral to her work, and traditional styles are subverted. With her fellow storytellers in cinema, dance, poetry,

---

[18] Glen Lowry, 'Gained in Translation', Art News, 5 (Mar 2006; accessible at http://www.artnews.com/2006/03/01/gained-in-translation/). See also Holland Cotter, 'What does Islamic Art Look Like?', *New York Times*, Feb 26, 2006 (accessible at http://www.nytimes.com/2006/02/26/arts/design/26cott.html).

20 *A Companion to Muslim Cultures*

photography and cyber-art, she fits into an ethos where not only cultural cosmopolitanism but also displacement and the power of memory are pervasive ... far beyond the familiar modern story of Palestine. The narrators of the *Hamzanama* would surely applaud.

Further Reading

Appiah, Kwame Anthony. *The Honor Code: How Moral Revolutions Happen*. New York, 2010.

Blizek, William L., ed. *The Continuum Companion to Religion and Film*. London, 2009.

Ernst, Carl and Richard Martin, ed. *Rethinking Islamic Studies: From Orientalism to Cosmopolitanism*. Columbia, SC, 2010.

Geertz, Clifford, 'Religion as a Cultural System', in Michael Banton, ed., *Anthropological Approaches to the Study of Religion*. New York, 1966, pp. 1–46.

Ibn Khaldun. *The Muqaddimah: An Introduction to History*, tr. Franz Rosenthal. Princeton and Oxford, 2005.

Mostafavi, Mohsen, ed. *Implicate & Explicate: Aga Khan Award for Architecture*. Baden, Switzerland, 2011.

Nusseibeh, Sari. *Once Upon a Country: A Palestinian Life*. London, 2007

Partridge, Christopher, 'Religion and Popular Culture', in Linda Woodhead, et al, ed. *Religions in the Modern World: Traditions and Transformations*, 2nd ed. New York, 2001, pp. 489–521.

Sajoo, Amyn B., ed. *Muslim Modernities: Expressions of the Civil Imagination*. London, 2008.

Saliba, George. *Islamic Science and the Making of the European Renaissance*. Cambridge, MA, 2007.

Sen, Amartya. *Identity and Violence: The Illusion of Destiny*. New York and London, 2006.

Sila-Khan, Dominique. *Crossing the Threshold: Understanding Religious Identities in South Asia*. London, 2004.

2

Everyday Tradition

Earle Waugh

From the earliest days of Islam, popular religious practices and the expressions of piety have been a matter of lively debate. After all, Islam was born in Mecca, a pilgrimage centre from pagan times that commanded the allegiance of people throughout the region. So Islam defined itself in relation to other religious practices of the time, and in its first days the community was in contention with various pagan rites. This was true also of the history of Judaism and Christianity, shared Abrahamic traditions with which Islam has both similarities and differences. Not surprisingly, the Quran has much to say about this. We can assume that during Muhammad's time, discussion about proper practice was very common, and hence vital in the making of 'tradition'.

What is important here is that both the Quran and the emerging tradition held that culture was not a neutral force in religious life. It had to be transformed in light of the new ethical standards. This was especially so with regard to pagan practices, which belonged to *jahiliyya*, the period of darkness before the light of the Revelation. At the same time, the Quran recognises that many prophets brought God's message to their lands and communities over the history of the world's peoples, and concludes that these messengers have sometimes been successful. The diverse religious cultures surrounding these messengers are fully acknowledged, even if the messages brought by these peoples are felt to have become distorted and in need of reform according to God's true word.

Muslim tradition, then, had a continuing place for religious cultures differing from that of Islam. The Quran is clear that all 'People of the Book' (notably Jews and Christians) were to be free to practise their faith. Early Muslim expansion frowned on any destruction by military forces of churches and synagogues. Rather, as was the case in Damascus, a large central church might be acquired (in this case by purchase) and converted to a mosque, while all others were left to their original congregations. Such communities were not subject to military service and contributed to the public good through special taxes, which made them part of a collective 'social contract'.

In this pluralist environment, religious markers became a vital aspect of the way identity was formed. To designate a practice as 'normative' or proper was one way of marking religious identity in relation to other traditions. When Muslims were challenged in this regard, their practices were tested against principles drawn from the Quran or the Prophet's practice (*Sunna*). If there was no authorised source to be found, then authorities deemed such practices non-Islamic. The upshot was that all practices within the Muslim religious environment had to be rooted either in the Quran or the *Sunna*. Practices that were not spelled out there had to have some kind of theological support, which also made reference to those primary sources for justification. There could be plenty of room for debate in these matters, and the process of legitimation might take a long time to sort out. Here, the Islamic legal system came to be an important mediator on matters of practice, and thus of what we may call the 'Muslim marker' system.

For Shia Muslims, the interpretation of the primary sources took place in the context of learned teachings associated with Ali (c. 598–661), who belonged to the immediate family of the Prophet, and later spiritual figures whose understanding was held to be inspired. Muhammad himself is said to have proclaimed, 'I am the city of knowledge and Ali is the door.' Hence, Shia theology prized a hierarchy of individuals who were specially honoured; this idea doubtless merged with or reinforced the growth of the Imamate, a central tenet in all the many branches of the Shia tradition. Piety and practice have been shaped by this reality, sometimes in response to the wider Sunni as well as Shia religious, social and political environment.

More generally, Muslim societies developed with state and religion closely entwined; there was an early tendency to see the 'official' cultural environment as either friendly or unfriendly to Islam. Even when there were no hostilities with non-believing neighbours, the view was that an Islamic cultural milieu (*dar al-Islam*) was best. This view had other implications too, as in the role of the official legal system in developing the sharia, including the status of non-Muslims therein. So the state played a critical role in shaping what a 'true' Muslim culture was supposed to be. Local practices could lose out to the perceived need for uniformity across Muslim lands, as is often the case with law.

Yet this could never be done easily when it came to culture. Elements of a tribal and popular sort always resisted 'universal' tendencies – even to our own day, no matter what the authorities say. As with all major religious traditions, Islam is a rich tapestry of cultures rather than a uniform set of beliefs and practices. This chapter offers a sampling of just how wide-ranging the pluralism of 'tradition' is for Muslims, both Sunni and Shia. Far from being a recent development, this diversity has enjoyed legitimacy from the earliest days, in matters both large and small.

Piety around the Quran

Devotion around the Quran has a rich culture of its own. Indeed, the scripture sets some of the proprieties about its own treatment, as in the sura al-Waqia (56:77–79): 'This is indeed a Quran most honourable, a Book well-guarded, which none shall touch, But those who are clean.' A popular reading has come to hold that one should not read the Quran without performing the ceremonial washing or *wudu*. Many other protocols have followed from this sacred status.

There are special practices that may not flow directly from the language of the Quran itself, but which appear to derive from its

24   *A Companion to Muslim Cultures*

unique position. These range from the special rules about its practical use, to how it is to be handled in the ordinary affairs of life. There are various stories of popular usage in this regard: Qurans being fixed to spears as a claim to cease hostilities between Muslims, or the authority of its verses serving to bring about compromise in a long dispute, or the reading of the Quran in its entirety during the month of Ramadan.

A stock of rules has grown around how the Quran is properly recited, known as the science of *tajwid*. Again, many of these rules stem from the special esteem for Quran-recital in public piety. Hence one should not merely recite a partial verse, thus taking part of the verse out of its context, or emphasising some aspect at the expense of the whole. Nor should one vary the text through lack of breath: published Qurans commonly give an indication of where one should pause for breath, and mark how much one must recite until the next pause.

There are social practices built upon particular types of piety. It is common that official religious gatherings begin with the recital of the Quran; otherwise they run the risk of being regarded as unofficial, and even un-Islamic. One will have the Quran recited at the wake of a beloved who has passed away. Families who are pleased at the birth of a child may well hire a Quran reciter as a way of expressing appreciation to God. Individuals may also recite certain verses for their perceived power to assist them in difficulties, such as selected verses for help in an exam. It was well-known in medieval Islam, and to some extent still today among some classes of believers, for verses to be written out on paper, dissolved in water and ingested as a way of invoking the Quran's curative powers. Verses may also be used as protection from adversity, and the practice of carrying verses on oneself when going into battle becomes a claim to divine assistance and protection. Likewise, verses may be inscribed and carried as amulets by believers. Some sections of the Quran have received special attention in the history of the text. The sura *al-Fatiha*, while the opening chapter in the Quran, has assumed the place of final benediction and blessing. Mystically-oriented believers have taken sustenance in the sura *al-Nur* (chapter 24), and have intoned its vivid passages for the special meanings that are seen there. During Ramadan, many place a great deal of emphasis on the night when the Quran was believed to have been first delivered to Muhammad, *laylat al-qadr* (chapter 97), and will remain awake in vigilant prayer all night for its special reward. There are verses that are regarded as potent in certain circumstances, such as in the face of a drought, and the community may gather to collectively recite these to bring rain.

Not surprisingly, there have long been verses that play vital legal and social roles in ceremonies such as marriage and divorce – notably sura *Nisaa* (chapter 4). The Quran also widely serves for the taking of an oath of veracity, much like the Bible. In this vein, passing under the Quran is an affirmation of one's integrity, a practice well known in some Iranian Shia communities. It implies a submission to the Quran's ethical standards, and the individual's invitation of divine judgment if one's character does not live up to the symbolic claim. Passing under the Quran may also be done before going on a long journey as a plea for protection from God.

Finally, there are everyday pieties on how the Quran should physically be treated. When reading it, for example, it is felt best to place it upon a stand; further, one should not hold one's place in the text with a vulgar marker. It should be closed when not in use, and must not be left on the ground or in an unkempt area. The Quran should not be ripped or ill-used, and when through normal use it falls apart, it must not be separated into sheets and left loose. An old or dismembered Quran is with appropriate ceremony to be burned or buried.

Piety around the Prophet

In a myriad of ways, the pious have sought to emulate the everyday practices of the Prophet. Muhammad was well known to be concerned about how an image becomes an object of worship. Hence, pictorial depictions have in mosques and other sacred spaces given way to the word.[1] Indeed, there is no 'official' portrait

---

[1] Fahmida Suleman, 'Art', in Amyn B. Sajoo, ed., *A Companion to Muslim Ethics*, (London, 2010), pp. 91-104.

26 *A Companion to Muslim Cultures*

of the Prophet himself. When images of him appear, such as in pictures of his life created by artisans for personal use of powerful patrons, the face may be veiled or appear without particular detail. Such drawings are especially common in the artistic cultures of Persia, Turkey and South Asia. In textual media, one may find elaborate descriptions, both of the appearance of Muhammad and of his character. Stories and poetry eulogising his character are greatly prized.[2] These became crucial in education where they provided justification for various kinds of normative behaviour. The actions of the Prophet, retained in the Sunna, are held to reflect both his personal life and his superior qualities as leader. His actions became a standard for conveying a divinely-sanctioned lifestyle. Scholars devoted lifetimes to recording these activities and then set out to understand what had been the context for such actions. The most authoritative of such reports passed into the great hadith collections, and became grist for the courts and for theologians, with direct results for the making of Muslim society.

Popular tales about Muhammad are often joined by those about all the prophets. This genre of writing is well known in Islam as the *Qisas al-anbiya* (*Stories of the Prophets*). These are adaptations of stories mentioned in the Quran, which are expanded by popular lore or other religious sources; and this was not just pious happenstance. The commitment of Abraham (Ibrahim in the Quran) to serving God even to the point of sacrificing his firstborn son Ismail is a key ingredient in the rites of pilgrimage. Both his temptation by Iblis (Satan) and wife Hagar's frantic search for water are crucial elements. The former is commemorated by the throwing of stones at the three stone Satans, and the latter by the seven running treks between the hills Safa and Marwa, recalling Hagar's traumatic experience in seeking water for her son on the verge of his dying from thirst.

Clearly, piety expanded its religious horizons very early to accommodate the need for more detail about how Muslims should under-

---

[2] Annemarie Schimmel, *And Muhammad Is His Messenger: The Veneration of the Prophet in Islamic Piety* (Chapel Hill, NC and London, 1985).

Everyday Tradition

stand their religious practices. In this way, doors were opened to many sources for help in grasping the nature of one's commitments to Islam. In Shia practice, the Prophet's family also served this need, most notably with regard to the role of Ali, but also the Prophet's daughter Fatima, and his martyred grandson Husayn. Ethical values of courage and wisdom have come to be especially attached to these figures.

Mere physical reportage of the Prophet's actions was not quite enough for the deeply pious. Muhammad was for many the very model of spirituality. To 'follow the Prophet' became the dedicated means to a deeper life in Islam, and out of the early asceticism of Muslims grew meditations on his life and work. Eventually, an aspect of this piety flowered into a full-fledged mystical orientation called Sufism in both the Sunni and Shia traditions, with enormous implications for faith, art and culture in the civilisations of Islam.

Recitations

Throughout Islamic history, a variety of forms have given voice to the inner longings of the heart. The rhythmic recitation of the Quran, the minaret call of the *muezzin*, the chants of the faithful while on pilgrimage to Mecca, the Sufi chanters who use song and incantation, all reflect a wider range of expression than the usual spoken word. These pious expressions have a musical content and shape, and they follow traditions of recital that have been specifically adopted for spiritual purposes. In all of them the goal is to carry the deeper messages of the heart in a medium that will appeal to the ordinary believer, whether Sunni or Shia.

Beyond these general practices, there is a complex network of recitals which are tied to more specific Muslim religious practices. Most of these have to do with the culture of communities as developed over time. A classic example is the activities that take place under the title of Muharram rites. These are carried out by Twelver Shia communities, from Iran, Iraq and Lebanon to India, Pakistan and the many other nations where such communities have settled. The rites involve a public *majlis* or lamentation assembly at which

28   *A Companion to Muslim Cultures*

the martyrdom of Imam Husayn in 680 is recalled by ritual acts and recitations. The rites begin on the first day of the month of Muharram, with community-wide activities for 10 days, complete with black and somber décor and dress. A *zakir* performs the recitations from traditional documents that narrate the events which led to the horrific deaths of Husayn and his closest relatives and associates at Karbala (in Iraq). The five principal figures – Muhammad, Fatima, Ali, Hasan and Husayn – are woven into a religious text that evokes the spiritual and physical costs of following God's true path. Of a similar tenor, but of more specialised piety are texts like the *Secret Words of Fatima* which reflect sensitivity to Shia values, and are recited in pious gatherings for the edification of the believers.

Sufism has its own well-developed culture of evocative spirituality, where the chanting of the sacred texts of *shaykh*s past and present has a central place. This mystical practice is enlivened by poetic forms and carries an especially potent spiritual message — a personal encounter with spiritual realities. The *shaykh*s are formidable figures who fashioned an Islam of the heart and created fraternities that spread throughout the Muslim world. Their texts usually carry the signature beliefs of the *shaykh*, and constitute a kind of creedal declaration of the spiritual life as understood by the founder and his followers. Often the texts are the main bearers of meditations called *dhikr* or remembrance, which usually proceeds with stylised movements. On occasion, the meditations are verses from the Quran that are knitted together into pious figurations. In all cases, *dhikr* indicates a spiritual language that is felt to bring one closer to God, the Prophet or the spiritual founder of the order.

In a similar vein, texts of spiritual edification are associated with the Ismaili branch of the Shia. At assemblies of prayers, special *ginan*s are recited. These devotional hymns evolved in the Indian subcontinent, and hence it comes as no surprise that they have much in common with the sacred culture of Hindu pious recitals. At the same time, they are deeply influenced by Sufi spirituality both in their ideas and language. Poetic in form, they contain allusions not only to special events of history but to the spiritual role of the Imams in leading the community aright.

Visitations

Rites of journey for spiritual purposes, such as the hajj or pilgrimage to Mecca, are enshrined in the culture of Islamic practice. Indeed, this rite is among the 'pillars.' But the importance of rites of journeying grew beyond this key event. The Quran diversified the performance of the hajj to include the *umra*, which is a less formal pilgrimage that stresses a visit to the holy places of Islam – a rite that may be undertaken at any time during the year, and is less rigidly structured. Visiting the sacred sites of early Islam continues to be regarded by Muslims as having special value, and increasingly groups travel throughout the Muslim world visiting such sacred spaces every year.

Pilgrimage rites themselves have been expanded by many communities to include journeying to sanctified sites. These may include shrines across the Near East and North Africa, but also in the wider Muslim world. To take one example, the Shia Dawoodi Bohras of South Asia include a 'domestic pilgrimage' where devotion is expressed at the shrines of key spiritual figures in that tradition. In this way, a Shia sacred geography is coupled with notions of a sacred cosmology. Women, in particular, often perform this rite and it is a source of much empowerment for these devotees, to whom a kind of 'family blessing' is attached that gives them a prime role in family life and decision-making when they arrive back home.

A variation of this is the Sufi journeying each year in celebration of the birthday of the founding *shaykh*s of their orders. Devotees travel to the shrines where they are buried, not only to beseech their aid with worldly difficulties but also to refresh themselves spiritually. The visitation is felt to put the devotee in touch with the *baraka* of the spiritual figure, grace that they possessed (and still project) by virtue of the mercy of the divine. A good example is the *mawlid* of Shaykh Ahmad al-Desouki in Tanta, Egypt. Hundred of thousands of devotees come every year to petition the *shaykh*'s aid. Such practice is not restricted to any single country: the rite is carried out wherever important spiritual figures of Islam are buried, including

North Africa, Pakistan and Iran. In India and Pakistan, this festival is called *urs*.

The veneration of exemplary figures is among popular Islam's great expressions, which often makes it the target of conservative criticism. The *karamat* or spiritual gifts associated with the saintly can inspire intense religiosity. It might include seeking out the current representative of the founders to request their benediction or aid, which the orthodox regard as deviation from Islamic norms. Petitions may be made at shrines for healing, for children and for prosperity. Sometimes the journey is made to thank the *shaykh* for some benefit deemed to have been received through a past request, and it is usually accompanied by a gift given in appreciation to the order. When one has received some result of this spiritual beneficence, it signals a permanent relationship with a sacred dimension of life that often empowers the believer to live a better Islamic life. Hence the practice is connected to both the spiritual and esoteric side of Islamic tradition.

In Shia tradition, such visitations can also involve a deeper journeying – a quest for meaning in the problems of human existence and the suffering of the righteous. Drawing on the texts and stories of the members of the Prophet's family, they seek to give public and ritual expression to matters that cannot easily be resolved by reason. Why did God allow the Prophet's family to suffer as they did and permit evil forces to triumph? How are humans to understand their own chaotic lives when the exemplary figures of Islamic history came to tragic ends? The rites offer a means of consolation, in which the events of 680 become a spiritual space that is physically attached to the actual sites of catastrophes.

Gendered Piety

The focus of some practices is overwhelmingly female, largely as a matter of evolving cultural preference rather than anything 'canonical'. In many locales, for example, few women attend Friday prayers at the mosque during the official gathering at midday. Such attendance was never forbidden outright; yet historically Muslim males tended to frown upon women's presence at these

Everyday Tradition

assemblies. It was males, as representatives of their families, who performed this 'official' prayer. Time and reformist movements have had an impact on these constraints. By contrast, in more traditionalist settings, there is an insistence that male resistance to women's attendance at Friday prayers is based on orthodoxy. Modern Shia women generally tend to reject such claims.

Similarly, with regard to the wearing of the veil in its various forms, the practice originated in early Islam as a feature of upper-class values. Women were felt to be guardians of family integrity in the public domain, and the veil offered a form of protection and personal freedom for those ends. It built upon verses of the Quran addressed to the Prophet's wives, the context of which was to set them apart from other women and society at large through specific dress codes.[3] How wide the application of these codes should be has been a point of contention. Indeed, both style and functionality have also played a role in the history of this practice.

In modern Islam, veiling is very much a matter of identity. For some Shia women in Iran, unveiling has been a symbol of western rejection of Islam, as it was during the 1979 revolution. Then, the hijab became an expression of resistance to what was seen as the Shah's pro-Western stance against it. At other times, throwing off the veil became a symbol of social progress, as in Egypt and Turkey during the early 20th century. Today, where the state sets out to regulate public veiling – from France and Belgium to Iran, Saudi Arabia and Turkey – piety can become highly political.

A more private set of practices relate to networks of Islamic piety. One example is the Zaynab sisterhood formed by Iraqi Shia women, with connections as far afield as the Netherlands; they practice ritual and spiritual observances that link their own post-Saddam plight to that of the granddaughter of the Prophet.[4] Just as Zaynab was the surviving keeper of the tragic narrative of Karbala

---

[3] Leila Ahmed, *Women and Gender in Islam* (London, 2010), especially pp. 54-56.

[4] Tayba Hassan Al Khalifa Sharif, 'Sacred Narratives linking Iraqi Shiite Women across Time and Space', in Miriam Cooke and Bruce Lawrence, ed., *Muslim Networks* (Chapel Hill, NC, 2005), pp. 132-154.

32 *A Companion to Muslim Cultures*

in 680, so these Iraqi women seek solace under the guidance of a *mullaya* or religious leader. Another example is the *zar*, a healing rite of chant and trance known throughout Egypt and parts of Africa. During these rites, female religious leaders help ill devotees to connect with spiritual sources in order to receive various kinds of blessings. There are considerable regional differences in these practices, but they all utilise 'Muslim' language and ideas in the service of practices which fall outside the bounds of 'official' Islam. As such, they tend to be viewed with suspicion both by conservatives and modernists alike in Muslim societies today.

Yet another class of rites that falls outside the canon – and strongly challenged today by women's rights advocates as well as state authorities – is associated with female circumcision. It is practised in a handful of Arab, African and Asian communities, including those of Christian and pagan conviction.[5] The rite is not necessarily an identity marker the way circumcision is for a Muslim male, but loosely relates to the need for control of women's sexuality. Normally the rite is carried out by a local Muslim woman, and the ceremony signals a girl's entire submission to religious behaviours. For others, it is 'female genital mutilation', a savage practice from the darkness of *jahiliyya* that should long ago have ceased.

Sacred Objects

A further area of popular piety is associated with the use of amulets and symbols of a religious nature. There are official symbols of Muslim identity that may be associated with this, such as the writing of pious verses around doorways and in shrines and mausoleums of the pious. These serve equally as Islamic markers as well as pious expressions.

One example is the use of the rosary or prayer beads. This relates to a longstanding tradition across the Muslim world of reciting the 99 'names of God' from the Quran, based on a rosary with at least 33 beads. A fixture within Sufi circles, it is also a

---

[5] Zayn Kassam, 'Gender', in Sajoo, ed., *A Companion to Muslim Ethics*, pp. 110-112.

Everyday Tradition 33

popular form of piety for many individuals in various branches of Islam. Quiet time is filled not with idle chatter but with meditation on the various names applied to God. The splendours of God's beneficence are brought to inner consciousness by reflection and recitation. In effect, the beads are another way of piously 'remembering' the divine in everyday life.

There are other everyday practices that are associated with less reassuring powers. Consider the status of the 'evil eye' in Muslim Egypt. At birth, a child does not just come into a family but into a whole culture. The evil eye is a belief that the culture has negative powers inherent in it. These forces can be destructive to the child's wellbeing. Steps must be taken to protect that child, and those steps are the subject of local lore. Boys may be dressed as girls to throw evil portends off their tracks; girls may be protected by the hanging of verses from the Quran in tiny containers around their necks, and so on. Moreover, representations of the eye of Horus from ancient Egypt may be placed on the walls as an effective means to protect the child, especially until the child is old enough for its parents not to fear its early death.

Examples of popular practices may be expanded greatly, drawing upon local customs and traditions within Muslim cultures. Students may recite the Quran before crucial tests, or visit a local shrine for help; mothers of girls may seek out a *shaykh* who is deemed able to effect the birth of boys for their next pregnancy. A vast array of acts related to health, wellbeing, prosperity and accomplishment can be found in the multi-layered tapestry of religious belief. These acts may not technically fall within the canon, yet they give hope and sustenance in times of difficulty, and thus find a place within Muslim piety. Many such acts are related to so-called 'Prophetic medicine', a traditional set of activities and popular ideas about health and wellbeing. These grew up outside the more official health practices espoused by the caliph's court, whose more 'scientific' model was passed on to medieval European medical

---

[6] See Ahmad Dallal, 'Science, Medicine, and Technology: The Making of a Scientific Culture', in John L. Esposito, ed., *The Oxford History of Islam* (New York, 1999), pp. 155-213.

schools.[6] Rather, such popular ideas and techniques continued to serve the public because either official medicine was not available or it was too expensive. These types of traditional practices still exist throughout the Muslim world.

Conclusion

There is a far richer tradition of piety in Islam than can be captured by assertions about the 'Five Pillars'. Nor will it do to try and reduce Islam to the sharia or legal regulations. The long and fruitful interaction of Muslims with their cultural surroundings has resulted in a lived tradition that is diverse, vigorous and colourful. Obviously Shia piety is just as complex as its Sunni counterpart.

This is why the question of what is 'canonical' or 'authentic' is constantly raised: tradition is not frozen in time, but remade in small and large ways by communities of Muslims the world over. Popular piety commonly intersects with contemporary issues of identity, as we have seen in this chapter – and this is not confined to Muslim communities in Europe and North America, or for that matter even just to Muslims. It is a global phenomenon, an essential part of the journey of modernity, notably with its embrace of the secular which challenges traditional ways in which the sacred shapes identity. Hence already we see pop culture Muslim rap on the music charts; so in the future it will be interesting to study the ways that Western popular culture intersects with Islam as that religion becomes 'Western'.

All of this indicates that, from the outset, Islamic civilisation has been highly pluralist in its encounters with other cultures, whose legitimacy has found a place in various ways in Muslim practice. No single model tells us how all Muslims relate to their tradition. On the contrary, popular piety suggests that Muslims interact variously with both 'the Tradition' and their own 'local' expression of Islam. Different meanings are attached to one's faith depending on the context. Popular piety has carved out its own influential path in Muslim cultures, and its practices form a living part of Islamic tradition today.

Further Reading

Aghaie, Kamran Scot, ed. *The Women of Karbala: Ritual Performance and Symbolic Discourses in Modern Shi' i Islam*. Austin, TX, 2005.

Asani, Ali. *Ecstasy and Enlightenment: The Ismaili Devotional Literature of South Asia*. London, 2002.

Cornell, Vincent J. 'Fruit of the Tree of Knowledge: The Relationship between Faith and Practice in Islam', in John L. Esposito, ed. *The Oxford History of Islam*. New York, 1999, pp. 63–105.

Kassam, Zayn. 'Ritual Life', in Andrew Rippin, ed. *The Islamic World*. New York, 2008, pp. 191–211.

Khan, Dominique-Sila. *Crossing the Threshold: Understanding Religious Identities in South Asia*. London, 2004.

Nelson, Felicitas H. *Talismans and Amulets of the World*. New York, 2000.

Padwick, Constance E. *Muslim Devotions*. London, 1961.

Partridge, Christopher. 'Religion and Popular Culture', in Linda Woodhead, et al, ed. *Religions in the Modern World: Traditions and Transformations*. 2nd ed. London, 2009, pp. 489–521.

Schubel, Vernon James. *Religious Performance in Contemporary Islam: Shi'i Devotional Rituals in South Asia*. Columbia, SC, 1993.

Suleman, Fahmida, ed. *Word of God, Art of Man: The Qur'an and its Creative Expressions*. Oxford, 2007.

Waugh, Earle H. *The Munshidin of Egypt: Their World and their Song*. Columbia, SC, 1989.

3

Modernity: Secular and Sacred

Abdullahi An-Naim

What is the place of faith in modern Muslim societies? Living by the ethical principles and traditions that form the sharia is at the heart of Muslim identity. How does this square with the secular idea of the state, in which diverse identities and cultures co-exist? Is the presence of public religion a barrier to political modernity? This chapter will discuss the nature of the relationship among the sharia, the state and the individual Muslim today, mindful of what history tells us about the lived experience of Islamic societies. We will see how the interface of sacred and secular drives the quest for a civic pluralism that can accommodate the legitimate aspirations of all citizens.

In essence, culture has a central place in how Muslims have come to understand the sharia, as well as in the emergence of the state as the formal space that individuals and communities inhabit. The diversity not only of Muslim but of all human societies – in the sheer variety of religious, social, political and economic choices – means that the constitution of each state is expected to reflect this reality. That is why we speak of human rights as central to modern life. For Muslims, human diversity is cherished as a gift in the Quran (49:13), not merely a demographic fact to be endured. And in keeping with the spirit of each individual seeking out the truth without compulsion (2:256), it is of the essence for Muslims to live by the ethics of the sharia as a matter of *voluntary* choice.

Calls for an 'Islamic state' to enforce the sharia are consistent neither with the spirit of the sharia itself, nor with the thrust of

38   *A Companion to Muslim Cultures*

the history of Muslim societies. Certainly, Muslim-majority countries may legitimately reflect this reality in their public life. But the strongest guarantee of religious freedom for individuals and communities comes from the separation of state and religion – in other words, a secular state. This does not imply secularism on the part of *society*, which is a matter of choice in public culture, with all the safeguards of a constitution that upholds human rights. It is these safeguards that allow for a modernity in which public religion has its rightful place.

The Nature of the Sharia

As the passageway into being a Muslim, the body of ethical principles and practices that form the sharia are a constant reminder of one's commitment to tawhid, or the 'unity' of God's creation. The sharia is derived from the quest of Muslims to interpret what the Quran and the Sunna or the traditions of the Prophet Muhammad mean for them. There is certainly more to Islam than the sharia, which is only a part of the rich experience of being a Muslim.

In principle, each Muslim is personally responsible for knowing and complying with what is required of him or her. The idea of individual moral responsibility is a recurring theme in the Quran (for example, 6:164; 17:15; 35:18; 39:7; 52:21; 74:38). When faced with a challenge in applying the sharia in practice, Muslims routinely seek advice and guidance from a figure such as a theologian, a Sufi leader or an imam. Hence, the framework of a particular school or tradition (*madhhab*) is engaged, in terms of doctrine and method of reasoning. What this means is that the wisdom of the Quran and Sunna are always filtered through the many layers of the experience and practice of earlier Muslims.

The belief that the Arabic text of the Quran that we read today is the actual one delivered by the Prophet in the seventh century is based on the fact that it has since been handed down from one generation to the next. This is also true of the Sunna – with all the controversies that attend the accuracy of many of the reports about what the Prophet did and said. In general, Muslims strive for consensus (*ijma*) as the basis of what is considered

Modernity: Secular and Sacred

foundational, and how to interpret such principles. The finality of the *text* of the Quran, and of Muhammad's role as Prophet, is for Muslims a matter of such consensus.

The sharia is the outcome of a process of reasoned reflection or *ijtihad* on how those primary sources apply to specific issues.[1] This also gave rise to a body of law, the *fiqh*, derived from the ethics of the sharia. The most dynamic periods in the development of the sharia and *fiqh* were those that valued the capacity of *ijtihad* to deliver innovation and change. The early Abbasid era (after 750 CE) was exemplary. It saw the flowering of pluralist schools of thought and law, and of sophisticated modes of reasoning (*usul al-fiqh*). In addition to the four major Sunni schools – Shafii, Hanafi, Maliki and Hanbali – the main Shia school, the Jafari, also emerged at this time. A host of social and political factors shaped the growth and spread of these schools, factors that likely also contributed to the reduction in the number of schools in the Sunni tradition and what is often called a 'closing of the gate of *ijtihad*' among the Sunni schools around the 10th century. Certainly, a conservative trend took hold in the face of instability and rapid flux in the Muslim world, leading to a long period of passivity in the unfolding of the sharia.

Two constraints that were imposed by scholars early on weighed heavily on the practice of *ijtihad*. First, it could only be exercised in matters not covered by clear textual guidance (*nass qati*) in the Quran and Sunna. Second, *ijtihad* could only be exercised by a scholar who met a rigorous list of qualifications, and was prepared to act in specified ways. By and large, patriarchy also ensured that few women had any role in the practice of *ijtihad*. These are, of course, all matters of human judgement in particular settings; there is nothing sacred about them. What is sacred is the responsibility of each individual for his or her moral choices, even if the individual chooses to seek guidance from others in this regard. It is the free exercise of this responsibility that deserves to be protected.

No reason or tradition stands in the way of Muslims reaching

---

[1] For a detailed account see Wael Hallaq, *Shari'a: Theory, Practice, Transformations* (Cambridge, 2009).

40 — A Companion to Muslim Cultures

a consensus around fresh readings of the Quran and Sunna, or methods of interpreting them. These could become a part of the *fiqh* or the sharia exactly as existing readings and methods did in the past. One must, of course, have the space for informed participation and the freedom of thought and expression to make the consensus meaningful. The validity of the results is judged by whether they gather a consensus of Muslims over time.

Sharia and the State

The authority of state institutions is exercised by individuals who act in their name. Legislation and public policy reflect the views of the governors at a particular time. A decision to punish the consumption of alcohol as a *hadd* (serious) crime, for example, or banning interest on loans (*riba*), is a political choice that is informed by what the governors think is in the public interest. Such decisions are secular, and there is nothing 'automatic' about them merely because a society happens to be Muslim.

Consider the experience of the Ottoman empire in this regard, which until 1917 was the world's largest 'Muslim territory'. Its rulers, the sultans, chose to make the Hanafi legal school the principal source of sharia-based legislation in the 19th century – the first time in history that the sharia as interpreted by a single school was codified and enacted as the official law of the land, called the *Majallah*. Then, as part of the empire's modernisation (*tanzimat*), the Ottomans borrowed from European legal codes and systems of governance in the name of strengthening the state and preserving Islam. Indeed, the *Majallah* itself was opened up for some selective borrowing from other Islamic schools. The result was a pragmatic code, secular in all the decisions that went into its making and enforcement, yet with claims of legitimacy that appealed to the sharia. It survived until the establishment of the Turkish Republic in 1923, which stripped away any claims to a 'religious' badge of state legitimacy.

But the Ottoman example cast a long shadow. The mix of 'Islamic' and Western sources, coupled with a claim to sharia-based legitimacy, became a trend in the Middle East after colonial

Modernity: Secular and Sacred 41

rule. A prime example was the work of the French-educated Egyptian jurist Abd al-Razzaq al-Sanhuri (1895–1971). His approach was based on the view that the sharia could no longer be reintroduced in its totality, given the demands of modernity. Sanhuri led the drafting of the Egyptian Civil Code of 1948, the Iraqi Code of 1951, the Libyan Code of 1953, and the Kuwaiti Civil Code and Commercial law of 1960/1; all were enacted as law without public debate. Clearly, the process of drafting, legislation and enforcement was fully secular.

Yet these initiatives also exposed the sharia more than ever to governors and judges in all its complexity. This included the intricacy of principles and practices that had evolved over centuries, and the strong differences of opinion among the various schools, Sunni and Shia. Further, official practice was often at variance with that of the majority of citizens: in Egypt and Sudan, for example, the inherited Ottoman Hanafi preference sat alongside the popular preference for Shafii and Maliki law. Since modern states can only operate on officially established principles of law of *general application*, sharia principles can hardly be enacted or enforced as the law of the land without selecting from competing frameworks that the sharia itself regards as equally legitimate. An 'Islamic state' faces the same hurdle, in enforcing its preferences as official in violation of the latitude allowed by the sharia itself.

Modernity has brought other shifts that radically alter the social context of the sharia. With the rapid growth of mass literacy, traditional religious scholars (*ulama*) no longer enjoy the intellectual leadership of their communities to which they were accustomed. Ordinary Muslims can and do question traditional interpretations of the sharia. While those with relevant learning will continue to have a greater impact on how the sharia is understood, more ordinary citizens than ever now regard themselves as capable of deciding for themselves how the sharia applies to the particulars of daily life, and also to express themselves on matters of public concern.

Finally, there is the shift in the nature of the state itself. Although established under colonial rule, the European model of the state has altered the pattern of social, political and economic

42 A Companion to Muslim Cultures

relations throughout the Muslim world. By keeping this form of organisation after independence, Muslim societies have chosen to be bound by the obligations of membership in a global community of states. These include obligations about what the national constitution must provide in terms of the human rights of all citizens, men and women, and their democratic governance. They are secular political rules, but as the Azhar scholar Ali Abd al-Raziq (1888–1996) famously noted in 1925, nothing in the history of Islamic civilisations is inconsistent with their observance.[2]

Civic Pluralism

Religion competes with other life philosophies in seeking to influence individuals, communities and public policy. We see this in matters as varied as choices about education, family life (marriage and divorce to child rearing, adoption and abortion), work, migration and social life. Longstanding traditions such as the sharia can shape choices at the individual, communal and institutional levels in many ways, even where the state is neutral in this regard and does not seek to impose 'religious' law. Indeed, as noted earlier, the Islamic ideal is one where free citizens and communities make life choices that are consistent with their understanding of the ethical principles of the sharia.

For the various religious and secular actors to negotiate on public issues while maintaining a stable national life, the 'rules of the game' must be agreed upon by all parties. 'Civility' requires a constant balancing of preferences in the name of the collective good. This is only likely to happen if the rules of the game do not favour one side over the other. And this is why the neutrality of the state needs to be guaranteed in a constitution which is secular, one that allows space for the negotiation of choices, public and private, among all citizens. It is not just religious actors or frame-

---

[2] *Islam and the Principles of Government* (Cairo, 1925); excerpted as 'Message Not Government, Religion Not State', in Charles Kurzman, ed. *Liberal Islam: A Sourcebook* (Oxford, 1998), pp. 29-36.

Modernity: Secular and Sacred

43

works that can upset the need for constitutional neutrality; secular forces such as cultural nationalism have often done as well.

One example is the French legislation that prohibits Muslim girls from wearing headscarves (hijab) in schools in the name of *laïcité* (official secularism). Here, priority is given to the assimilation of immigrants into 'French' cultural citizenship, rather than to a multicultural one as in North America. In this republican version of secularism, which favours a uniform way of being French, religion is treated as a permanent threat rather than a partner with whom choices can be negotiated. The result is to cast Muslim citizens as outsiders in society, with limited access to the public institutions that should protect their free exercise of citizenship. It is ironic that the same approach has been espoused by Turkey toward citizens who wear the Muslim headscarf. In both cases, the pursuit of a cultural preference by the state, in the name of secularism, violates the pluralist neutrality in which secularism is rooted.[3]

Although a secular framework offers the best assurance of civic pluralism, its neutrality leaves it unable to provide guidance on important ethical problems that affect the lives of citizens. Indeed, that is not the business of the state. Secular *philosophies* (like religious ones) can have plenty to say about ethical problems, but it is not for the state to embrace particular philosophies. For many believers, the commitment to a secular civic pluralism will be sought in faith traditions; there is certainly plenty of support in Islam on this score. Equal citizenship for non-Muslims, for example, is far more likely to be achieved with the aid of justifications rooted within Islam.

The primary task of a secular framework, then, is to uphold the separation of religion and state in pursuit of a pluralist civic space, one that is inclusive of all its citizens. A secularism that forces a choice between faith and citizenship loses its claim to

---

[3] Nilüfer Göle, 'Forbidden Modernities: Islam in Public', pp. 119-136, and Eva Schubert, 'Modern Citizenship, Multiple Identities', pp. 161-182, in Amyn B. Sajoo, ed., *Muslim Modernities: Expressions of the Civil Imagination* (London, 2008).

44 *A Companion to Muslim Cultures*

democratic governance. The former Soviet Union provides a classic example of the failure of a state-sponsored theology – atheism – to survive without the use of force. After its demise, the former Soviet republics, including Russia, have seen a massive resurgence in both Christian and Muslim affiliation.

Civic pluralism, in other words, cannot be about taking religion out of public life. Politics and faith do not operate in distinct realms. When Muslim societies as well as non-Muslim ones face issues of public policy and private choice, religious faith must typically contend with secular reasons on the way to a decision. This puts a premium on *informed* choice, in religious and secular matters alike. An informed citizenry is surely more likely to exist where it has access to pluralist sources of knowledge and modes of applying them. The interface of secular and religious, then, is a richer field than either in isolation for the flourishing of 'civic reason'.

Ultimately, there is no escaping the mutual dependence of the roles of religious authority and autonomy on the one hand, and of the political authority and legal powers of the state on the other. Religious communities need the cooperation of the state in order to further their own mission. Indeed, the more organised and successful a religious community, the more likely it is to compete with the state for influence over the aspects of public policy, including the implications for electoral choices. Charitable donations to such communities are often exempted from taxes by the state. The state also acts as the arbiter in conflicts between religious groups, and sometimes within them: they have recourse to the rule of law.

But the state will also seek ways of limiting how 'religious' influence is exercised. It may do so through control of funding for the upkeep of religious places or schools. It may, as in most Muslim states, disallow political parties to be formed on the basis of religious affiliations. Claims for charitable tax exemptions can be conditioned on staying away from political activity. From Nigeria, Egypt and Turkey to Pakistan, Malaysia and Indonesia, the relationship between religious and state institutions is an ongoing reality. Where religious actors entirely lose

Modernity: Secular and Sacred 45

their autonomy from the state, as happened for a long period in Turkey and Iraq, secularism becomes an ideology whose democratic legitimacy is undercut. No less troubling, of course, is the collusion between state and religion, as in Saudi Arabia, where the result is a 'political Islam'. Another version of political Islam has resulted in the triumph of religion over the state in Iran. All these societies are in flux as various models of civic life are tested – much as they were for centuries in the West. The contests at hand are part of a global narrative of political evolution, a very secular reality.

Faith and Citizenship

Whatever one may think of its legacy, European colonialism and its aftermath have drastically altered the basis and the nature of political and social organisation within and among the 'territorial states' where all Muslims live. For the modern state and its institutions penetrate and shape the lives of citizens in a thoroughgoing way, in private and public matters alike. And this puts citizenship at the very core of the individual's relationship to society and the state, including the freedom and space to practice one's faith.

'Citizenship' here refers to one's membership in the political community of a territorial state, with all the rights and responsibilities that go with it. It exists alongside other ties and identities that relate to professional, religious, social and political memberships. Indeed, these will often shape how one treats citizenship. But what is special about being a citizen is that it 'frames' all those other memberships, to which it gives us access in ways that we constantly seek to make meaningful. Thus for a Muslim to perform the pilgrimage (hajj) to Mecca, she/he will require a visa issued by the government of Saudi Arabia – which involves one's status as the citizen of another country. The exception would be if I lived in Saudi Arabia, which reinforces the point that belonging to a territorial state is central to all the choices in modern life.

Today, citizenship is very much about civic equality and access

46 A Companion to Muslim Cultures

to participation in public life.[4] This reflects a long (and ongoing) global quest for effective inclusion, notably on the part of various minorities and women. Historically, inclusion was also the driving force in the emergence of the Muslim umma, which broke out of the confines of tribe, clan, class and gender: anyone could join the community of believers as an equal. There was a civic dimension to this, in that all who committed themselves to the Medina constitution (c.622 CE) were deemed members of a single community.

Religious minorities in the Muslim tradition were deemed protected or *dhimma*, a status that recognised Christians and Jews as part of the Abrahamic family which included Muslims. The state ruled by Muslims assured the members of a *dhimmi* community security of their persons and property, the freedom to practise their religion and to govern their communal affairs. In exchange, that community gave its allegiance to the state, and paid a special tax (*jizya*). The precise terms of each *dhimma* compact could vary according to context, as the early Muslim umma grew into a multitude of domains covering numerous faith traditions. Often, the status of *dhimma* was extended to 'non-Abrahamic' communities, and on occasion, *dhimmi*s were treated as if they were part of the Muslim community.

When considered in its proper historical context, the *dhimma* system compared favourably to any other at the time. True, there were pragmatic merits to this system as a mode of governance; yet the sharia and *fiqh* also invested it with moral meaning, in the pluralist spirit of the Revelation. Christian domains could hardly make the same claim, as European travellers often noted in the Middle Ages.[5]

Yet this scheme came to be frozen in time as part of the 'tradi-

---

[4] As set forth in the *International Covenant on Civil and Political Rights*, adopted by the United Nations in 1966; virtually all Muslim states are party to this treaty.

[5] See, for example, Maria Rosa Menocal, *The Ornament of the World: How Muslims, Jews, and Christians Created a Culture of Tolerance in Medieval Spain* (Boston, 2002).

Modernity: Secular and Sacred 47

tion' in many parts of the Muslim world. What was once intended to be inclusive and humane gradually fell out of step with the political evolution of the state, where membership could not be tied to religion. For this would violate the universal tenet of non-discrimination, a cornerstone of human rights law. In effect, equal and participatory citizenship implies the constitutional separation of the state and religion.

Two examples serve to show how traditional civic membership has adapted to modern secular citizenship, even as religion continues to have a vital place in the public domain.[6] Let us begin with India, which is host to the world's largest Muslim minority – one which was part of the ruling class for many centuries in the Indian subcontinent. With their own diverse origins (Afghan-Turkic, Arab, Persian and various 'indigenous' ethnicities), India's Muslims gradually evolved traditions of toleration and coexistence that complemented Hindu traditions in this regard. Yet membership in society was less about equal citizenship than peaceful accommodation, usually involving feudal lords and other elite groups that were Hindu. Indeed, citizenship as we know it existed nowhere in the Middle Ages; empires everywhere grappled with 'managing' co-existence.

Under the Mughal emperor Akbar (1542–1605), the system of state administration came to include all the various civic groups and interests – though they had to fit into a hierarchy which privileged Muslims. Eventually, the flourishing civic life of the Mughal empire fell victim to civil wars, regional invasions and stagnation, even before the start of the British colonial conquest in the 18th century. Efforts to halt the colonial advance through strands of 'political Islam' (a sharia state, jihad, and so on) such as those led by Shah Wali Allah (1703–1772), Sayyid Ahmad Barelwi (1786–1831), Hajji Shariat Allah (1781–1840) and Hajji Muhsin (1819–1862) all failed. With the British prevailing as rulers, Muslim leaders like Sayyid Ahmad Khan (1817–1898) encouraged a

---

[6] For a more detailed discussion of these examples, see Abdullahi An-Naim, *Islam and the Secular State: Negotiating the Future of Shari'a* (Cambridge, MS, 2008), chapters 4 (India) and 5 (Turkey).

48 *A Companion to Muslim Cultures*

co-operative attitude toward the new political and social regime as the best route to modernity. But this was at odds with how Khan saw the role of popular institutions and a genuinely equal citizenship. At the same time, Hindu elites were resentful of their Muslim counterparts, especially with the fresh legacy of Mughal rule and the old hierarchy of 'citizenship'. These tensions became a precursor to the politics of the struggle for independence that culminated in the partition of India and Pakistan in 1947.

India has since evolved a formal commitment to equal citizenship under a constitution which upholds a firm separation of state and religion. In a country with a large Hindu majority but also substantial minorities of Buddhists, Sikhs, Christians and Muslims (and sub-minorities of Hindus), a secular framework of governance and citizenship is clearly sensible. India's version of secularism has not excluded religion from public life, in which Islam and Muslims play a visible role. The constitution guarantees the right of minorities to manage their religious institutions, and to equal treatment by the state in granting them aid.

But the *practice* of equal citizenship, with the assurance of access without discrimination to public institutions, has eluded India's Muslims. In the aftermath of several episodes of serious communal violence directed at Muslim citizens, a public commission of inquiry was asked in 2005 to report on the social, economic and educational status of this community of well over 100 million (just over 10 per cent of the national population). The report of the commission, chaired by the eminent judge Rajinder Sachar, was sobering in its portrayal of how unequal India's Muslims were in their access to employment, health and educational institutions; overwhelmingly, they were among the poorest Indians.[7]

While India is to be commended for taking the Sachar report's findings seriously, a key lesson has been the shift in the neutrality of the state over the years.[8] In 1949, when communal conflict

---

[7] Text and follow-up at http://minorityaffairs.gov.in/sachar

[8] See Subrata K. Mitra, 'Desecularising the State: Religion and Politics in India after Independence', *Comparative Studies in Society and History*, 33 (1991), pp. 755-777.

Modernity: Secular and Sacred 49

flared over the 16th century Babri Masjid in Ayodhya, which is also a revered site for Hindus, the state successfully defused the tensions. But it failed to do so in 1992, when despite assurances to the Supreme Court of India, politicians and religious leaders incited Hindus to destroy the Masjid; Muslims were the majority of the thousands killed.

Earlier, in a very different episode, a 62-year old Muslim woman, Shah Bano, had sought a judicial order of maintenance against her divorced husband. She was ultimately able to elicit this from the Supreme Court as a statutory right of all citizens – though the court also sought to justify this on the basis of Quranic and Sunna traditions. The Muslim community was split on the merits of the judgement. In the face of agitation by some Muslim organisations, parliament passed the Muslim Women (Protection of Rights on Divorce) Act of 1986, which took away the right of maintenance for Muslim women, except during the *idda* (waiting period) of four months in sharia tradition.

The Ayodhya and Shah Bano episodes speak to the cost of abandoning the neutrality of the state in matters of faith. Hindu nationalists capitalised on the 1986 legislation by rousing public sentiment against Muslim influence on the state (which on the evidence of the Sachar report was sadly lacking), while the fall of the Babri Masjid came close to triggering a civil war. It is true that communal identity is an important aspect of civil life in much of the world, and India is no exception. But it cannot trump equal citizenship as the basis of constitutional governance. Where the state fails to defend it, the prospects for civic pluralism are squandered.

There are also lessons about state neutrality in our second example, that of Turkey in its emergence from the Ottoman empire. Like Akbar's India, the Ottomans evolved a tolerant system of governing their diverse minorities as *millet*s (autonomous communities), a far-reaching innovation from the hierarchy of the *dhimmi* system. In the face of European and then Arab nationalism, as well as pressures from rival empires, the autonomy of the *millet*s (covering Armenian, Jewish, Syrian Orthodox and a host of Muslim communities) progressed rapidly in the modern period. The reform

A Companion to Muslim Cultures

(*tanzimat*) decree of 1839 marked the official affirmation of the legal equality of all non-Muslim and Muslim subjects of the sultan. An 1856 decree abolished the traditional tax on non-Muslims (*jizya*), and disallowed any derogatory reference to minority communities. When the empire yielded to the Turkish republic under Kemal Atatürk, the full equality of all citizens was enshrined in the 1926 constitution.

The Kemalist secular constitution soon became a model across the Muslim world as a template for political modernity, including gender equality. But it had its own tensions. The Turkish state took it upon itself to administer all the country's mosques and imams (who became salaried civil servants); another official agency was placed in charge of religious charitable foundations (*waqfs*). All religious education and charitable activities were to treat secularism as a first principle under the watchful eye of the state. Yet the country's Alevi and Shia Muslims were taught the Sunni Islam of the majority. 'Designated' minorities such as Armenian and Greek Orthodox Christians and Jews enjoyed autonomy; but other Christian denominations, and groups such as the Bahais and Yezidis have not been recognised. Sufi orders have no official standing either, though the rules have been relaxed since the early Kemalist ban on them.

Turkey's bid for membership in the European Union has induced a loosening of the state's control on some aspects of religious status and practice, but not in the matter of women's headscarves in public institutions. Indeed, the European Court of Human Rights upheld the ban in its 2005 ruling in Leyla Şahin v. Turkey, on the basis that secularism would otherwise be compromised. Yet other secular states have not found such a ban to be necessary. The court was less sympathetic to the state's controlling ways in its 2008 ruling in Zengin v. Turkey, where the mandatory teaching of Sunni Islam to Alevis was challenged. Such an approach was found to be a violation of the religious freedom and pluralism to which all citizens were entitled. Secularism can, of course, become a doctrine as rigid and intolerant as a hardline version of any religion. To insist that there is only one way to be a citizen of Turkey, defined by the Kemalist ethos, simply leaves out in the name of

Modernity: Secular and Sacred 51

secularism those whose piety or ethnicity or faith is outside the mainstream. Kurds, Alevis and women wearing the hijab pose a test to Turkey's professed ideals as a modern Muslim society. Indeed, the stakes are high in this regard beyond its borders, for Turkey is still looked upon widely as a leading model of governance across the Muslim world.[9] On a personal level, during my visit to launch a book in Indonesia, which has the world's largest Muslim population, Turkey's record was invoked at each of five different events.

And the example of India as a non-western model of growing global status is no less vital.

Concluding Reflections: In Search of Cultural Legitimacy

Whether it is the political culture that shapes the institutions of governance, or the wider social culture in which individual and collective lives intersect, it is in this domain that societies make the religious and secular choices that form their identities. Hence the remarkable diversity of Muslim societies not only in their political and economic lives but also in how they understand and practice Islam. Muslim communities in the Indian subcontinent have more in common with Hindu or Sikh ones than with Muslims in Bosnia or Senegal. Religion does not determine identity – and neither religion nor identity is fixed in the changing domain of culture.

This puts an extremely high premium on the kind of cultural space that a society offers. Does it value diversity in language, the interpretation of faith and of collective memories? Are individual and communal choices in this regard protected by the frameworks of civility and law, and is there fair access to them for all in society? How does the cultural space allow for accountability of the governors as well as of other public, and private, actors? Since these elements are central to all societies, there is a shared perspective

---

[9] On a personal level, during my visit to launch a book in Indonesia, which has the world's largest Muslim population, Turkey's record was invoked at each of five different events.

52   *A Companion to Muslim Cultures*

on the modern framework in which they can thrive: secular constitutional government, civic pluralism and equal citizenship.

Yet paper-guarantees alone of rights and freedoms are worth little. What is it that gives real meaning to constitutions and citizenship? Experience tells us that it is the existence of civil society which makes the difference. It is here that citizens can foster the public good, hold governors accountable, and participate in the making of peaceful social change. All this requires both the state and civil society to uphold the rule of law, which implies respect for an independent judiciary. But how is the *trust* that makes for such civil give-and-take to be established, especially if it has been lacking in the past? This is often a major challenge for societies in postcolonial Asia and Africa, where many years of authoritarian culture have eroded trust between governors and the governed.

In Muslim societies, it is often non-secular actors such as imams, sharia-related bodies and religious fraternities that enjoy the trust of individuals and communities. This makes them essential partners in the making of political modernity alongside secular actors. Indeed, secularism is commonly linked in public memory with the burdens of European colonialism; it needs new legitimacy to take root as a positive influence. Without the help of religious actors, secularism would have to be imposed – hardly the route to legitimacy.

Once again, it is the domain of culture where such legitimacy is fostered. A culturally legitimate value or practice has the respect of communities and societies because it meets their needs or purposes in life. The giving of alms (*zakat*) and of endowments (*waqf*), for example, enjoys such legitimacy among Muslims: they are tied to values of equity and generosity which are not only universal but also deeply *localised* in diverse communities. Legitimacy needs credible *insiders* to the culture to validate choices, in ways that are meaningful locally. *Zakat* and *waqf* in Mali, Tunisia, Qatar and Malaysia – societies so varied in their social organisation – require trust to be channelled through indigenous actors and processes. Their credibility is necessary for the practices to thrive locally.

In this vein, ideals like constitutionalism and civic pluralism must find cultural legitimacy in each locality, no matter how high their global ranking as 'pillars of modernity'. This is not to say that the outside world has no part to play. Rather, it is to recognise that unless social change is to be forced upon a society, in which case legitimacy will be elusive, positive influence from the outside is best channelled through support for positive local trends and movements. Even where global standards have been agreed upon, local legitimacy is essential.[10]

The cost of imposing what is locally seen as a foreign political agenda was evident in post-September 11 Iraq. Only gradually did the country's western rulers come to appreciate the folly of ignoring domestic realities, in which a new order must take root. Whether the lessons learned there will be applied sensibly in post-Taliban Afghanistan remains to be seen. But the evidence in both cases also shows that social and political culture is malleable. The status of minorities, women and of public religion have all been negotiable, not captive to what a dominant group claims is 'the Islamic way' as a mask for mere self-interest.

Indonesia's recent history also shows the extent to which secular and religious choices are filtered through the changing realities of public culture. As with Turkey, secularism became an authoritarian state ideology in post-independence Indonesia under Sukarno (1945–1967) and Suharto (1967–1998). There were positive aspects to the secularist doctrine of *pancasila*, which was made part of the constitution from the outset. *Pancasila* sought to honour the diversity of a far-flung archipelago with scores of languages and ethnicities, and to anchor an inclusive citizenship.[11] Yet as part of an official ideology, it also often served as a tool of political and social control.

Pluralist Muslim actors like Nurcolish Madjid and Abdurrahman

---

[10] Richard Falk, 'Cultural Foundations for the International Protection of Human Rights', in Abdullahi An-Naim, ed. *Human Rights in Cross-Cultural Perspectives* (Philadelphia, 1992), pp. 44-64.

[11] An-Naim, 'Indonesia: Diversity and Pluralism', in *Islam and the Secular State*, pp. 259-260. The five formal principles of *pancasila* are humanism, nationalism, democracy, social justice and monotheism.

54   *A Companion to Muslim Cultures*

Wahid – the latter serving as president from 1999 to 2001 – worked hard to persuade Indonesians to adopt aspects of the secular legacy as part of their new democratic culture. Some have called for the adoption of Islam as a 'total way of life', and cast 'secularism' as the arch enemy. But for Madjid and his colleagues, a secular public life is not about excluding Islam at all; rather, it avoids imposing it through the machinery of the state.[12] The struggle to legitimise this view occurs today in a cultural space that is relatively open, amid the waves of political Islam since September 11.

From Central Asia to West Africa and the diaspora in the West, Muslim communities are rethinking the future of the sharia, and its relationship with politics. Despite the claims of radical actors, it is obvious to most Muslims that the state best serves this process by widening the space for it. In the final analysis, this vindicates the central message of the sharia itself – and indeed of the Quran – that ethical responsibility rests with the individual alone. It is not a responsibility that can or should be passed on to the state, with its very worldly concerns in a globalised age. The great diversity of societies today puts the onus on the state to ensure that it upholds the equal dignity of all faith traditions within its borders; this would also be in keeping with Islam's pluralist spirit.

Further Reading

Akbarzadeh, Shahram and Benjamin MacQueen, ed. *Islam and Human Rights in Practice: Perspectives across the Ummah.* London and New York, 2008.

An-Naim, Abdullahi. *Islam and the Secular State: Negotiating the Future of Shari'a.* Cambridge, MS, 2008.

Bhargava, Rajeev, ed. *Secularism and its Critics.* Oxford, 1998.

Bremer, Louis, ed. *Muslim Identity and Social Change in Sub-Saharan Africa.* Bloomington, IN, 1993.

---

[12] Robert Hefner, 'Varieties of Muslim Politics: Civil versus Statist Islam', in F. Jabali and J. Makruf, ed., *Islam in Indonesia: Islamic Studies and Social Transformation* (Montreal, 2002), pp. 36-151.

Modernity: Secular and Sacred

Feldman, Noah. *The Fall and Rise of the Islamic State.* Princeton, NJ, 2008.

Hashmi, Sohail H., ed. *Islamic Political Ethics: Civil Society, Pluralism, and Conflict.* Princeton, NJ, 2002.

Mandaville, Peter. *Global Political Islam.* London and New York, 2007.

Mir-Hosseini, Ziba and Richard Tapper. *Islam and Democracy in Iran.* London, 2006.

Sachedina, Abdulaziz. *The Islamic Roots of Democratic Pluralism.* Oxford, 2001.

Sajoo, Amyn B. ed. *Civil Society in the Muslim World: Contemporary Perspectives.* London, 2002.

Sen, Amartya. 'Religious Affiliations in Muslim History', in *Identity and Violence: The Illusion of Destiny.* New York, 2006, pp. 59–83.

Yavuz, Hakan and John L. Esposito, ed. *Turkish Islam and the Secular State.* Syracuse, NY, 2003.

4

Spiritual Life

Carl W. Ernst

Spirituality is often contrasted with religion as being more personal, less authoritative, and definitely more interesting. Parallel to spirituality is mysticism. St. Teresa of Avila and Meister Eckhart are exemplars of both spirituality and mysticism: their meditations and experiences are voiced in poetry and prose of extraordinary quality. These medieval Christians were not 'independent' mystics but belonged to highly organised and disciplined monastic orders firmly under church authority.

Islam's mysticism is widely equated with Sufism, which has its own institutional history. 'Sufi' is from the Arabic word for wool (*suf*), the rough garment of ascetics and prophets in the Near East, symbolising self-denial. Sufism's most popular exemplar today is the classical Persian poet Jalal al-Din Rumi (1207–1273), who is often represented as someone who transcended all religions. Sufi spiritual circles used a religious vocabulary based almost entirely on Arabic and Islamic sources. Yet with the coming of modernity, Muslim reformist thinkers and movements saw Sufism as something apart from Islam, an unwelcome innovation and intrusion that stood in the way of rationalist change. This mirrored the view of European scholars who also thought that Sufism was separated at birth from Islam – but saw Sufism as a positive force. In fact, for most of Islamic history, this form of spirituality and mystical practice has been a major feature of Muslim societies.

58   *A Companion to Muslim Cultures*

Beginnings

Muslim spiritual life starts with the Quran and the Prophet Muhammad, inextricably linked with each other from the outset. As an example, one may cite the famous Quranic passage on 'the Night of Power' (*laylat al-qadr*), regarded as the night on which the revelation of the Quran was delivered to the Prophet:

> Truly We caused it to descend on the Night of Power.
> And what shall inform you of the Night of Power?
> The Night of Power is better than a thousand months.
> On it descended the angels, and the Spirit,
> With the permission of their Lord, with every command.
> It is peace, until the break of day (97:1–5).

The act of revelation is shown as the descent of the Spirit, which elicits a corresponding ascent on the part of the Prophet through the heavens to meet God. This dialectic of divine presence and prophetic ascent became the model of spiritual experience for later generations of Muslims. Muhammad in particular is the exemplar of spirituality for Sufis, who strive to imitate him both in his outward religious practice and in his inner spiritual states. His oft-quoted saying, 'I was sent to perfect good character', affirms his role as a guide. Sufis came to view Muhammad as the being of light whose mission was fully universal.

Joined to the basis of mystical experience was the notion of spiritual community, which the Sufis trace back to the 'People of the Bench', a group of Muslims in the early Medina community whose only home was a portico in the mosque. They stand as the first example of organised spiritual life based on a community that shared everything. The earliest Sufi circles formed around individuals of intense piety who brought an ascetic impulse to their meditation upon the Quran. This turn away from worldly enticements was significant at a time when the early Arab empire enjoyed an unparalleled concentration of wealth and power. Early figures like Hasan al-Basri (642–728) had a major effect on their contemporaries, through public preaching and through their writ-

Spiritual Life 59

ings. They drew attention to the need for psychological introspection and moral analysis as part of obedience to the commands of God. These leaders formed relations with followers and associates that were informal and highly personal, but they were initially known as ascetics and devotees; the term Sufi did not come into general use until about the year 800.

The outstanding Sufi leaders of the ninth and 10th centuries, such as Abu Yazid al-Bistami and Junayd al-Baghdadi, later came to be regarded as the central organisers of the Sufi movement. The growth of this movement led to the development of a biographical and historical account of Sufism, in which early ascetics and pious leaders were viewed as a chain of masters and disciples, who had safeguarded and transmitted a mystical knowledge that had originated with the Prophet. The early theorists of Sufism had described it as parallel to the standard Islamic religious sciences, to which it added the internal knowledge of divine realities. By the 14th century, leading scholars like Ibn Khaldun acknowledged Sufism as an integral part of religious knowledge. The spiritual practices of this movement were not, however, carried out by isolated individuals in a spontaneous and unconnected fashion. There was a gradual accumulation of shared knowledge and practice over centuries by large numbers of people who committed themselves to intensifying and internalising their relationship with God and the Prophet. It is this collective historical tradition that we describe by the name of Sufism.

Shia Spirituality

Sufism was not the only form of spiritual expression among Muslims. Philosophy, though pursued by a relatively small number of specialists, was an important resource for reflection on theology and prophecy. The mystical tendencies of Greek philosophers like Plotinus found their echo in the meditations and speculations of Muslim philosophers such as Ibn Sina (c.980–1037), Suhrawardi (1097–1168) and Mulla Sadra (c.1571–1641). A much more extensive form of Muslim spirituality took form in the various Shia movements of the early Islamic centuries. At its heart, the Sunni-Shia debate over

60 *A Companion to Muslim Cultures*

the succession to the Prophet was about the spiritual basis of authority over the community of Muslims.

What distinguished the Shia was the conviction that Muhammad had clearly bequeathed his authority to his cousin and son-in-law Ali. Eventually, Ali was to gain universal recognition as the fourth caliph, though the Umayyad family (from the old Meccan aristocracy) opposed him – and after his assassination turned the caliphate into a royal Umayyad dynasty. The opposition between the rightful religious leader (Imam) of the community and the de facto ruling caliph became a central tenet in the historical development of Shia Islam. The Imams descended from Ali and his early successors were figures widely renowned for their piety. Yet they frequently spent their lives in virtual captivity under the caliphs, who for the Shia were nothing more than military or political commanders.

There are several major branches among the Shia, for whom the Imams are the rightful successors of the Prophet; they have diverged mostly over questions of succession to the office of the Imam. These include the Twelver Shia, who believe in twelve Imams beginning with Ali, and predominate in Iran;[1] the Nizari Ismailis who are mainly in Central and South Asia, with significant communities across the Middle East, Europe and North America, and whose present Imam, the Aga Khan, is the 49th hereditary successor to the Prophet in this lineage;[2] and the Dawoodi Bohras, a community of perhaps one million people centred in western India, whose present leader, Syedna Mohammed Burhanuddin, is the 52nd successor to the Fatimid Caliph-Imam al-Amir (d. 1124) and his son al-Tayyib in this tradition.[3] Other branches among

---

[1] The historical persecution and suffering of the Imams has a particular place in Twelver Shia theology, giving rise to rituals of lamentation that recall the redemptive role of that suffering – not unlike the Christian view of the suffering of Jesus. Indeed, the 12th Imam, al-Mahdi (b. 869), is believed to have gone into occultation (hidden by the divine) and will return to redeem mankind.

[2] The classic account is Farhad Daftary, *The Ismā'īlīs: Their History and Doctrines* (Cambridge, 1990; 2nd ed., Cambridge, 2007).

[3] A fine recent study is Jonah Blank, *Mullahs on the Mainframe: Islam and Modernity among the Daudi Bohras* (Chicago, 2001).

the Shia include the Zaydis, the Nusayris, otherwise known as Alevis, mainly in Turkey and Syria, and the Druze of Lebanon and Israel.

Central to the vision of Shia Islam is the Imam as a figure endowed with exalted wisdom and authority. As remarked previously, it is a basic tenet here that God will not deny the grace of divine guidance to humanity. The finality of Muhammad's prophethood is a given; there is at the same time an ongoing need for guidance as a logical and existential reality. It is the Imams who fulfil that need for continuing aid, and their sayings form a supplementary body of hadith. The prayers, writings and speeches attributed to Ali, compiled in the 10th century under the title *Nahj al-balagha* (*Peak of Eloquence*) are a vital resource. Shia Muslims also regard Fatima, the Prophet's daughter and Ali's spouse, with reverence; she is said to have been created, like the Imams, from a primordial light, and her life filled with extraordinary events. Scholars have compared her role to the position of the Virgin Mary for Roman Catholics.[4]

The logic of spiritual mediation calls for some comment, because of the tremendous success of Protestantism in levelling the notion of spiritual hierarchies and elites. While Catholic and Orthodox Christians still accept the idea that God can single out saints and endow them with extraordinary grace, Protestants insist that all human beings have equal access to God. On the other hand, sainthood demands an appreciation of the idea that some people can be closer to God than others. They are as it were spiritual athletes, who through a combination of effort and divine grace have achieved special status. To put it another way, there are keepers of the gate on the path to the inner sanctum. The strength of the personal relationships that many Muslims feel with the Imams and saints is certainly remarkable.

Just as the Protestant movement in England sought to destroy the Catholic monasteries and shrines, so Islam's puritanical 'reformers' undertook a campaign against the tombs of saints and

---

[4] See Mohammad Ali Amir-Moezzi and Jean Calmard, 'Fatema', *Encyclopaedia Iranica* (Costa Mesa, CA, 1999).

62   *A Companion to Muslim Cultures*

Imams where reverence is shown for their spiritual authority. In 1801, the forces of the movement founded by Abd al-Wahhab (1703–1792) raided Iraq and destroyed the dome of the tomb of Imam Husayn in Karbala. Over a century later, a massive demolition ensued of all the tombs in Medina, particularly the tombs of Imams and members of the family of Muhammad. By some accounts, consideration was given to razing the tomb of the Prophet himself, but the structure was preserved as part of the original mosque of Medina. While the disagreement over intercession and mediation is a serious one, there are likely political aspects to it. The shrines of both Shia Imams and Sufi saints were centres of power and wealth, linked to income derived from pious donations as well as land taxation. Their eradication was a potent symbol of the extension of local authority over all Muslims in the sacred domains of Arabia.

Later Sufism

In the maturing of Sufism, one important institutional feature was the tomb of a 'Friend of God', as Sufi manuals described saintly figures; these tombs became a focus of local pilgrimage. Sainthood here took as its model the sanctity of Imams in Shia Islam. Saintly figures – *shaykh*s and *pir*s – were spiritual supports of our world, men and women under God's grace. Even if direct guidance from such figures was rarely obtained during their lifetime, there was nothing to prevent people of all classes from seeking aid after their demise. Such *shaykh*s and *pir*s 'lived on' as intercessors on behalf of the devotees.

The tombs of many Sufi saints were typically erected at or near their homes. In Islamic legal tradition, ownership and maintenance of the tombs fell to family members and descendants, who may or may not have had any spiritual aspirations. In later generations, the devotion of pilgrims supported a class of hereditary custodians who were in charge of the upkeep of the tomb-shrines, which could include a hospice where Sufi teaching took place, and other institutions such as mosques, religious academies or open kitchens. Increasingly, the tomb became an independent

Spiritual Life

institution, in some cases serving as the centre of a massive pilgrimage at the annual festival of the saint. These festivals were variously described as the saint's birthday (*mawlid*) in the Mediterranean region, or 'wedding' (*urs*) in Iran and India where the saint's death anniversary was observed as the soul's union with God. Tombs of especially popular saints often came to be surrounded by royal burial grounds: kings and members of the nobility would erect their own tombs to gain a borrowed holiness or to benefit in the afterlife from the devotion of pilgrims. Examples of this kind of necropolis include the shrines of Khuldabad and Gulbarga in the Indian Deccan, Tatta in Pakistan and the many graveyards of Cairo.

Often the tombs and hospices became centres for poetry and music. One regularly hears the Arabic poetry of Ibn al-Farid (c.1181–1235) before mass audiences at his tomb in Cairo, notably at his annual festival. India's Chishti shrines are centres for *qawwali*, a colourful recital of musical religious poetry. At major festivals across South Asia, such as that of Baba Farid (c.1173–1266) in Pakistan, dozens of singers compete for the honour of reciting at the saint's tomb, mixing Persian lyrics with Punjabi, Sindhi, Hindi and other languages. Distinctive traditions emerged in Turkish shrines and hospices, with styles different from that of the courts. A classic example was the measured dance of the Mevlevi Sufis or 'whirling dervishes', very much alive to this day. In North Africa, other distinctive styles developed that used ancient Greek ideas of the four humours to effect healing, based on the bodily 'sympathies' of certain musical modes. In West Africa, the Senegalese order of the Mouridiyya has developed a strong tradition of devotional praise, which in turn has influenced popular music through performers like Youssou N'Dour. The Mouridiyya also use visual arts to engage their devotees.

The decisive institution in the making of Sufism, however, was the establishment of 'orders'. While the comparison with monastic Christian orders such as the Dominicans and Franciscans is tempting, Sufi orders are quite different. They do not observe celibacy and are less centralised in their structure, with a more fluid hierarchy. As well, they originated in a less formal fashion.

64   *A Companion to Muslim Cultures*

A number of outstanding personalities of the 12th and 13th centuries lent their names to associations which evolved distinct spiritual 'ways' or *tariqa*s, including special formulations of the names of God for meditative repetition (*dhikr*).

Each of these associations became known as a *tariqa* – or indeed as a 'chain' (*silsila*) in which masters and disciples were the links. The chains were traced back in time, always ending with the Prophet Muhammad, usually through Ali. There are parallel chains that include the early Shia Imams, who are commonly revered in Sufi circles even if their orientation is Sunni. An interesting variation occurs with the Naqshbandi order, which reaches the Prophet through Abu Bakr as his first caliphal successor (r.632–634), preserving an anti-Shi'i tonality that is unusual in Sufism. Still, the Naqshbandi include the eighth of the Twelve Shia Imams in their lineage.

The major religious impact of the Sufi orders was to popularise their spirituality on a mass scale. What had earlier been a 'private' movement was now made available to a wider public, which could partake in instruction through recitation of the names of God, in the circulation of accounts of holy lives and in shrine rituals. Initiation rituals took place in which the master's presentation of articles such as a dervish cloak, hat or staff would signify the disciple's admission. A common feature was the requirement that the disciple copy out by hand the genealogical tree of the order, linking the disciple to the entire chain of masters back to the Prophet. Interestingly, the practice of multiple initiations took hold from the 15th century, so individual Sufis could receive instruction in the ways of several different orders while maintaining a primary allegiance to one.

Sufi orders like the Qadiriyya (named after Abd al-Qadir Jilani, 1071–1166) are spread across the Islamic lands from North Africa to Southeast Asia. Others are more regional, like the North African Shadhiliyya (named after Abu al-Hasan al-Shadhili, 1196–1258) and the South Asian Chishtiyya (named after Muin al-Din Chishti, c.1141–1236). Some are known for distinctive practices, such as the Rifaiyya's loud recitation of the *dhikr,* in contrast to the Naqshbandiyya's silent one. Sufi leaders such as the early Chishti

Spiritual Life 65

masters sought to keep politics at arm's length and advised their followers to refuse offers of land endowment. Some Sufi masters showed their disdain of the material world by refusing to entertain rulers or visit them at court.

Yet other orders have a history of association with political life. The Suhrawardiyya and the Naqshbandiyya in India and Iran felt it important to influence rulers in the proper religious direction, while the Bektashiyya had strong links to the elite Ottoman troops known as the Janissaries. When much of the Islamic world fell under European domination in the 19th century, Sufi institutions played varied roles. Hereditary custodians of Sufi shrines in places like the Indian Punjab were treated as important local landlords by colonial officials, and were further entrenched as political leaders by British patronage. Ironically, the cooperation of these Sufi leaders later became an essential part of the successful movement for independence from Britain. Similarly, the Senegalese Muridiyya became heavily involved in peanut cultivation, with the support of French colonial authorities, and emerged in the postcolonial order as a major social institution. With the overthrow of traditional elites by European conquest, Sufi orders in some regions remained the only surviving Islamic social structures and furnished leadership for anticolonial struggles in Algeria, the Caucasus, China and Libya. French administrators in North Africa viewed Sufi orders with suspicion, and colonial scholars produced police dossiers on the orders to predict their reactions to official policies.

In the postcolonial period, Sufi orders and institutions have had an ambiguous position. Governments in many Muslim countries, such as Egypt and Pakistan, have sought to bring the orders and shrines under state control. Officials often appear at Sufi festivals, seeking to link popular reverence for saints with support for the regime. Still, many of the most significant Sufi orders flourish without official recognition. But contemporary fundamentalist movements attack Sufism with a passion and condemn its pilgrimages to shrines as idolatry. Modernists and secularists also criticise Sufism for many of the same activities, but in their minds the problem is medieval superstition and the manipulation of credulous masses.

66   *A Companion to Muslim Cultures*

In Turkey's secularist course under Kemal Atatürk (r.1923–1938), Sufi orders were banned outright. To this day, the performance of rituals such as the 'whirling dervish' dance of the Mevlevis is mainly tolerated as a cultural activity, and exported through touring companies and sound recordings. The tomb of Rumi, which many visitors treat as a shrine, is officially a museum. Sufi activities are also not publicly tolerated in Saudi Arabia and Iran, since they could easily become an unacceptable alternative religious authority. Yet the founders of certain fundamentalist movements, such as the Muslim Brotherhood in Egypt and the Jamat-i Islami in India, were exposed to Sufi orders in their youth, and seem to have adapted certain organisational techniques and leadership styles from Sufism. The key difference is that these movements replace Sufi spirituality with ideology in order to become mass political parties in the modern nation-state.

In recent years, Sufi orders from Asia and the Middle East have reached out to major urban centres across Europe and North America. While many groups have a firm grounding in Islamic tradition and may even adhere to the clothing and customs of their original homeland, other groups present Sufism as a mystical universal religion that may be pursued through chanting and dance, without the practice of ritual prayer or other observance of traditional duties. It is too soon to predict the future of Sufism in the West, but it has already taken on such local aspects of life as the joint participation of men and women. At the same time, there is a striving to preserve distinctive traits of traditional Sufism such as tombs of Sufi masters – notably those who have died in the West – which have become pilgrimage sites.

Tradition is also advanced as the poetry of Rumi finds new expression in western translations that have become massively popular. Other major figures like Ibn Arabi are also becoming well known in this way. The cultural products of Sufism, especially in the form of music, have generated an international following in the category of 'world music', through outstanding performers like the late Nusrat Fateh Ali Khan (1948–1997). While some may find institutional Sufism to be authoritarian, the charting of the inner

Spiritual Life 67

range of spiritual experience in Sufism offers a resource that has a wide appeal today.

Art and Spirituality

Across the ages, spirituality has often found expression in various forms of artistic creativity. Certainly the history of Christian spirituality cannot be divorced from its expression in architecture, painting and other arts. One expects no less in relation to the cultures of the Islamic world, in all their diversity.[5] Indeed, this is very much part of the tradition in the spirit of the Prophet's observation that 'God is beautiful and loves beauty'.

'Islamic art' has become a widely used phrase. Yet as art historians have noted, 'It is easier to say what Islamic art is not than what it is', for it 'refers neither to art of a specific era nor to that of a particular place or people'; it was not necessarily made by Muslims, and could even be made by Muslims for Christians or Jews.[6] The category of 'Islamic art' was created by non-Muslim scholars in order to describe beautiful artifacts coming from Muslim countries. There is no equivalent term in premodern Muslim cultures, though in modern times the European phrase 'fine arts' has been translated directly into Arabic and other languages. From an early date, artisans in different Muslim countries produced objects of high quality both for daily use and for the luxury market; at various times, especially after the 17th century, Europeans were greatly interested in collecting and even imitating high quality artifacts from Muslim regions.

To a great extent, this artistic production simply continued the traditions of existing arts from those regions (such as Egypt, India, Persia and Syria). There was not necessarily anything about them that was directly related to Islam as faith – though pottery and metalwork came to include wise sayings and advice written in

---

[5] For an excellent introduction to Islamic spirituality and art in the broadest sense, see John Renard, *Seven Doors to the House of Islam: Spirituality and the Religious Life of Muslims* (Berkeley, CA, 1996).
[6] Jonathan Bloom and Sheila Blair, *Islamic Arts* (London, 1997), p.1.

68   *A Companion to Muslim Cultures*

Arabic, which could have some religious content. In the same way, monuments of Islamic architecture made use of forms that were already current throughout the ancient world (the dome, the octagon, pillared galleries). With the possible exception of *muqarnas*, the delicate geometrical tracery found in transition zones from domes to walls, there is hardly a single architectural element that could be considered exclusively Islamic.

In Europe for the past two hundred years, 'art' has generally meant fine art objects not intended for use, in contrast to 'crafts' which are produced for everyday needs. Yet in major collections of Islamic art in the museums of New York or Washington, alongside miniature paintings one finds a huge variety of beautiful but everyday objects, ranging from pencil cases to candlesticks, inkwells, metalwork, book bindings, carpets, coins, swords and jewellery. There has been a tendency to consider all the products of Muslim societies as 'Islamic', though we would not refer to ordinary crafts produced in medieval Europe as 'Christian'. The larger civilisational space of Islam can be called 'Islamicate', to include non-religious activities or material culture.[7]

One could also distinguish religious art and sacred art. The latter would consist of objects used in the practice of the faith, such as calligraphed Qurans and prayer books, ornate mosque lamps, prayer carpets and the architecture of the mosque itself. Islamic religious art would include books with miniature illustrations, offering stories about prophets and saints. Paintings with religious content relating to Islam are not empty of religious significance, but since they have no function in religious practice, they are not quite sacred. Everyday items produced by artisans in majority Muslim countries are best called 'Islamicate', both because they lack direct religious significance and because they can be produced and consumed by Muslims as well as non-Muslims.

Again, culture and faith are closely entwined in the much-discussed issue of the 'prohibition' of images in Islam. It is often thought that the legal tradition forbids depicting living creatures,

---

[7] Marshall Hodgson, *The Venture of Islam: Conscience and History in a World Civilization*, vol. 1 (Chicago, 1974), pp. 56-60.

Spiritual Life   69

on the grounds that this may encourage idolatry, and also usurps the unique creative authority of the divine. But the history of Islamic art shows that pictorial art has a long and vigorous tradition which is quite complex.[8] The Quran makes no direct reference to painting and the visual arts, though like the Hebrew Bible it firmly rejects idolatrous worship. Hadith reported from the Prophet is said to show his distaste for specific objects with images of humans or animals, but it is debated whether this extended to images at large. He was distressed, for example, when curtains embroidered with figures distracted from prayer, but had no objection to them being trimmed and used as pillow cases.

In secular settings, from mural paintings in royal palaces to book illustrations in the sciences, history and poetry, Muslims have widely used images. Yet it is true that in sacred spaces, Muslims have generally rejected them. There are important exceptions, like the eighth-century Umayyad mosque of Damascus, with mosaics of a heavenly landscape of trees, rivers and buildings; but it contains no humans or animal figures. This absence of images in sacred art has a parallel in the iconoclastic movement of eastern Christianity, which saw a large-scale rejection of image worship at roughly the same time as the beginning phase of Muslim civilisation in the eighth and ninth centuries.

Artistic (and spiritual) creativity found particular expression in non-figural forms. Whether in small decorated objects or major monuments, calligraphy, geometric patterns and vegetal ornamentation became the hallmarks of Islamic art. Arabesque – infinitely repeating patterns of vegetal ornamentation and geometry – fill the margins of books and the walls of buildings with a constant reminder of the beauty and order that is the basis of the universe. Calligraphy derives its prestige from the Quran itself. Although the Arabic script existed in pre-Islamic times, it became a highly developed art form over a period of centuries in both sacred and secular contexts. As the vehicle for the word of God,

---

[8] See Oliver Leaman, *Islamic Aesthetics: An Introduction* (Edinburgh, 2004); and Fahmida Suleman, 'Art', in Amyn B. Sajoo, ed., *A Companion to Muslim Ethics* (London, 2010), pp. 91-104.

70   *A Companion to Muslim Cultures*

Arabic script was employed in Qurans to permit the contemplation of divine beauty, and this formed the basis for a calligraphic aesthetic in multiple styles that extended to all languages that used the Arabic script (Persian, Turkish, Urdu).

The messages conveyed by the texts spelled out in Arabic script were also vital to the meaning of the buildings they adorned. The Dome of the Rock in Jerusalem quotes verses from the Quran on the human nature of Jesus; hence the monument stands as a statement against the Christian ideology of the rival Byzantine empire. In the margins of the enormous gateway of the Taj Mahal, Quranic verses describe the garden of paradise at the resurrection; while tourist guidebooks explain the building as a Mughal emperor's gesture of love for his wife, art historians argue that it represents the mystical interpretation of the afterlife according to Ibn Arabi.[9] The spectacular calligraphic decoration of the Alhambra palace in Granada includes not only pious sentiments but also Arabic court poetry that subtly celebrates the imperial authority of the Moorish ruler.

Islamicate art was often made by and for non-Muslims, in ways that blur religious identities. In 15th century India, a Sanskrit manual for Hindu architects gave instructions on how to build a mosque, described as a temple without images which is dedicated to the formless supreme God. It also appears that Hindu architects who restored the Qutb Minar in Delhi in 1368 had their own theological understanding of the mosque structure.[10] When the Spanish Christian king Pedro the Cruel (also known as Pedro the Just) built a new palace in Seville in 1351, he employed workmen from the Moorish kingdom of Granada who filled the monument with Arabic calligraphy and arabesque design. Pedro was aware of their religious content and implications. His use of Moorish architectural style seems to have been based on the desire to emulate the most convincing available model of imperial authority, rather

---

[9] Wayne Begley, 'The Myth of the Taj-Mahal and a New Theory of its Symbolic Meaning', *Art Bulletin*, 61 (March, 1979), pp. 7–37.

[10] Carl W. Ernst, *Eternal Garden: Mysticism, History, and Politics at a South Asian Sufi Centre* (Albany, NY, 1992), pp. 32-33

Spiritual Life 71

than on any idea of interreligious understanding. Despite the centuries-long anti-Muslim Christian militancy of the Reconquista, Spanish Christians used artistic styles and motifs of the Moors even after their expulsion and forced conversion from 1492 onward. This so-called *mudejar* art (a Spanish term from the Arabic *mudajjan*, a Moorish subject in Christian territory) was a Christian appropriation of Islamicate culture.[11]

Orientalism

A different kind of European appropriation of Islamicate culture was in the Orientalist school of painting, which came to the fore in the mid-19th century, about the same time as the new technique of photography. Orientalist painting was created by artists (especially French) who had travelled to the countries of North Africa or the Near East. For Europe at that time, 'Oriental' defined the immediate East, primarily the Ottoman empire, as a stand-in for the Muslim world. With the growth of printing and the immense popularity of travel literature, pictorial representations of exotic cultures had become a staple of visual illustration.

Yet neither the travel books nor the illustrations of faraway countries provided genuine encounters with other cultures. Travellers tended to take with them deeply ingrained prejudices, frequently based on the reading of earlier travel books rather than their own observations. Illustrations were often commissioned by publishers, frequently recycling stock images on the basis of well-established stereotypes. Ironically, works of fantasy tended to be much more eagerly accepted as authentic representations of remote lands. This tendency had been seen in medieval times, when the travel narrative of Marco Polo was generally considered far inferior to the outrageous adventures of Sir John Mandeville, which are filled with Sinbad-like encounters with fabulous beasts and monsters. The imagined Orient was a counter-image against which Europe defined itself.

---

[11] Ciclo Internacional de Exposiciones Museo Sin Fronteras, *Spain: Mudejar Art – Islamic Aesthetics in Christian Art* (London, 2002).

72   *A Companion to Muslim Cultures*

Even before European colonialism established its supremacy over the Ottoman empire and other Muslim lands, European authors took a regal and superior attitude toward the Orient, as shown by this declaration from an early-18th century collection of pictures from the Near East:

> The reader imagines himself inspecting the other inhabitants of the Earth, and exercising over them a kind of sovereignty, he examines them with attention, approves or condemns their choice of customs, amuses himself and often laughs at the oddness of some, sometimes admires the beauty and majesty of others, always preferring the customs of the country where he was born.[12]

The impulse to depict the Orient in visual form received a major boost with Napoleon's 1798 expedition to Egypt. It resulted in the publication of the massive *Description de l'Égypte* (1803–1828) by a team of French scholars, with numerous maps and illustrations of ancient and modern Egypt. A striking aspect of the Orientalist imagination was the way in which it collapsed the present into the ancient past, invariably regarding the Oriental as trapped in a time warp that prevented him from being part of today. This powerful metaphor has become an omnipresent cliché in travel writing and journalism. How often must one read that visiting country X was like travelling back in time 500 years?

A feature of the Orientalist view that reinforced this time-warp was the questing of Protestant Christian pilgrims for places in the Holy Land where the life of Jesus had taken place. Contemporary Arab Bedouin costume, for example, was viewed as the equivalent of Biblical garb. So American travellers who rarely could converse with Arab Christians or Muslims imagined themselves transported back in time, or understood the Near East to exist in a timeless realm unaffected by history. The very real effects of the

---

[12] Jean-Baptiste Vanmour, *100 Prints Representing Different Nations of the Levant* (Paris, 1712-13), quoted in Lisa Small, 'Western Eyes, Eastern Visions', in *A Distant Muse: An Orientalist Work from the Dahesh Museum of Art* (New York, 2000), p. 9.

Spiritual Life 73

19th-century version of globalising trade (of which Euro-American tourism was a manifestation) by then had intimately linked Muslim lands with the economies of Europe and America. Yet these connections were glossed over by powerful images of 'East is East, and West is West'. The legacy of these Orientalist views was to play out in a host of public settings in the 20th century and in our own time, as shown in Edward Said's seminal work *Orientalism* (1978).

Contemporary Expressions

Spiritual life finds expression today in media ranging from cinema and photography to abstract art. Iranian films have often creatively departed from Hollywood styles, to global acclaim: examples include Mohsen Makhmalbaf's *Gabbeh* (1996), depicting love and beauty among the nomadic tribes of southern Persia with lyrical intensity, and Majid Majidi's *The Color of Paradise* (1999), with its rich evocation of the spirituality of children. Then there are the thoroughly contemporary styles of abstract painting of Iranian women artists like Feeroozeh Golmohammadi, and of Bangladeshi artists whose compositions would be hard to distinguish from the abstractionism of Japanese or Dutch artists. Can these productions be called Islamicate, when they partake so robustly of global trends in style and conception?

There is also the matter of how the modern proliferation of images through technology has involved styles of mass political art. To take an example from Tehran, the new mausoleum of Ayatollah Khomeini (1900–1989), like many other shrines in Iran, contains gigantic free-standing portraits of Khomeini and his martyred son Ahmad. Similarly, cemeteries devoted to martyrs of the Iranian revolution or the Iran-Iraq war are filled with photographs of the departed. Likewise, one sees here pictures in various sizes of the Prophet, Ali and Husayn. While some Muslims elsewhere may object to all this, Iranians do not appear to share such views.

A powerful counter-impulse has arisen in certain extreme manifestations of Islamist ideology in recent years. In part, this

74 *A Companion to Muslim Cultures*

rejection of images may be seen as a deeply ambivalent response to the global proliferation of images as a means of advertising. This is especially disturbing to those who have opted to define sexuality through rigidly separate spaces for males and females. But there are other factors at play.

Most dramatically, the Taliban of Afghanistan demonstrated their extreme abhorrence of images when in 2001 they destroyed the colossal Buddhas of Bamiyan, which had stood there since the sixth century. The demolition of these statues was only the most spectacular event in a campaign that also reduced the contents of the Kabul Museum to practically nothing. In short order, the Taliban had annihilated (or sold on the black market) treasures from the many cultures that traversed the Silk Road over the ages. They also proclaimed their unprecedented austerity by outlawing all photographs (except ID cards) and all forms of music except recitation of the Quran. Such perspectives, sometimes shared in parts of the Middle East, come at the cost of a flourishing spiritual life.

What may, in all its varied forms, be called Islamic art testifies to centuries of development of the sense of beauty within Muslim cultures. Even the European appropriation and objectification of Islamic art, like the participation of Muslims in international modern art, engages the aesthetic joys of creativity. Like the Sufi orders that survive despite the obstacles thrown in their way by modernity, these varying forms of expression act as channels that both preserve the heritage of the past and strive to make possible a more direct personal access to higher rewards.

Further Reading

Amir-Moezzi, M. A. *The Spirituality of Shi'i Islam: Beliefs and Practices.* London, 2011.

Barks, Coleman. *The Soul of Rumi: A New Collection of Ecstatic Poems.* San Francisco, 2001.

Cooke, Miriam and Bruce Lawrence, ed. *Muslim Networks: From*

Hajj to Hip Hop. Chapel Hill, NC, 2005.

Ernst, Carl W. *Sufism: An Introduction to the Mystical Tradition of Islam.* Boston, MA, 2011.

Fernea, Elizabeth Warnock. *Guests of the Sheikh: An Ethnography of an Iraqi Village.* New York, 1989.

James, William. *The Varieties of Religious Experience.* Cambridge, MA, 1985.

Karamustafa, Ahmet. *Sufism: The Formative Period.* Berkeley, CA, 2007.

Renard, John. *Windows on the House of Islam: Muslim Sources on Spirituality and Religious Life.* Berkeley, CA, 1998.

Schimmel, Annemarie. *Mystical Dimensions of Islam.* Chapel Hill, NC, 1975.

Shah-Kazemi, Reza. *Justice and Remembrance: Introducing the Spirituality of Imam 'Ali.* London, 2006.

5

Gender and Identity

Elena Caprioni and Eva Sajoo

Women's subordinate status is primarily a cultural phenom-
enon and extends, in both temporal and geographical terms,
far beyond religions, at least those which are traditionally blamed
for keeping women in an inferior position. If accusations are
to be made, criticisms should be levelled against men for having
been unable or unwilling to change cultural traditions and
prejudices, whether religion-based or otherwise.
Abdelfattah Amor, 'Civil and Political Rights,
including the question of Religious Intolerance.'[1]

Much has been written about Islam and women. As female
equality becomes a watchword in global charters and social frameworks, new debates have emerged on what equality means in
various societies. In what might be called the 'Muslim world', the
unequal treatment of women is often linked to religion. But is the
status of women always tied to religious principles? Is there anything
positive about the identities offered to women in faith traditions
– specifically Islam? Female social identity or gender is something
that all societies construct, and which must change as cultural and
social conditions do. Modernity, with all its rapid energy, hastens
the processes of change. Yet it appears not to have lessened the
unequal status of Muslim women.

This chapter will examine the lived experiences of women in

---

[1] *Report for UN Commission on Human Rights* (New York, 2009), p. 7.

78   *A Companion to Muslim Cultures*

two neighbouring Muslim regions: Afghanistan and Xinjiang in north-west China. Both are going through deep transformation as part of a modernising process. We explore the politics of identity and gender, and sources of female emancipation that are non-Western. In understanding these case studies, we attend to the relationship between 'religion' and 'cultural tradition', and the factors that shape both. As these case studies illustrate, barriers to women's equality can hardly be explained by religion alone; gender roles are tightly linked to larger struggles for identity within particular social and political contexts.

Islam and Its Interpretations

How the ethical demands of a religious message are heard depends very much on the ears that receive it. This is as true today as it was in the time of Prophet Muhammad. Culture – as captured in the customs, traditions, values and views of a people – permeates all aspects of life. It influences how religion is practised and understood. The sheer diversity of practices across Muslim societies and communities offers ample evidence of how religion takes on local colours and interpretations. This is especially true with regard to women. When existing social customs privilege certain members of society at the expense of others, any teaching that challenges this will encounter resistance.

Fatima Mernissi recounts that even in Muhammad's time, the ethical voice of Islam was constantly tested by Arabia's patriarchal filters. Pre-existing beliefs about female impurity and inferiority found their way into hadiths of dubious lineage; misogynistic sentiments sought the backing of the Quran and the Prophet. Such reports were at variance with what we know about Muhammad's life and teachings; yet they still provide an excuse to ignore the more challenging ethical demands of Islam in favour of traditions more palatable to patriarchal interests. Modern scholarship has shown the dominant impact that male interpreters of the Quran have had historically in the shaping of the theological and legal traditions alike. The upshot is the legitimation of practices that keep women in subordinate positions in secular and religious life.

Gender and Identity 79

The situation has been further complicated by the aftermath of the colonial period. As Leila Ahmed points out, while colonial authorities were rarely interested in genuine female equality, they were keen to use the veiling and treatment of Muslim women as evidence of cultural inferiority, and as justification for their own intervention. This has resulted in a focus on those very aspects as somehow critical to Muslim identity – by Muslims and westerners alike. In the post-colonial era, this is reflected in a discourse of identity that has pervaded even countries without direct colonial experience.[2] Mernissi notes that the resurgent emphasis on female veiling in Islam occurred at the end of the 20th century, 'when Muslims in search of identity put the accent on the confinement of women as the solution for a pressing crisis. Protecting women from change by veiling them and shutting them out of the world has echoes of closing the community to protect it from the West.'[3]

This emphasis on women is not unique to Muslim societies. Women have routinely been used as ideological markers by political and religious groups, from Soviet Communists to Christian fundamentalists. The construction of women as bearers of collective identity and culture – with the 'forced identities' this often implies – is explored at length by Nira Yuval Davis in *Gender and Nation* (1997) and *Woman-Nation-State* (1989). As societies experience increased urbanisation and encounters with foreign influences, women are caught at the centre of renewed definitions of cultural identity, often framed in religious terms.

Muslim women, however, have not simply accepted the choice of either a constrained identity defined by conservatives, or a complete break with cultural and religious markers in the name of emancipation. Across the Muslim world, many have defined ways of keeping the faith while rejecting the assertions of its patriarchal interpreters. Margot Badran has charted the rise of Islamic feminism, which demands the equitable treatment of women on

---

[2] Leila Ahmed, *Women and Gender in Islam* (New Haven and London, 1992).
[3] Fatima Mernissi, *Women and Islam: An Historical and Theological Inquiry*, tr. Mary Jo Lakeland (Oxford, 1991), p. 99.

80   *A Companion to Muslim Cultures*

the basis of religious principles. 'Islamic feminists who articulate an egalitarian form of Islam should not be confused with Islamist women who promote political Islam and its patriarchal version of the religion', notes Badran.[4] There are also Muslim women who espouse a solely secular feminism.

As women navigate the rapid social changes of modernising societies, and the contending versions of gender identity they produce, they confront inequalities that are perpetuated by tradition and social factors. We turn now to the particular situations of women in Xinjiang and Afghanistan, and to how their circumstances have shaped the ways in which female identity is defined.

Xinjiang

Uyghurs are an ancient Turkic ethnic group living in the north-western region of the People's Republic of China (PRC) which is today officially referred to as the Xinjiang Uyghur Autonomous Region. For Uyghur nationalists and diasporas abroad, the region is 'Eastern Turkistan', which signals a territorial and cultural attachment to Russian Turkestan.

Uyghurs are identified as one of China's 56 ethnic groups, representing 46 per cent (9.8 million) of the population of Xinjiang.[5] They speak a Turkic language that falls within the 'Chagatai' linguistic group, and is written in Arabian-Persian script. Most are Sunni Muslims of the Hanafi school.

Originally, 'Uyghur' referred to a Turko-Mongolian tribe from the Mongolian heartlands of the Orkhon river valley. They mainly followed a shamanist religion called 'Tengrism', and also had contact with the Nestorian Christians, Buddhists and Manichaeans. In 774, they established the Uyghur Khaganate (744–840) in central Mongolia and extending to the eastern oases along the Silk Road

---

[4] Margot Badran, *Feminism in Islam: Secular and Religious Convergences* (Oxford, 2009), p.6

[5] Xinjiang Weiwuer Zizhiqu Tongjiju, *2009 Nian Xinjiang Tongji Nianjian* [2009 Xinjiang Statistical Yearbook], (Beijing: Zhongguo tongji chubanshe, 2009), p.78.

Gender and Identity 81

(the Tarim Basin and the Turfan Depression) to the Ferghana Valley. After a massive attack from the nomadic Kyrgyz, the Uyghurs were forced to move to the south-west of today's Xinjiang, where they mixed with the local population and adopted a sedentary lifestyle. Here, their ancient religion was enriched first with Buddhist elements, then with Sufi ones; Christianity was generally tolerated. Simultaneously, the Karakhanids (a confederation of Turkic tribes) established their kingdom (840–1211) in what is presently Kazakhstan and Kyrgyzstan. After the conversion of the Karakhanid ruler, Satuq Bughra, in the 10th century, the western Tarim basin was linked to the Muslim world of Transoxiana. By the mid-15th century, most Uyghurs had converted to Islam through a variety of paths – voluntary individual and group conversions (including through adoption and marriage) and occasionally involuntary ones.

Xinjiang was annexed to the Qing empire (1644–1911) as a 'protectorate' in 1759, then became a 'province' in 1884. It was incorporated into the PRC in 1955. The present borders of this territory were established only after 1759; previously, the region that Chinese scholars and officials knew as part of the Xiyu or Western Regions was rarely a politically united entity.

There is remarkably little Chinese scholarship on the conditions of Uyghur women, though it is common to hear that Islam is the sole cause of misogyny among them. This provides a way to ignore the fundamental question of why inequality still exists in this region, despite the longstanding policy of the Chinese Communist Party (CCP) to promote the emancipation of women. Instead, our aim here is to recompose the fragments of the history of Uyghur women, and the articulation of the roles of both sexes, to clarify how the status of women is influenced by local values, religion and Han reforms.

Uyghur women's lives differ considerably from place to place, and no stereotypical 'Uyghur woman' exists. Life in the region's main city of Urumqi is quite different from that in the more traditional and populous city of Kashgar, and both differ from the rural areas of Xinjiang. Through field work in the region, and the study of both primary and secondary sources, very different views

82   *A Companion to Muslim Cultures*

of female identity and history emerge. A key aspect of this case study is how Uyghur women, within and outside Xinjiang, today see life under Communist rule since 1949 in comparison with the pre-Communist period (1912–1949). This will tell us much about the varying impact of faith, culture and politics in the shaping of identity and gender.

Before Mao's Revolution

Expatriate Uyghur women describe the pre-Communist era as a harmonious period in which there was minimal contact (and hence friction) with Han Chinese. Uyghur society generally was based on a separation of roles and responsibilities between men and women, which was ascribed to their understanding of Islamic principles. Men dealt mainly with farming and prayed at the mosque or at the family tomb; women were primary caregivers and housekeepers, praying at home. At the same time, women had the right to be supported by men. Women could choose to study and/or work, to dress and beautify themselves as they pleased, and to spend time with their friends without being judged. They could initiate divorce and even remarry, as stated in the Quran. Men respected them, reciprocating their devotion with clothing and jewellery. In fact, the refusal of a man to observe this custom gave his wife grounds for divorce.

In this account, while men and women had very different roles and duties, they considered themselves as equals because they each believed they could not exist without the other. Their words suggest that 'equality' does not imply that women must imitate men, submitting themselves to masculinising either their appearance or responsibilities. Rather, equality meant mutual respect as a result of complementary roles.

The women interviewed as well as the written sources available establish that women were responsible for the family and the home. However, the oral and written accounts diverge regarding women's behaviour in the larger community. The written accounts, unlike the oral ones, do not depict women as being politically and economically active, nor as a group free to wear make-up or go

Gender and Identity

out. According to some written accounts, only women belonging to the upper class were dedicated to the role of housekeeper because the family had enough money to support them. In rural areas and amongst the lower classes, women were both housekeepers and labourers outside the home. In a text from the 1930s regarding the daily life of women and men in the countryside, women's duties are listed as follows: reciting prayers in the morning, caring for the house and children, sewing clothes, cooking and serving meals, milking the cow, managing the family economy and helping the husband in the fields.[6] The divergence between written and oral reports can be explained through the fact that some of the women interviewed had not lived in Xinjiang during the pre-Communist era. In fact, their history of this time was passed down through the stories of their mothers and grandmothers.

Many women living in Xinjiang reverse this view, asserting that the status of women was tightly linked to the principles of the Quran, and quote some verses to 'demonstrate' their subordinate social status. Yet the Quran also proclaims the absolute moral equality of the two sexes; indeed, Muslim feminists rely heavily on the text to challenge what they see as its patriarchal manipulation.[7] The traditionalist interpretations of the text claim that it essentially requires women to take care of the home and produce children, as noted in the following Uyghur idioms used at that time: *Qišniŋ rahiti oton, ärniŋ rahiti xoton* (Firewood serves for winter, a wife serves for her husband's pleasure) or *Xotun kiši tüt tamniñ quli* (Woman is the slave of the house). Wives were not allowed to make decisions independently, but had

---

[6] Gunnar Jarring, *Material to the Knowledge of Eastern Turki: Tales, Poetry, Proverbs, Riddles, Ethnological and Historical Texts from the Southern Parts of Eastern Turkestan* (Lund, Sweden, 1951).

[7] For example: 'To whoever, male or female, does good deeds and has faith, We shall give a good life and reward according to the best of their actions' (Quran 16:97); 'People, be mindful of your Lord, who created you from a single soul, and from it created its mate, and from the pair of them spread countless men and women far and wide' (Quran 4:1). See Fatima Mernissi, *The Veil and the Male Elite: A Feminist Interpretation of Women's Rights in Islam* (Paris,1987).

84   *A Companion to Muslim Cultures*

to follow their husbands: *Ayalniñ pütün xudasi XUDA, yärim Xudasi är* (Allah is God for a woman, the husband is half God). In general, a woman could not speak with a man in public without being labelled immoral; she could only meet her future husband, chosen by her paternal family, just a few days before marriage, which usually happened when she was between 14 and 16 years old. She had to wear a veil and accept that her husband could have other consorts.

Despite the denial of many of the interviewees, the existence of polygyny seems to be supported by writings in Uyghur culture. There are many references to *palančiniŋ čoŋ xotuni* (the big wife), *palančiniŋ ikkinči xotuni* (the second wife), *palančiniŋ kičik xotuni* (the small wife), and to the sentiment *birgä täkkän yaxši, ikkigä täkkän baxši, üčkä täkkän paxši* (the first wife is a good woman, the second a witch, and the third a prostitute). However, no references to polyandrous terms, such as *palančiniŋ kičik eri* (the small husband) are to be found.

Uyghur women can be divided into two different orientations regarding their status, one which typifies expatriate women, and the other, local women. Among the former, there may be an attempt to preserve and possibly embellish pre-Communist Uyghur society, creating a more romanticised oral memory. Indeed, the oral records, especially when the sampling is made up of immigrants, refuges and the exiled, should be approached with caution. We should keep in mind that the literature available on Uyghur diasporas – which praises their society and motherland before the arrival of Hans and despises them after – has played its own role in influencing these oral sources. Memory is fallible and can be selected and ordered according to the present-day perspective and concerns of the respondents. On the other side, local women tend to justify the aggressiveness of men and the inferiority of women exclusively through religion. Again, we should keep in mind that these oral sources may have been influenced by Communist ideology which until the 1980s classified all religions as popular superstitions that corrupted scientific thinking. After Deng Xiaoping's reforms, even if the government became more tolerant of spiritual expression and guaranteed the

Gender and Identity

freedom of religious belief, it still insisted that 'party members are atheists and should energetically attempt to spread atheism' in the region.[8]

After Mao

The founding figure of the People's Republic of China, Mao Zedong, famously said: 'Women hold up half of the sky'. The Maoist Revolution witnessed a new era for women by persuading them to accept the twin roles of housekeeper and worker, while condemning those who held on to a 'Confucian mentality' about women's inferiority. If before 1949 'woman' was synonymous with the weaker sex, after the revolution her image was smilingly dressed as a man, equal to his working tasks. In the new ideology, women could gain social, political, juridical, cultural and moral independence inside and outside the house only through their economic independence. This was held to inaugurate the inclusion of women in the world of work because all the reproductive forces, regardless of gender or ethnicity, should seek to build the socialist society.

The Chinese Communist Party committed itself to promoting equality between men and women throughout Xinjiang as well. Yet the Party's efforts to erode the ways of Uyghur culture and substitute the official one appear to have failed. Several Chinese scholars and journalists insist that the state of subordination of Uyghur women is rooted in Islamic doctrine. They claim that this subordination was reinvigorated after the break-up of the Soviet Union into independent nations in 1991, notably in Muslim Central Asia. Chinese officials label the Islam of today's Xinjiang as conservative and radical under the impact of fundamentalist forces in

---

[8] 'Guanyu wo guo shehuizhuyi shiqi zongjiao wenti de juben guandian he jiben zhengce' [Concerning the Basic Viewpoint and Policy toward the Question of Religion during China's Socialist Period] (March 1982), in Central Committee of the Chinese Communist Party, *Xinshiqi tongyi zhanxian wenxian xuanbian* [Selection of Documents on the United Front in Recent Times], (Beijing, November 1985), p. 1225.

86   *A Companion to Muslim Cultures*

the former Soviet Union, which they cast as incompatible with modernisation.

However, the status of women even in other areas of China where there is no Islamic influence is not especially different from that in Xinjiang. The prolonged effort to eradicate the Confucian tradition amid massive economic modernisation has left unchanged the reality that in much of China sons are still preferred, mainly for their superior earning power. Female infanticide and sex-selective abortions are common. This has led to an elevated male-to-female sex ratio in the country, at about 120 boys to 100 girls in provinces such as Shandong, Shaanxi, Henan, Anhui, Zhejiang, Jiangxi, Fujian and Guangdong. Yet this is absent among Uyghurs (110 boys to 110 girls) because, according to some respondents, they show no preference for male children; women even retain their original surnames after marriage.[9]

The Chinese model of equality of roles and responsibilities between the sexes was received differently by Uyghurs, depending on their social and cultural backgrounds. For example, in Urumqi the use of cosmetics and fashion accessories make Uyghur women resemble other women around the world; while in Kashgar and Khotan the link with local values is still evident in the preference for brown veils and working at home (see Plate 3). These seem obvious examples of the process of globalisation, rather than any denial of Uyghur identity.

Expatriate Uyghurs see Han migration as having fed a decline in the status of women in Xinjiang. The entry of women into the workforce is seen as an imperative that is dictated by the Chinese government. In this account, women are expected to work as long as men, to separate themselves from their children, to cut their hair, to wear the same blue uniform as men in order to camouflage their

---

[9] Li Jiang and Wei Feldman, 'Female Child Survival in China: Past, Present, and Prospects for the Future', paper presented at the Centre Population et Développement – Committee for International Cooperation in National Research in Demography – Institut national d'études démographiques Seminar on Female Deficit in Asia: Trends and Perspectives, Singapore, (December 5-7), 2005.

Gender and Identity 87

femininity, and to avoid using cosmetics and jewellery. Rebiya Kadeer, who heads the World Uyghur Congress, noted in a 2006 personal interview that, 'Han imposed new policies, changing and destroying Uyghur values and culture, giving women a masculine connotation'. Indeed, even Chinese women criticise the state for what they see as its attempt to suppress femininity.[10]

In the cities, however, women more easily accepted the Chinese idea of equality. According to Kadeer, the role and responsibilities of women changed because they have had to work like men and tend to waste their earnings on parties and other unworthy purposes instead of using it for their children's education. Meanwhile, in remote rural areas, Kadeer says that women still embody the ethical values of Uyghur culture, but most of them remain uneducated because their families cannot pay for their schooling. She laments that rather than help poor farmers to educate their daughters, the Chinese government 'invites' them to send these girls to work in mainland China, or risk losing their government supply of fertilisers and water.

By and large, women in urban areas report that they enjoy a decidedly better life than their mothers and grandmothers, despite the constant problem with gender issues in the region. These women can attend school at all levels, achieving better results than men with the encouragement of their parents to study hard. Between 1995 and 2008, the number of girls finishing secondary school increased fivefold, according to official Chinese sources. The number going to university has risen to unprecedented levels, surpassing males in Xinjiang. Participation in the workforce has also increased dramatically, from 17 per cent of women working in 1957 to 41.5 per cent in 2009. Most work as teachers, some in areas like farming, forestry and animal husbandry, a small number in public management and social organisations.

In the political sphere, women are also increasingly well represented at the county, provincial and prefecture levels. According to a 2006 report by the International Uyghur Human Rights and

---

[10] Cristina Gilmartin, et al., ed., *Engendering China: Women, Culture, and the State* (London, 1994).

88   *A Companion to Muslim Cultures*

Democracy Foundation, 16 women held important governmental posts in the 14 prefectures of Xinjiang. In addition, government sources report a sharp rise in the number of female deputies in the People's Congress of Xinjiang, as well as the People's Political Consultative Conference of Xinjiang. While the numbers speak of an elevated female presence in Xinjiang's public space (economic and political), they do not indicate the ratio of Han to Uyghur women, or how this new status is viewed by Uyghur communities.

Overall the political and economic integration of women in Xinjiang seems to be a slow and arduous process. A sense of the relative weakness of women in Uyghur society is conveyed by proverbs such as these which are still part of everyday usage: *Qizi barniñ därdi bar* (A family with many women will be miserable); *Qiziñ Öyde ärsiz uzaq turmiğay, ölärsän puşaymanda sän ağirmay* (Let your daughter marry or you will die of regret instead of illness); *Xotun xäqniñ çeçi uzun, ä qli qisqa* (Woman: long hair, short wit); *Ärsiz xotun, yugänsiz baytal* (A woman without a husband is like a horse without a halter); *Är jeni bilän, xişri äri bilän* (Men rely on life, a wife relies on her husband).

In the countryside, the stereotype of illiterate woman confined to the four walls of the home can still prevail. The official illiteracy rate is 3 per cent, but government records show that 37 per cent of people end their studying after primary school. Typically for rural women, the day begins with prayer at dawn, followed by the daily routine of domestic chores.

Official criticism of certain Uyghur customs has had the effect of reinvigorating them. For example, the Chinese government fought against the ritual of gifts that husbands present publicly to their wives, to reduce the gap between lower and upper classes. But wives insist on continuing this as a demonstration of respect and affection towards their families.

Again, the introduction of the one-child policy has reinforced traditional Uyghur practices. The one-child policy, introduced in 1979 by Deng Xiaoping to halt demographic growth, permits only one child per family in the city and two per family in the countryside in the case of a handicapped or female infant. National

Gender and Identity

minorities, however, are entitled to at least two children no matter where they live.

Before 1949, an Uyghur woman had the right to give birth to her first two children in her natal home, and successive births in the husband's hometown, where she was assisted by him and/or by her in-laws. Husbands opposed their wives giving birth in their natal home for reasons of control; yet these same husbands now encourage their wives to return to their family homes in order to keep the birth a secret.[11]

In visits to rural areas, a large majority of Uyghur girls were seen wearing the romal (a brown veil) to gain respect, uphold their history and religion, and avoid 'playing' like Chinese girls. It is understandable that for a girl born in a land that she considers under foreign occupation, wearing the romal is a way to assert her identity and cultural pride.

Identity vs. Status

Patriarchal traditions, education levels and cultural nationalism all play a part in shaping the status of women in Xinjiang. Often it is men who tend to vigilantly maintain Uyghur traditions. Since the large-scale arrival of the Han was a traumatic and threatening event for them, the 'emancipation' of women can easily be experienced as a further incursion by the Chinese government.

In general, women living in Xinjiang seem satisfied with their growing roles in public life. They ascribe to local traditions and male prejudice the relatively low level of social change in rural areas. The views of expatriate Uyghurs are more complicated. Many women idealise the pre-Communist period and view Han Chinese policies as an unqualified negative influence. The idea that traditions must be preserved seems largely a reaction to the influx of the Han and to their perceived attempt to weaken religion and Uyghur culture by replacing them with Han habits and customs.

---

[11] See Ildiko Beller-Hann, 'Work and Gender among Uyghur Villagers in Southern Xinjiang', *Cahiers d'études sur la Méditerranée orientale et le monde turco-iranien*, 25 (1998), pp. 93-114.

90   *A Companion to Muslim Cultures*

Ironically, as expatriates, they are removed from the setting in which their traditions and customs can be preserved. They inhabit societies in which women have much greater social and political freedom. Yet given the political tensions that have caused much emigration, it is perhaps unsurprising that these communities would view Han policies in stark terms. Neither of these groups of Uyghurs shares the view of Chinese scholars that Islam alone explains the subordination of women in Xinjiang. In reality, the condition of Uyghur women seems linked most closely to local values of cultural identity and its preservation – influenced by Islamic traditions, but also by the onset of profound and rapid socio-economic change driven by official policy and globalisation. Female identity is buffeted by competing impulses: to find an anchor in the old ways and to modernise, mindful of the ways of both Han women and those of the West. Even the inattentive visitor to the cities and countryside of Xinjiang sees that there is no typical Uyghur woman. Her heterogeneous world includes veiled, westernised, traditionalist and Sinicised women.

Afghanistan

Afghanistan has long been linked to other parts of the Muslim world. Its forbidding mountain passes were traversed by traders, travellers and scholars, bearing diverse customs and cultural products as they made their way along the Silk Road, which connected countries as diverse as China, Turkey and Italy for nearly thirteen centuries. Bordered by modern Iran, Pakistan, Tajikistan, Uzbekistan, Turkmenistan and China, Afghanistan shares ethnic populations and cultural influences with all of these nations.

Today, in the shadow of Taliban rule and a long period of civil strife, it is a country often associated with ceaseless violence and turbaned religious extremism. Its recent history has been especially dark for women, who have been systematically denied education, health, independence and public life. Afghan women face many challenges as they strive for a place in their nation's reconstruction. Whether it is walking to school or running for parliament, many are exposed to intimidation and physical danger.

Gender and Identity 91

What are the sources of the barriers placed before them? Is westernisation the only way to improve the treatment of Afghan women? This case study examines the history of women and reform in Afghanistan, before analysing current conditions and their causes.

When we speak of women in Afghanistan, it is important to recognise just how diverse they are in cultural and social terms. The country has over 50 ethnicities spread over 34 provinces. The lives of Kuchi nomads are markedly different from those of settled ethnic Tajiks in Badakhshan, Hazaras in Bamiyan, or the urbanised population of Kabul. They also vary in religious tradition and practice. The Hazaras and many Tajiks are Shia Muslims, while the southern Pashtun tribes are Sunni. However, the worst legalised oppression of women was conducted by the Taliban, who emerged from Kandahar, in the ethnic Pashtun heartland, and ruled the country from 1996–2001.

History

The rulers of Afghanistan have traditionally come from the Pashtun tribes of the south. At 42 per cent of the population, they are the single largest ethnic group. Yet they have not always been associated with the kind of extreme misogyny demonstrated by the Taliban: urban and rural divisions have proved more significant than other markers. Under the monarch Amanullah Khan (r. 1919–1929), a national marriage law was introduced in 1924. It established a minimum age for marriage, prohibited forced marriage, and created legal recourse for women with abusive husbands. Amanullah established co-ed schools, even teaching classes himself on occasion. His queen, Sorayah Tarzi, built girls' schools and argued that the equality of Muslim women was firmly based on Quranic principles. These reforms were further advanced under the reign of Zahir Shah who, in 1935, made primary education compulsory and free for all children.

Controversially, Amanullah supported unveiling and Sorayah herself set the example in an attempt to shift social norms. This sparked resentment among more conservative religious leaders, who eventually forced the king from power. The modernising

92 *A Companion to Muslim Cultures*

ways of the royal couple had outstripped the social flexibility of some segments of the population for whom certain ways of dressing and behaving were integral to culture and identity.

Amanullah was not the only reformer. Under Prime Minister Daoud Khan (1953–1963) women were encouraged to pursue higher education, and some were included in international delegations. The 1964 Constitution, introduced by Zahir Shah, guaranteed the equal status of women, giving them the right to vote and placing the first four women in Parliament. During this period many studied at Kabul University. Significantly, women not only took up careers in teaching and nursing, but also became surgeons, doctors, and professors of mathematics and physics. According to Arlene Lederman, who lived in Kabul with her husband, an engineering professor during this period, there were more female members of the Faculty of Science at Kabul University in 1965 than in most American universities.[12] The city looked like many European capitals, with women wearing lipstick and miniskirts on public buses. Prime Minister Daoud also instituted a forcible unveiling campaign across the country by penalising covered women and those who provided services to them in public. This may not have caused much stir in Kabul, but the rest of the country was a vastly different matter. Daoud soon faced an emerging fundamentalist movement, whose members he began to arrest and otherwise restrain.

Prime Minister Daoud was forced from office in 1978 by Marxist army officers. In 1979 the Soviet Union invaded the country to end infighting between the two Afghan Communist parties, and to ensure that a unified government was in place to suppress the Islamist movement which was now actively supported by Pakistan's Inter-Services Intelligence Agency (ISI). For women, this was a 'radical' phase. In keeping with Communist principles, the government upheld gender equality throughout the country. Literacy teams went into rural areas, knocking on doors and taking women, by force if necessary, to the local literacy class. How much literacy

---

[12] Arlene Lederman, 'The Zan of Afghanistan' in S. Mehta, ed., *Women for Afghan Women* (New York, 2002).

Gender and Identity

was spread in this fashion is an interesting question, but what it did produce was deep resentment over the invasion of homes and state coercion in the name of an anti-religious ideology.

The Soviet presence also caused alarm for its Cold War rival, the United States. Concerned only with the expulsion of Soviet troops, President Ronald Reagan decided to arm and support Afghan insurgents. The intermediary for this was Pakistan, which then selected which groups would receive support and how much. A major outcome was the strategy of creating a chain of *madrassa*s and training camps for the resistance in Pakistan's Northwest Frontier Provinces and the Federally Administered Tribal Areas. These lay along the border with southern Afghanistan, a frontier known as the Durand Line that was quite arbitrarily created by the British in 1893. The Pashtun population on both sides is ethnically and linguistically indistinct and regularly crosses a boundary not recognised by Afghanistan.[13]

Many of the Pashtun insurgents who fought the Soviets in Afghanistan rotated through this part of Pakistan, equipped not only with guns and anti-tank missiles but a militant ethno-religious ideology. They called themselves mujahideen (those who wage jihad). After the Soviets withdrew in 1989, the insurgent groups struggled amongst themselves for control of the country – a lawless period of civil war, which saw widespread theft, massacres and rape of the population. Much of the infrastructure for education and health services was completely destroyed.

The Taliban were Pashtun, former mujahideen determined to rid the country of warlord control and institute rule of law under an 'Islamic state'. Their name comes from the word *talib*, meaning religious student, though many Muslims would regard them as religiously illiterate. This is a reference to the *madrassa*s many attended in Pakistan, which were dedicated to producing mujahideen. When they took Kabul in 1996, they were at first welcomed by a population traumatised by civil war. But the Taliban's version of sharia as

---

[13] For a detailed account of these events and recent Afghan history see Ahmed Rashid, *Descent into Chaos: The United States and the Failure of Nation-building in Pakistan, Afghanistan, and Central Asia* (New York, 2008).

94   *A Companion to Muslim Cultures*

public law banned education and employment for women, involved stoning and flogging for all manner of acts, and introduced draconian rules on dress and behaviour for men and women, including a ban on music and dance. Women were confined to the home, unless covered in a burqa and accompanied by a male relative. They were forbidden access to male doctors, which often meant denial of medical treatment entirely, since few female doctors could work. Taliban rule from 1996–2001 ranks as an extraordinarily bleak period for Afghan women, and its scars remain.

Since the overthrow of the Taliban by international forces, there have been significant improvements for Afghan women. Their equality is once again upheld in the Constitution (2004), which guarantees them 25 per cent of the seats in the Lower House of Parliament (Wolesi Jirga). Bamiyan province became the first to have a female governor, and women in many places have returned to work and school. But women are far from equal in practice in Afghanistan. The extent of the inequality and insecurity they face varies by region.

What are the reasons for the often extreme forms of misogyny that Afghanistan has witnessed? Is it part of Afghan culture? It is because of Islam? Is it a localised set of tribal Pashtun codes? How do Afghan women see themselves, their culture, and their future?

Identity: Between Politics and Culture

The notion that the Taliban represent some indigenous, traditional set of Afghan, or at least Pashtun, values with regard to women ignores the evidence. After the fall of the Taliban, the Back to School Campaign (2002–2003) saw the greatest recorded enrolment levels in Afghan history, with 33 per cent of the national figure being female, according to the Afghan Ministry of Education. This included the Pashtun provinces of the south, which while not achieving the 98 per cent female enrolment levels of provinces like Badakhshan and Herat, nevertheless demonstrated an eagerness to educate their daughters.[14]

---

[14] Sara Amiryar, Ed Kissam and Mohammed Eisa, 'Afghanistan's Primary Education Systems' (Washington, DC, 2004).

Gender and Identity

It is true that *pashtunwali* (the traditional tribal code of the Pashtun) tends to view women as chattel to be owned and traded, but this is not an adequate explanation for the ongoing barriers that Afghan women face. Culture is malleable; its practices and norms adapt to changing conditions. This is evident in the different social norms of urban environments, which tend to innovate faster than their rural counterparts. Kabul has always been very different from rural Zabul.

The changing nature of culture can work in reverse as well. When social conditions deteriorate markedly, certain patterns of behaviour are manifest in response. Girls' attendance in school is poor from Rwanda and northern Uganda to Kosovo and southern Afghanistan.[15] What these places share, in addition to low female attendance, is a recent history of lawlessness and violence. When physical security is threatened, parents act to protect their children, and girls are more frequent targets of kidnapping and abuse than boys. In Afghanistan, the extreme forms of oppression women have faced have much to do with thirty years of war and instability. As Deniz Kandiyoti argues, 'what to Western eyes looks like "tradition" is, in many instances, the manifestation of new and more brutal forms of subjugation of the weak made possible by a commodified criminal economy, total lack of security and the erosion of bonds of trust and solidarity that were tested to the limit by war, social upheaval and poverty.'[16]

Practices like child marriage are reinforced in low-security situations where girls are at risk of kidnapping or sexual abuse. Confining women to the home is also a custom which gains strength in lawless circumstances. In Afghanistan, the widespread kidnapping and rape which took place during the 1990–1996 civil war emphasised the vulnerability of women, and renewed conservative

---

[15] Jackie Kirk, 'Women in Contexts of Crisis: Gender and Conflict', Paper for UNESCO *Education for All Global Monitoring Report 2003/4* (Paris, 2003).
[16] Deniz Kandiyoti, 'The Lures and Perils of Gender Activism in Afghanistan', Anthony Hyman Memorial Lecture, SOAS (London, 2009), p.9. Available at: http://www.soas.ac.uk/cccac/events/anthonyhyman/16mar2009-2009-the-lures-and-perils-of-gender-activism-in-afghanistan.html

96 · *A Companion to Muslim Cultures*

customs that might otherwise have waned. These tendencies were heightened in the refugee camps in Pakistan and Iran, which according to the UN housed 4.5 million Afghans beginning in the 1980s. Further, the Taliban insurgency which emerged in 2003 and has since gained in strength and range has targeted women for intimidation. Even in urban Kabul, and as far north as Kunduz, women who teach and work in or for government or NGOs have received death threats from the Taliban for daring to step outside the home. Such activities are typically termed 'un-Islamic' in night letters (*shabnameh*) delivered in secret to terrorise recipients. The characterisation reveals something of the politics of identity in Afghanistan.

The Taliban are not the only voices claiming that a misogynistic, extreme form of religious practice is both 'Islamic' and Afghan. True, the country has ratified the Convention on Elimination of all forms of Discrimination Against Women (1981) and affirmed the equal status of women in the Constitution (Article 22); but the reality is another matter. Even in provinces with a sufficient police force and judicial system, the law is frequently applied in ways that reinforce female inequality rather than address it. Women are routinely jailed for fleeing their family or marital homes regardless of the cause; those reporting rape are at risk of being charged with 'adultery', which covers all extramarital sex. In 2009, under pressure from powerful mullahs, President Hamid Karzai approved the 'Shia Personal Status Law' to garner political support. It allowed a man to withhold food and water from his wife if she failed to cooperate with his sexual demands, and required her to gain her husband's consent before leaving the house.[17]

Other powerful voices in the struggle for Afghan identity include the Islamic Council of Clerics, which has urged the government to re-establish *hudud* punishments (such as stoning, amputations and flogging). The Council also monitors the country's emerging television stations for 'improper' broadcasts, and claims that music

---

[17] See Article 133(4) and Article 177 of *Shiite Personal Status Law* (Afghanistan), March 2009, available at: http://www.unhcr.org/refworld/docid/4a24ed5b2.html.

Gender and Identity 97

is 'un-Islamic'.[18] The recent appearance of female vocalists on the popular television talent show 'Afghan Star' has generated great controversy, and even death threats.

Yet these are not the only voices with a claim to authenticity. Music and dance are no more 'un-Afghan' than roast lamb. Among the many instruments which are embedded in the rich musical traditions of Afghanistan are lutes such as the *dutar, tanbur, dambura, rubab, setar* and *sarinda*, along with the *ghaichak* (a type of fiddle) and the *zirbaghali, daireh, dohol* and *soorna* (various drums). The Pashtun *neemakai* is a form of song composed by women, while in Herat the harmonium as well as drums such the *daireh* and *tabla* were played at women's wedding celebrations by female troupes. At other festive occasions, women have customarily sung and played the *chang* (harp) and tambourine, even if for women-only audiences. They have also engaged in various forms of dance in private settings: the *ghamzagi, natsa, ishala* and *khaghazbadbazi* are solo dances performed by women (Plate 4), while the *attan* and *khattak* are group dances which may be performed by men or women, but not together.[19]

With the advent of Radio Kabul in 1960, which broadcasts across the country, female vocalists began to acquire mass co-ed popularity. Among them was Ferida Mawash, who was awarded the honorary title of Ustad (music master) by the Afghan government in 1976. The Kabul School of Music was established in 1974. Many musicians fled Afghanistan during the 1990s, when the civil war plunged the country into chaos and brought in severe musical

---

[18] Sayed Salahuddin, 'Islamic clerics seek return to strict Islamic law', Reuters, 10 August 2010. Available at: http://www.reuters.com/article/idUSTRE67B2QA20100812 . See also Andrew Tkach, 'Fight for future of Afghan culture plays out on TV', CNN, 6 August 2009. Available at http://edition.cnn.com/2009/WORLD/asiapcf/08/06/generation.islam.afghan.star/index.html.

[19] John Baily, 'Can you stop the birds singing? The Censorship of Music in Afghanistan', Report for the World Forum on Music and Censorship (Copenhagen, 2001), accessible at www.freemuse.org; and Hafizullah Emadi, *The Culture and Customs of Afghanistan* (Westwood, CT, 2005).

98 *A Companion to Muslim Cultures*

censorship, first under President Burhanuddin Rabbani (1990–1996) and then under the Taliban (1996–2001).

Models of Womanhood

Conservative claims about the role of women are similarly weakened by the historical record. Afghanistan has a long tradition of fearless, independent women. Malalai, a woman killed on the battlefield in the Anglo-Afghan War (1839–1842), has achieved national renown. Amid the blight of civil strife in recent times, defending women's participation in society has called for heroic measures at all levels. Meena Kashwar Kamal was 20 years old when she founded the Revolutionary Association for the Women of Afghanistan (RAWA) in 1977. Among its goals was the equality of men and women, and a democratic culture in Afghanistan. She established schools for Afghan refugees who flooded into Pakistan after the Soviet invasion, and declared that Afghan women, once awakened, could change their country.[20] Suhaila Seddiqi, an ethnic Tajik who was appointed Minister of Health in 2001, has been the country's top surgeon for several decades. Even the Taliban found themselves unable to dispense with her skills, and reinstated her as head of surgery at Wazir Akhbar Khan Hospital in Kabul eight months after dismissing her.

There are many who risked death by establishing and attending secret schools for girls during the Taliban period and in the aftermath of growing insurgent attacks on girls' schools. As Shamsia Husseini, a victim of an acid attack put it: 'My parents told me to keep coming to school, even if I am killed.'[21] Others protested in the streets of Kabul, when news of the Shia Personal Status Law broke, braving a hail of stones thrown by supporters of the instigating mullah.

---

[20] Aryn Baker, 'Meena Kashwar Kemal', in *60 Years of Asian Heroes. Time Magazine* (2006). Available at: http://www.time.com/time/asia/2006/heroes/in_meena.html. See also 'The Revolutionary Association of the Women of Afghanistan' at: www.rawa.org/rawa.html.

[21] Quoted in Dexter Filkins, 'Afghan Girls Undeterred by Attack', *The New York Times*, 13 January, 2009.

Gender and Identity

Is Islam the barrier to female equality in Afghanistan? Not according to Suhaila Seddiqi: 'Afghan women would like freedom within the framework of Islam. I don't like the freedom of women in the West. I think Islam has a lot of respect for women. Men and women are equal in Islam, but the Taliban worked against Islamic values.'[22]

While religious claims are frequently made to justify extreme forms of misogyny in Afghanistan, what is actually being defended is an extreme version of the Pashtun customary code, warped by years of conflict and wrapped in the vocabulary of religion. As Carol Mann points out, 'The ubiquitous burqa has become the symbol and uniform of this new kind of ethnicised Islamism, ubiquitous even in areas such as Northern Afghanistan which had scarcely worn it before the Taliban made it compulsory.'[23]

Afghan women have been faced with competing models of identity, in which their appearance and role is a key symbol. For King Amanullah, like his contemporaries Mustafa Kemal in Turkey and Reza Shah Pahlavi in Iran, unveiled women were the mark of a modernised nation. Under the Soviets, women became tokens of Communist ideology. Today, Afghan women who dare to work outside their homes are often accused of being 'western', of having abandoned an Afghan, Muslim identity which demands their silence and submission. The social advancement of women has been characterised by its detractors as a foreign agenda. To the extent that western countries persist in portraying Islam as inherently misogynistic and human rights as an exclusively western idea, they only increase the strength of conservative voices. For Afghan women, the challenge lies in defining a pluralist identity which takes into account the interplay of culture, faith and human rights in a changing world.

---

[22] MSNBC Interview, December 21, 2001.
[23] Carol Mann, *Models and Realities of Afghan Womanhood: A Retrospective and Prospects*. Paper prepared for the Gender Equality and Development Section, UNESCO (Paris, 2005), p.11.

Conclusion

Women face competing claims about culture and the ways in which it ought to shape their lives, even if the degree of female subordination varies from place. This is hardly peculiar to Muslim women at this stage in modernity and globalisation. For Xinjiang's Uyghur women, greater political and economic freedoms have become available to them in recent decades, along with an influx of Han migrants. This version of modernity, centred on a Chinese cultural model, is not sympathetic to religious identity. It is hardly surprising that Uyghur men and some women react to this state of affairs in ways that are defensive, and reassert the patriarchy of old. Yet there is also a positive sense that something of real cultural value is worth retrieving in navigating the choices that are thrown up by modernity.

In Afghanistan, the ongoing effects of thirty years of conflict have destroyed the social and economic gains that women enjoyed from the 1950s to the late 1970s. While there was some promotion of women's rights under Communist rule from 1979–1992, this linked female equality to an anti-religious ideology. The lawlessness of civil war and the ensuing rise of religious extremists silenced and paralysed women's social progress. A rural, Pashtun code of behaviour that claims to be an authentic version of Islam has been elevated to the status of 'Afghan culture'. Attempts to challenge entrenched patriarchal customs involve great personal risk. But this need not be regarded as a hopeless situation.

Other societies have abandoned misogynistic prescriptions supposedly linked to religion. In England, for example, women faced enormous barriers to political and economic participation well into the 20th century. While they began entering the formal workplace during the Industrial Revolution as factory workers, it was only during World War I that they were encouraged to work because of national economic necessity. They achieved the vote shortly afterward, in 1928, yet social barriers remained formidable until the aftermath of World War II. The 'traditions' invoked earlier to exclude women were now reinterpreted to allow for the practical demands of modernity – and the remaking of tradition.

Gender and Identity

Religion is inexorably bound up with culture. More often than not, cultural claims are voiced in religious terms, and religious demands are always filtered through a cultural context. Yet culture is not static but malleable, adapting and reacting to social changes. For women in Xinjiang and Afghanistan, as in so many other parts of the world, the challenge is to locate the ethical resources to support equality from within their religious and cultural contexts, claiming lives that cannot be reduced to a simple choice between identity and freedom.

Further Reading

Al-Hibri, Aziza. 'Women and Social Change', in Amyn B. Sajoo, ed., *A Companion to the Muslim World*. London, 2009, pp. 133–156.

Badran, Margot. *Feminism in Islam: Secular and Religious Convergences*. Oxford, 2009.

Beller-Hann, Ildiko. 'Customary Law under Socialism: the Uyghur in Xinjiang.' Paper presented at the conference on *Central Asian Law: An Historical Overview*, in Leiden, 13–17 Oct 2003; available at www.iias.nl/iiasn/july04/socialism.pdf.

Caprioni, Elena. 'A Look Inside the Heterogeneous World of Women in Northwestern China', *The International Journal of Interdisciplinary Social Studies*, 3 (2008), pp.149–159.

Emadi, Hafizullah. *Culture and Customs of Afghanistan*. Westwood CT, 2005.

Gilmartin, Christina K., G. Hershatter, L. Rofel and T. White, ed. *Engendering China: Women, Culture, and the State*. London, 1994.

Gladney, Dru. *Muslim Chinese: Ethnic Nationalism in the People's Republic*. 2nd ed. Cambridge, MA, 1996.

MacInnis, Donald E. *Religious Policy and Practice in Communist China*. New York, 1972.

Mann, Carol. 'Models and Realities of Afghan Womanhood: A Retrospective and Prospects'. Paper prepared for the Gender Equality and Development Section, UNESCO. Paris, 2005.

Mernissi, Fatima. *Women and Islam: An Historical and Theological Inquiry*, tr. Mary Jo Lakeland. Oxford, 1991.

Millward, James A. *Eurasian Crossroads: A History of Xinjiang*. New York, 2007.

Rashid, Ahmed. *Descent into Chaos: The Failure of US Nation-building in Pakistan, Afghanistan, and Central Asia*. New York, 2008.

6

Science and Social Change

Morgan Clarke

The Nobel Prize for Medicine was awarded to Robert Edwards in 2010 for his pioneering work on *in vitro* fertilisation (IVF) many years ago with Patrick Steptoe. By uniting sperm and egg outside of the human body under laboratory conditions, and then transferring resulting embryos to a woman's uterus, IVF has offered the hope of a solution to many instances of infertility. The world's first 'test-tube baby', Louise Brown, was born in the UK in 1978. With the eventual globalisation of IVF and allied assisted reproductive technologies (ARTs), it is estimated that more than four million more babies have been born with their aid worldwide, in what has become a multi-billion dollar market.

The Middle East has proved especially receptive: the first IVF centre in the Arab world was established in Saudi Arabia, closely followed by centres in Jordan and Egypt, in 1986. The first birth was claimed by Egypt in 1987, leading to wider acceptance and the establishment of clinics across the region. IVF has been more or less controversial wherever it has travelled, and such controversies in the Middle East have most often been seen as requiring religious guidance. Indeed, these ethical dilemmas thereby offer an area where religious traditions can assert their relevance to the modern, technological world.

Our focus here is on the response of Muslim scholars, who commonly observe that Islam is not opposed to science and biomedicine as the secularist stereotype would have one believe. Rather, Islam honours the pursuit of knowledge in the service of humanity, as the glories of medieval Islamic science testify. The

104   *A Companion to Muslim Cultures*

Christian churches have their own distinctive positions, as do Jewish rabbinic legal specialists. The latter debates are notably rich, in part because of Israel's public funding of IVF for infertile citizens. This reminds us that political and cultural factors have a large role to play in how new technologies are received and practised. After describing the ethical challenges that IVF poses and the responses to them by Muslim scholars, I will briefly discuss the situation in practice in religiously-diverse Lebanon today.

The Challenges of Assisted Reproduction

Artificial intervention in such supposedly natural processes as the making of children initially raised deep-seated and familiar worries about the hubris of modern science. The media's rapid dubbing of children conceived by IVF as 'test-tube babies' only served to deepen public misconceptions of what was involved. But such procedures have now become routine, and those worries have subsided. Nevertheless, a number of serious questions remain.

The process itself is gruelling. Women must first be given doses of hormones to stimulate 'superovulation', and eggs that develop then removed. Originally this was done by means of laparoscopy, a surgical procedure where an optical tool, the laparoscope, was inserted to view the ovaries and control the collection of the eggs, which were removed by passing a hollow needle through the abdomen. Today this has been superseded by a process where an ultrasound probe with a fine hollow needle is inserted into the vagina, and the needle is then advanced into the ovary where the eggs are retrieved by a suction device. Next, the eggs are prepared and selected for fertilisation with the man's sperm, which must be screened and 'washed'. Resulting embryos can be transferred to the woman's body by guiding a catheter through her cervix and flushing them into her uterus.

Success rates for such procedures are not high. The UK average live birth rate after IVF in 2008, according to the Human Fertilisation and Embryology Authority, ranged from 33.3 per cent for women under 35, down to just 2.6 per cent for those over 44. Women, especially older women, may have to undergo multiple cycles of IVF,

Science and Social Change

often without success. One must ask whether hopes are, in many cases, being unfairly raised for what can be very costly treatment. Younger women may be better advised to persist with trying to conceive without medical intervention; older women might be told that their chances of success are poor. A controversial way of improving the chances of successful implantation in the uterus is to transfer multiple embryos. This raises the prospect of potentially dangerous multiple pregnancies – which for an otherwise infertile couple may seem like a positive outcome, but involves associated risks to both babies and mother. Many regulatory bodies have sought to limit the number of embryos that can be transferred at one time.

Another means to improve the chances for an infertile couple to obtain a child, especially in the hardest cases, is to use the sperm or eggs of a third party. In earlier times, the use of donor sperm was the only solution for many cases of male infertility, artificially introduced into the women's uterus in so-called 'donor insemination'. Donor sperm can also be used in IVF, although this has become much less common due to the advent of ICSI (intracytoplasmic sperm injection), a variant of IVF where individual sperm are injected into ova through 'micro-manipulation' under a high-powered microscope. Just one sperm is sufficient for conception, providing a solution to many previously insoluble cases of male infertility.

For women (notably older women) whose eggs are not considered viable for successful conception, using the eggs of another woman may improve the chances. These eggs can be fertilised with the partner's sperm through IVF and the resulting embryo then transferred to the uterus. Where the problem lies with the woman's ability to carry a foetus to term, however, a 'surrogate' uterus is required. In 'traditional' surrogacy, another woman would conceive with the man's sperm and the baby would then be handed over to the couple. With the advent of IVF and 'gestational' surrogacy, an embryo constituted from the egg of the woman and her partner's sperm can be transferred to another woman's uterus and then carried to term and handed over to the couple. In this variant, the baby will be the receiving couple's genetic child, which generally makes it a much preferred choice.

106 *A Companion to Muslim Cultures*

A number of issues arise here, beginning with the source of donor gametes (egg or sperm) and the identity of surrogates. Willing donors and surrogates may, for instance, be found within the family, yet the ensuing family relationships could become very complicated indeed. Further, who would properly be considered the parents of the child? Should the genetic tie be paramount and the child considered to be related to the provider of the sperm or egg, that is, the donor in the case of donor gamete procedures? Or should the couple hoping for a child and making use of this genetic material be considered the parents? Should the identity of the donor be known or anonymous? As well, the prospect of different women providing the genetic material *and* carrying the resulting foetus in the womb raises the question as to which of these roles constitutes motherhood. Such techniques can also be utilised by single women and men, and gay and lesbian couples, giving rise to unconventional families.

It is sometimes argued that the sheer complexity of these issues should preclude allowing such procedures at all. Where they are allowed, further problems arise as to the propriety of payments being made for the services rendered. Some have also raised concerns about the possibility for women to conceive at far later ages than before. And as gametes and embryos can be frozen and then used many years later, posthumous parentage – using the sperm of a dead man, for instance – has become not only a possibility but a reality, provoking sharp debate.

Many more embryos may be brought into being than are eventually made use of, which opens the possibility of donating unused embryos to other couples in need. Can – indeed, should – the remainder be preserved through freezing, or destroyed? Pre-implantation genetic diagnosis (PGD) allows the selection of embryos for transplantation according to a number of criteria, which may also be seen as ethically challenging. PGD lets embryos be screened for genetic diseases, which implies the discarding of unhealthy ones. Sex-selection is also facilitated, along with screening for compatibility with existing children in dire need of therapeutic transplants, to give so-called 'saviour siblings'.

Contemporary Muslim Responses

Even before the new reproductive techniques had become established in the Middle East and elsewhere in the Muslim world, scholars began to consider their implications. IVF thus found its place alongside a host of other bioethical issues such as organ transplants and brain death, in a burgeoning Islamic jurisprudence of medicine (*fiqh al-tibb*). Some early responses were clearly influenced by media portrayals. Egypt's Shaykh Abd al-Halim Mahmud, for instance, felt that 'growing babies in test tubes' would leave them devoid of humanity, love and compassion, and wondered why such practices were mooted in an overpopulated world.[1] 'Test-tube babies' (*atfal al-anabib*) has stuck as the commonest term for IVF in the Islamic legal discourse, alongside 'artificial conception' (*al-taqlih al-sinai*). But what is actually involved was soon well understood, along with the stakes. A consensus quickly emerged that this was a potential boon for infertile couples, whose longing for the blessing of children is recognised and sanctioned by the Quran (18:46): 'Wealth and children are the ornament of this life (*al-mal wa-l-banun zinat al-hayat al-dunya*).'

In principle then, there is no objection to using modern medicine, including IVF, to address problems of infertility. This was the position taken in an official opinion (*fatwa*) in 1980 by the then Grand Mufti of Egypt, Shaykh Jad al-Haqq Ali Jad al-Haqq of Cairo's al-Azhar university,[2] just two years after the birth of Louise Brown. For Jad al-Haqq, as for almost all other Muslim scholars, IVF is permitted. It is commonly noted that care must be taken with regard to potentially problematic issues, such as uncovering and handling of the woman's body by the medical practitioner, and masturbation for providing a sperm sample. The necessity of undertaking infertility treatment, where such need is

---

[1] '*Fi talqih atfal al-anabib*', in *Fatawa al-Imam Abd al-Halim Mahmud* (Cairo, 1981–1982), vol. 2, pp. 245–246.

[2] '*Al-talqih al-sinai fi-l-islam*', in Ministry of Religious Endowments, ed., *Al-fatawa al-islamiyya* (2nd ed., Cairo, 1997), vol. 9, pp. 3213–3228.

108 *A Companion to Muslim Cultures*

established, generally provides sufficient grounds. Female medical specialists are often preferred.

At the same time, Shaykh Jad al-Haqq placed limits on the practice of IVF, most importantly on the involvement of parties other than a husband and wife. In particular, the use of another man's sperm was seen as falling 'within the meaning and consequences of *zina*' (adultery and broadly illegitimate sexual relations), a most serious offence under the sharia. Here, Jad al-Haqq echoes the view held long before the advent of IVF by his predecessor at al-Azhar, Shaykh Mahmud Shaltut, on donor insemination.[3]

The subsequent debate has backed away somewhat from such a ready identification of these medical procedures with *zina* proper. There are clear and stringent criteria for the establishment of such an offence, including the witnessing of the sexual act; donor insemination and IVF using donor sperm do not meet those criteria. Alternative grounds for opposing these techniques might include the blocking of avenues for potential evil (*sadd al-dharai*). Some Shia scholars use the *hadith* (saying of the Prophet) that promises the worst torments in the hereafter to 'the man who placed his seed in a womb forbidden to him'. But others then observe that, while that might apply to donor insemination, in IVF one transfers an embryo rather than introducing semen into the woman's uterus. IVF using donor sperm is thus for some, such as Ayatollah Yousef Sanei of Iran, less clearly ruled out.[4]

In the case of donor eggs, the sharia's allowing of polygamy may offer a ready solution: the husband can choose to marry the donor of the egg. The same would apply for a surrogate mother, or 'hired womb' (*rahim mustajir*) as the literature often puts it (and some scholars go on to discuss whether such an arrange-

---

[3] '[A]n abominable sin, and a mighty one. It meets with *zina* in one frame: their essence is one': *Al-fatawa: dirasa li-mushkilat al-muslim al-muasir fi hayat al-yawmiyya wa-l-amma* (Cairo, 1965), p. 328.

[4] See the correspondence quoted in Morgan Clarke, 'Children of the Revolution: Ayatollah Khamene'i's "Liberal" Views on *In Vitro* Fertilisation', *British Journal of Middle Eastern Studies*, 34 (2007), p. 299.

Science and Social Change

ment does indeed fulfil the requirements of a sound contract of hire). Here it would seem that no question of *zina* arises. A 1984 fatwa from the Islamic Legal Council (al-Majma al-Fiqhi al-Islami) of the Muslim World League, based in Mecca, allowed procedures involving two wives, married to the same man. But that permission was reversed the following year. The broad consensus among Sunni scholars is that the involvement of parties other than a husband and one wife is not permissible, above all because it entails a 'confounding of kinship relations' (*ikhtilat al-ansab*). The same is generally thought to apply to the posthumous use of gametes as well.

Shia scholars, while initially as cautious as their Sunni counterparts, have become more receptive to the permissibility of donor egg procedures and surrogacy arrangements, aided by the possibility of temporary marriage contracts in their tradition. For an egg donation, the husband may enter a temporary marriage contract with the donor for the duration of the procedure, perhaps for 24 to 48 hours. The same holds for a surrogacy arrangement – though rather longer – as ruled by Lebanon's late Ayatollah Muhammad Husayn Fadlallah, for example.[5] Some scholars have dropped even this requirement, among them Ayatollah Ali al-Khamenei, presently Supreme Leader of the Islamic Republic of Iran, who also allows posthumous gamete use.[6]

Ayatollah Khamenei's opinion on the use of donor sperm is quite unique, in that he finds it to be permissible both by IVF and insemination. He adds that, 'if a child is born in this way, it is not related to the husband, but to the producer of the sperm and to the woman, who is [here] the owner of the egg and the womb'. This is a vital point. For the many scholars who find the procedure unacceptable, it is an open question as to whether any legal kinship relation (*nasab*) is established at all. In husband and (one) wife IVF, all are agreed in finding the offspring fully legitimate. But for those who see donor situations as analogous to *zina*, such children may resemble those of *zina* in lacking a legit-

---

[5] Muhammad Husayn Fadlallah, *Fiqh al-sharia* (Beirut, 2003), vol. 3, p. 523.

[6] Ali al-Husayni al-Khamenei, *Ajwibat al-istiftaat* (Beirut, 2003), pp. 69–71.

110 *A Companion to Muslim Cultures*

imate father. The implications for the children's social as well as legal standing are obviously highly significant.

Where scholars do not perceive such a close correspondence with *zina*, if the child is to be given a father, should it be the donor, that is, the provider of the sperm, or the husband of the woman recipient, the 'social father' (not a term used in Muslim legal debates)? It should be noted that while the fostering of orphans is strongly encouraged in Islamic tradition, full adoption is generally ruled out, as a 'falsification' of the child's true origins. A legal resource would nevertheless seem to exist for allowing the husband to take on the mantle of legal father here: the assumption of paternity within marriage. So even in the classical stance on adultery and a subsequent pregnancy, for instance, unless the husband repudiates his wife and her child (which he is fully entitled to do), a child born during their marriage is considered his. The adulterer gets no such right over the child. This might lend itself to the use of donor sperm, but Muslim scholars seem largely agreed in finding that possibility distasteful.

The issue is still more complicated for motherhood in the case of donor egg procedures and surrogacy arrangements. Here scholars note that motherhood could be awarded to the woman who provides the egg, the genetic mother; or to the woman who carries the child in her womb and delivers it; or jointly to both; or to neither. The last two options are rarely favoured. Those who prefer the second option, perhaps the majority of Sunni scholars (while recalling that for them these procedures are largely ruled out) and a good number of Shia ones, most commonly rely on the Quranic verses, 'Their mothers are those only who gave birth to them (*waladna-hum*)' (58:2), and 'With much pain his mother bears him, and with much pain she brings him into the world' (46:15). Others, now perhaps the majority of Shia scholars, award motherhood to the provider of the egg, the genetic mother, deeming the Arabic verb used in the former verse, *walada*, as ambiguous and not referring unequivocally to childbirth itself, but to reproduction more generally.

These are not merely technical issues. If the donor is to be considered the parent, then all sorts of potential problems arise.

Science and Social Change

Will there be inheritance rights between the child and the donor? Can the child inherit from their 'social father', the husband? Even where the techniques themselves are forbidden, some scholars note that it is only the children of *zina* proper who can be denied inheritance, not the offspring of these medical procedures. Others oppose any inheritance rights at all.

There is also the matter of domestic life. If the child is considered to be related to the donor rather than the recipient, what about the intimacies of the home? Many Muslims observe the injunction that women who have reached the age of majority should veil before unrelated men. In the case of a girl born from donor sperm, she would on maturity have to veil before her 'social father', the husband of the couple. In the case of a boy born from donor eggs, the wife, who had carried him to term and delivered him, would have to veil before him when he came of age.

Muslim scholars have found a means for extricating oneself from some of these problems: the now somewhat obscure institution of *rida*, or 'milk kinship', created through breastfeeding between the suckling woman and the child suckled. While the 'milk mother' and 'milk child' do not have full kinship rights with respect to each other – they do not inherit from one another, for example – they do owe each other respect and compassion, and the rules of veiling and intimacy are relaxed. Where a woman has used donor eggs and carried the child to term, she will then likely breastfeed the child, creating a milk kinship relation which removes the problem. Some scholars even see the woman's nurture of the child in the womb as in itself creating a relationship analogous to that of *rida*, through her vital contribution to the physical sustenance of the child. A daughter of donor sperm can be considered as the husband's ward (*rabiba*), his wife's child, and thus not required to veil before him. As for inheritance, this can be resolved by making gifts and bequests to the child.

In view of the classical Islamic perspective that the 'ensoulment' of the embryo takes place much later than conception, the destruction of surplus embryos is less troubling for Muslims than it is for Christians, most notably Catholics. As well, Muslim scholars often adopt a relaxed stance with regard to PGD and

112   *A Companion to Muslim Cultures*

'sex selection', finding it acceptable for 'family balancing' in individual cases, though discouraged as a general rule. Indeed, there is even a willingness to consider the possibility, as yet unrealised, of human cloning and artificial wombs.

The Example of Lebanon

The theological openness toward opportunities that IVF offers has proved a welcome boon for many infertile Muslim couples. Middle Eastern societies, for instance, can be robustly pronatal, encouraging and expecting couples to have children right after marriage. For many, this can be stressful. In my research in religiously diverse Lebanon in 2003–4, doctors reported that couples come within months of marriage, sometimes even before, to seek advice and even treatment. When in case of genuine need treatment is advised, many Muslims derive comfort from the explicit rulings that are given by their religious experts, which in this instance tend to be enabling rather than restricting. Christian (and especially Catholic) opinion is, we should say, rather different. Broadly, the Vatican rules out all artificial interventions in human reproduction. Orthodox leaders (in Lebanon at least) initially took a similar stance, but have reportedly softened their position to allow IVF between husband and wife.

Public opinion at large has tended to lag behind not only the medical advances in this field, but also much of the religious debate. IVF was slow to acquire widespread social acceptance in Lebanon and patients were very reluctant to advertise their treatment, even travelling some distance to conceal it. With the stigma attached to infertility, and hence to addressing it through medical techniques such as IVF, treatment would often be kept secret, even from close friends and family. But extensive media coverage of the issue, along with soap operas, has led to much greater public awareness. Secrecy is still the rule for donor procedures, however, which carry a strong association of sexual impropriety. In the Middle East as a whole the procedures are not readily available, given the broad Sunni consensus against them. But they are available in Lebanon, which attracts patients from across the region.

Science and Social Change 113

This availability is no doubt due to Lebanon's striking religious diversity. Any party seeking legislation to prohibit donor procedures must contend with getting the agreement of all eighteen of Lebanon's official religious communities: besides the many different Christian denominations, there are the Sunnis, Twelver Shia, Druze, Ismailis and Alawis. Among Shia scholars alone, there is much diversity of opinion on these matters. Thus Lebanon's own late Ayatollah Fadlallah allowed the involvement of more than one woman in the use of temporary marriage, while Iran's Ayatollah Khamenei, influential in Lebanon due to the prominence of the Lebanese Hezbollah, does not require such marriages at all, and also allows the use of donor sperm. Ayatollah Ali Sistani of Iraq, who has a wide following in the region and beyond, has a different opinion again.

Since there is no national law in place, doctors are left free to practise as they see best. Many choose to follow the professional guidelines of the European and North American settings where they mostly specialised, and which frequently allow such procedures for infertile couples. Yet such paths can be highly challenging for patients on a personal level even if religious permission is in place. At this juncture, donor procedures are not at all common in practice.

The only other country in the region where these techniques are available is Iran, where a law permits egg and embryo donation. Sperm donation remains beyond the pale, despite the Supreme Leader's permission of it, one should note. Iran's relatively open attitude towards these and other treatments has helped nurture an important reproductive technology sector, alongside associated scientific programmes such as research into stem cell technologies. In a globalised world of biotechnology, opportunity as well as controversy flows to where local bioethical stances facilitate it. One may thus discern a distinctly political aspect to such debates.

Conclusion

It is not enough simply to invoke 'the Islamic position' on the science of reproduction and its implications for individuals and societies. There is rich diversity in a field that involves secular as

114   *A Companion to Muslim Cultures*

well as theological debate across the Muslim world and beyond. Where ordinary people such as infertility patients turn to clerics for advice, it is offered on an individual basis; after all, the facts may vary significantly from case to case. On the other hand, the medical profession and governments want something different: standardised regulation.

The emergence of Muslim legal committees, such as al-Majma al-Fiqhi al-Islami, allows the production of something closer to the latter need, in the form of a series of resolutions that take into account the opinions of all the Islamic legal schools. But it is the interface between Islamic legal (and other religious) scholarship and medical and state legal expertise that produces effective regulation. For example, the reasons why donor egg procedures are possible in Lebanon and Iran are very different. They have more to do with the distinctive legislative realities of those countries than with individual Islamic legal opinions as such.

Further, many argue that for a genuine 'Islamic medical ethics' to emerge, the debate needs to move beyond these legalistic approaches and towards training morally grounded doctors. Amid the unfolding of fresh advances and choices in modern medicine, Muslim scholars must thus grapple not only with the demands of their individual followers and the changing cultural contexts in which they live, but also with the demands of the state and other political actors – including the scientific and medical establishments that enjoy power and prestige in the modern world.

Further Reading

Atighetchi, Dariusch. *Islamic Bioethics: Problems and Perspectives.* Dordrecht, 2007.

Brockopp, Jonathan and Thomas Eich. *Muslim Medical Ethics: From Theory to Practice.* Columbia, South Carolina, 2008.

Clarke, Morgan. *Islam and New Kinship: Reproductive Technology and the Shariah in Lebanon.* New York, 2009.

Inhorn, Marcia. *Quest for Conception: Gender, Infertility, and Egyptian Medical Traditions.* Philadelphia, 1994.

Science and Social Change   115

— *Local Babies, Global Science: Gender, Religion, and In Vitro Fertilization in Egypt*. New York, 2003.

Inhorn, Marcia and Soraya Tremayne, ed. *Islam and the Biotechnologies of Human Life*. New York, in press.

Rispler-Chaim, Vardit. *Islamic Medical Ethics in the Twentieth Century*. Leiden, 1993.

Sachedina, Abdulaziz. *Islamic Biomedical Ethics: Principles and Application*. New York, 2009.

Salama, Ziyad. *Atfal al-anabib: bayna-l-ilm wa-l-sharia*. Amman, 1998.

al-Sistani, Muhammad Rida. *Wasail al-injab al-sinaiyya*. Beirut, 2004.

7

Architecture and Community

Hussein Keshani

In the old cities of the Islamic world, *masjid*s (mosques) were places where people, especially men, came together as a community to pray. Prominent works of *masjid* architecture were not only monuments of faith or dynastic power but also a means to reinforce, if not idealise, the community of the faithful. Yet *masjid* architecture was not the only kind that built such bonds. Urban fortifications, palace-complexes, walled gardens, funerary monuments, public works, commercial spaces and architectural ornament also fostered alternate, overlapping senses of community and, over time, distinctive identities. Civic and religious identities remain closely bound-up in architectural settings, as part of a deeply shared ethos that plays itself out in towns and cities as far apart as Samarkand, Isfahan, Fez and Zanzibar.

The role of architecture in shaping the public expression of this ethos is enormous: the grace and functionality of styles leaps across rigid divisions between 'secular' and 'religious' spaces. This fluidity is part of what makes a living heritage, where culture is not merely a showpiece but rather is integral to the everyday life of a community. The built environment has been a field of remarkably imaginative expression of Muslim identities in all their local and global diversity. This chapter will explore the historical unfolding of some key architectural forms which have laid the foundations of civic landscapes in the Muslim world, and the contemporary quest to make that heritage meaningful for diverse communities.[1]

---

[1] On the particular roles of cities and mosques as 'living heritage', see the chapters respectively by Amira Bennison and Hasan-Uddin Khan in Sajoo, ed., *A Companion to the Muslim World*.

Urban Fortifications

As with cities elsewhere, walls gave a sense of security and communal identity to Muslim communities that engaged in masonry-building. Many cities were extensively fortified with imposing bastioned walls and monumental gateways that restricted access. Both the royal and administrative precincts and the surrounding urban fabric, dense with the property of nobles and merchants, were typically fortified.

One dramatic example of early urban fortifications from the eighth century is the horseshoe-shaped wall of the Abbasid city of al-Rafiqa, which adjoined the earlier Syrian city of al-Raqqa and is now in ruins. In the Islamic Mediterranean, ancient Roman fortifications loomed large, inspiring rulers and builders such as those who built the stunning citadel of Aleppo in Syria, with its steep ramparts and limestone walls. Just as impressive are fortifications in the 14th-century South Asian city Daulatabad, which was located around a large granite outcrop and boasted four concentric rings of fortress walls. Later Mughal rulers and their allies were also prolific builders of fortifications. Though masonry fortification appears to be less common in sub-Saharan Africa, some examples exist as do ones made of earth. Earthen ramparts could be just as imposing as stone walls; the walled city of Birni N'gazargamo, capital of the Saifawa dynasty of Kanem/Bornu in modern Nigeria, was built in 1470 with walls seven metres high and two kilometres long.

These examples only hint at the widespread use of urban and palace fortifications across the Islamic world and are strong reminders that security against rivals and invading forces were a constant concern for patrons and builders of pre-modern Islamic architecture. But urban walls also forged a strong sense of a common urban identity and belonging. Walls that divided people also brought them together in both spatial and psychological realms.

Palace Communities

Warfare and semi-nomadic lifestyles meant that rulers and military elites were often on the move. When they slowed down, however, palace-complexes located within city walls, on their outskirts or in the countryside, were scenes of intricate daily life. The largest palace-complexes tended to be cities within cities, courtly communities within larger communities that typically combined separate households for elite women, their children and their servants, with administrative headquarters for government officials and courtiers.

Architectural historian Gulru Necipoglu has highlighted how various types of palace-complex architecture are thought to have existed in the mainly masonry-building regions of the Islamic world.[2] Drawing on Byzantine, Roman, Mesopotamian and Sassanian examples, the Umayyads and Abbasids experimented with agricultural villas in the Greater Syrian and Iraqi countrysides. The Abbasids tried out urban palace-mosque complexes as well – and refined the idea of a luxurious, sprawling multi-court suburban garden palace which inspired many later dynasties to come. The vast scale of the palace complex of Caliph al-Mutasim at Samarra, for example, which spans 145 hectares, evokes the spectacular concentrations of wealth and power achieved by the dynasty.

The Turkic migrations and the spread of Turkic dynasties were accompanied by the rise of the fortified urban citadel from the 11th century on, such as the one built at Aleppo. The concept can even be observed on the East African coast in southern Tanzania near Kilwa, where the Husuni Kubwa palace complex – a collection of stone courts overlooking the Indian Ocean, similar to ones in the Arabian Gulf – once stood.[3] After the Mongol invasions in

---

[2] See Gulru Necipoglu, ed., Special Issue on Pre-Modern Islamic Palaces *Ars Orientalis*, 23 (1993).

[3] The name of this 14th-century complex derives from the Arabic *husn*, a fortified enclosure, and the Kiswahili *kubwa* for large (the smaller one, Husuni Ndogo, being about 80 metres to the east of the palace).

120   *A Companion to Muslim Cultures*

Central Asia and Greater Iran, the urban citadel and multi-court palace were synthesised in unique ways, and later exploited to their full potential in the capitals of the Safavid, Ottoman and Mughal empires. In contrast, the palace-complexes of the mainly wood-building Southeast Asian sultanates generally lacked fortifications. Looking to Indian, Chinese and indigenous traditions for inspiration, their courts emanated symmetrically from the centrally-located ruler's residence; an axial alignment with local mountains was felt to be auspicious.

The multi-court palace concept often included a variety of enclosed garden courts, with pavilions on the perimeter that could be used for both functional and recreational purposes. The elegant garden courts of the Alhambra palace complex in Granada, though heavily restored, offer a glimpse into how Roman gardens were adapted in Islamic architecture – and more significantly, the westward diffusion of Persian garden design ideas such as the *chahar bagh*, a four-quartered garden subdivided by water channels. Reflecting pools were also used in the garden courts of the Alhambra, and to the east, as in the court of the Chihil Sutun (40 Pillars), one of two surviving pavilions from the multi-court Safavid palace precinct that adjoined Isfahan's *maydan* (square).

The walled *chahar bagh* came to be extremely popular in Central Asia, Iran and South Asia. The spread of the idea from Central Asia to India was encouraged by the founder of the Mughal dynasty, Babur (r. 1526–1530), who disliked the gardens of earlier Muslim rulers in northern India. The walled *chahar bagh* would become the preferred setting for Mughal tomb architecture. The *chahar bagh* even served as the underlying planning principle for the new cities of Safavid Isfahan and Mughal Shahjahanabad; both sported a long axial avenue with a continuous water channel.

Enclosed gardens were not confined to palace precincts, and sometimes they stood alone in urban areas. The variants of the *chahar bagh* included parterres of flowers, trickling fountains, reflecting pools and water channels running down steps; their uses extended to agriculture, staging encampments, holding court and hosting parties, as well as the performance of religious rites. Islamic gardens are often said to be mirrors of paradise, striving to recreate

Architecture and Community   121

on earth the pleasures of heaven mentioned in the Quran. Yet it is important not to lose sight of the more worldly aspects of Islamic gardens as practical sites and social spaces in the lives of Muslim communities.

Walled and elevated palace-complexes could serve to separate elites from the larger society by creating distinct courtly worlds. But they were also essential catalysts for surrounding development. The palatial communities served as crucial nodes around which cities evolved, creating tangible architectural symbols of authority and luxury.

Lively Tombs

In one of history's intriguing twists, tombs that were built to commemorate the deceased would in many regions become vital centres of Muslim life, alternate sites of religious devotion and places to socialise. Tradition typically called for the deceased to be laid in the ground perpendicular to the direction of Mecca, so that their faces could be turned toward the Kaaba (the direction of ritual prayer). It was appropriate to bury the deceased in a family dwelling, a suburban cemetery, or later near or within a religious institution such as a *masjid* or *madrassa*. Rural and village landscapes abounded with graves and tombs as well.

Building tombs over graves is an old practice in the Muslim world, perhaps dating to the time of Prophet Muhammad, and likely influenced by Byzantine Syrian shrines for saints and relics. No tomb was built for the Prophet himself, who was said to have been buried in his home, which was also the Medina *masjid*. Centuries later, rebuildings of the Medina *masjid* by the Mamluks and Ottomans led to architectural embellishment of the Prophet's gravesite with a large dome, which was integrated into the *masjid*. The tomb and *masjid*, which have been extensively expanded in the late-20th century, form the second most important pilgrimage destination for pious Muslims after the Kaaba.

Graves of the deceased were originally no more than unmarked mounds, but these gave way to the use of grave markers of many varieties. After the ninth century, tomb construction seems to

122   *A Companion to Muslim Cultures*

have also risen in popularity, perhaps tied to the growing religious authority of saintly individuals and the venerative practices which their personas attracted.[4] Tomb-building stems in part from this urge to commemorate exceptional saintly souls. Earlier on, it was the Companions of the Prophet, the Shia Imams, and Old and New Testament figures whose gravesites were distinguished by tombs. Later, those of celebrated Muslim mystics, religious scholars and frontier soldiers credited with expanding Islam's reach attracted tombs. The 14th century Central Asian ruler Timur, after a pilgrimage to the small shrine of the 12th century mystic Ahmad Yasavi, commissioned a monumental tomb and religious centre for the shaykh, credited with bringing Islam to Kazakhstan, pioneering Turkic poetry and establishing his own Sufi order. The belief that blessings could be derived from visiting the graves of saintly souls was an impetus for building tombs, and the formation of pilgrimage networks that – along with trade networks – helped tie together disparate regions of the Muslim world.

The Egyptian towns of Fustat and Aswan offer two important groups of early tombs dating from the 10th century and later, which signal a growing interest in commemorating the deceased, saintly or otherwise. The small scale was typical of earlier funerary works, but after the Turkic and Mongol conquests tomb-building took on more monumental proportions and was closely tied with ruling figures and elites, a preference of the Mamluks as attested by the domed tombs of Cairo's historic skyline. But it was the successor empires of Genghis Khan (the Ilkhanids, Timurids and Mughals) who built tombs on an unprecedented grand scale to serve as dynastic and imperial monuments cared for by legions of attendants. A highpoint in this love affair is undoubtedly the Taj Mahal in Agra. Set within a vast garden enclosure, the marble-clad domed edifice was built by the Mughal emperor Shah Jahan for his favourite wife in 1631, though he is also buried there.

Tombs were not lifeless monuments; along with graves, they attracted ritual prayer activity for many reasons. Their explicit orientation towards Mecca, the use of *mihrab* (prayer niche)

---

[4] See further the chapter by Earle Waugh in this volume.

imagery, the belief in the aura of the gravesites of charismatic religious individuals, the custom of visiting graves annually and the practice of employing Quran readers at gravesites, all brought people to gravesites and made them vibrant centres of activity. The most common form for a tomb was a domed cube, though this varied. Anatolia and Iran are known for their distinctive tomb towers with conical roofs, which grew in popularity from the late 10th to the 13th century. An impressive example is the Gunbad-i Qabus, completed with baked brick in 1006. Another interesting variation found in Damascus and Baghdad is the *muqarnas* tomb, in which the roof is made up of a series of honeycomb-like arched niches that create stunning optical effects.

Tombs were not always independent structures. Mamluk Cairo and its environs show that tombs could be integrated into religious institutions like the *masjid* or *madrassa*, securing perpetual prayers for the souls of the deceased. Such hybrid structures still incorporated prominent funerary domes and roofs that served as an eternal marker of one's spirit on the cityscape. Tombs with large endowments and donations, as well as reputations for spiritual blessings, attracted all kinds of people locally and regionally. They became nodes for crossroads communities and were often woven into civic life. Indeed, just as palace-complexes were triggers of urban development, so too were tombs for the growth of communities.

Civic Architecture

In the historic cities of the Islamic world, communities also formed around a variety of civic architectural works that offered useful social services. These included the *madrassa*, small hospitals (*bimaristans*) and bathhouses (*hammams*). As societies grew more complex, institutions dedicated to teaching and learning evolved beyond the *masjid* and the homes of scholars. These first emerged around the 10th century in eastern Iran, where they were favoured by the westward-expanding Turkic dynasty, the Saljuqs, who likely used them to disseminate and institutionalise their own doctrinal convictions in a heterodox environment.

124   *A Companion to Muslim Cultures*

Madrassas were primarily devoted to the Islamic religious sciences – Quran interpretation, hadith scholarship, and legal studies – but mathematics and science had their place in these institutions too. They could stand alone or be joined to *masjids* or tombs, and generally stood one or two stories high, with small chambers surrounding a central rectangular court that was usually open to the sky (but could in some regions be covered with a dome). Typically, halls for students and teachers to perform their daily prayers were incorporated.

In the late 12th century, before the Mongol invasions put an end to the Abbasid dynasty, Baghdad's *madrassas* included the impressive al-Mustansirriya, named after the caliph. Mamluk Cairo was also enthralled with *madrassas*. Domed tombs for rulers and elites frequently adjoined these lavishly ornamented buildings. The funerary *madrassa* of the 15th century sultan Qaitbay is a good example of this marriage of death and learning. Among the grandest *madrassas* ever built are those in the Timurid Central Asian capital Samarkand, famed for its religious scholars. The city's Registan Square consists of a group of three monumental *madrassas* (the Ulugh Beg, Shir Dar and Tilla Kari) built between the 15th and 17th centuries, which together form a pleasing urban ensemble (Plate 5). Likewise, the Ottoman sultan Suleyman included at least four *madrassas* around his monumental 16th century mosque in Istanbul.

Muslim societies inherited a long tradition of medical science from the Greeks, the Persians and the Indians, so it is no surprise that hospitals could be found in many of the historic cities of the Islamic world. While the Abbasids were active patrons, surviving examples are scarce; later ones dating after the Turkic migrations began do survive in fine condition. One example is Mamluk Aleppo's premier hospital, the Maristan of Arghun al-Kamili, built in 1354. With its open court and reflecting pool, it was a tranquil place to be treated for one's ailments. Equally pleasing is the hospital of Ottoman Sultan Bayazid II in Edirne, where music was reportedly one form of treatment prescribed for the mentally ill.

Public bathhouses were also a common feature in many Muslim cities, a legacy in part of Romano-Byzantine architecture.

Architecture and Community 125

Bathhouses could be important generators of revenue – a fact not lost on the Il-Khanid ruler Ghazan Khan (r.1295–1304), who ordered a *hammam* to be built with every *masjid* in the villages of Iran to help finance *masjid* operations. The Yalbugha Hammam in Aleppo, rebuilt by a Mamluk governor in the 15th century and creatively restored in the 20th century, preserves the subterranean atmosphere of domed bathhouses lit with starlike openings (Plate 6). The charming twin-baths commissioned in Ottoman Istanbul by Suleyman's famous spouse, Hürrem Sultan, cleverly separates men and women while sharing the heating facilities. It was in such places that ordinary people relaxed and socialised; rulers and elites, after all, could build private baths in their homes.

In general, commissioning religious and civic works was considered pious work, the kind rulers and elites were expected to undertake on behalf of Muslim societies. This responsibility extended to waterworks, public water facilities and bridge-building, the elements of flourishing cities and agricultural districts. Isfahan's Khawju bridge and weir, built by the Safavids in the 18th century, shows how public works could on occasion combine architectural ingenuity with beauty (Plate 7).

Commerce

Dotted along the Muslim world's vast trade networks were commercial buildings, several of which were built upon existing military outposts. Spaces for commerce were routinely encouraged by rulers and elites who saw the benefits in bringing in revenue. Most buildings followed a courtyard plan, varying by region in details and quality. In coastal cities, urban bazaars and commercial buildings on land routes flourished, accommodating merchants and animals laden with goods. These multi-purpose spaces were known by names such as *funduq*, *khan* and *caravanserai*.[5] Remote hinterland facilities provided fortified overnight accommodations and animal stables, while urban facilities focused more on warehousing and shops.

---

[5] On the social ethos of these institutions see Bruce Lawrence's chapter, 'Networks of Solidarity', in Sajoo, ed., *A Companion to the Muslim World*.

126 *A Companion to Muslim Cultures*

Numerous examples survive after the rise of the Saljuqs, notably in Iran. Especially grand with its elaborate vaulting is the Khan Mirjan of Baghdad, whose revenue was intended to finance a neighbouring *madrassa*'s operations. Then there is the Rustam Pasha urban *caravanserai* in Edirne, which stood on one of the major trade routes linking Asia with Europe. Commissioned by Suleyman's trusted vizier, it was built by the Ottomans' greatest architect, Sinan. Modern restorers have sought to give this building a new lease on life by converting it into a hotel.

Bazaars proliferated across West Asia and the Islamic Mediterranean, with covered streets called souks, but these are difficult to date. Long tracts of single room shops lined narrow streets that were sometimes arranged in multiple rows. More established areas would cover the streets with materials like cloth, reeds, brick and stone. Among the most elaborate examples of this style of commercial development taken to its logical extreme is the Grand Bazaar of Istanbul, which includes two large 15th century commercial storage buildings (*bedestans*) surrounded by a maze of covered streets forming one large superstructure.

These works of architecture brought together merchants and fostered trade networks that spanned continents. Within cities, they created yet another urban space where people could engage with each other. It is often said that commerce is the lifeblood of cities. If so, then commercial spaces were among the vital organs that helped historic Islamic cities flourish.

Minorities

Christians, Jews, Hindus and others frequently lived alongside Muslims not only as tolerated minorities but even as majorities (Istanbul being a prime instance for much of its history) in the Islamic world. Hence, we have non-Muslim monumental architecture that drew upon the architectural vocabulary of Muslim societies. In 17th century Isfahan, Shah Abbas had the suburb of New Julfa built for the Armenian Christian community, which enacted the remarkable Vank cathedral using the architectural idiom of the Safavids. In Old Cairo, the restored 19th-century Ben

Architecture and Community 127

Ezra Synagogue was a reconstruction of an historic 11th-century synagogue which was attended by the renowned medieval Jewish philosopher Maimonides. At times, Muslim communities were conquered by outsiders and became minorities, as in 12th-century Sicily under the Norman Crusaders, 13th century Iran under the Mongols, and 16th-century Christian Spain. Here, the building traditions nurtured by Muslim societies generally continued to be employed and adapted.

It is worth remembering that there was no universal archetype of the Islamic city; the architectural works that helped define cities were not always separate entities. At various times and locations, different combinations of spaces and building types with common affinities took place. These combinations included fusing *masjid*s with palaces, *madrassa*s with tombs, commercial with residential spaces, *hammam*s with *masjid*s, tombs with *masjid*s, and hospitals with *madrassa*s. Such hybrid architectural spaces combined not only different functions, but different kinds of communities as well.

These genres of architecture and their hybrids were the locus around which settlement occurred. In societies that came to adopt Near Eastern cultural values, a common feature in the design of homes was the ability to uphold the segregation of the sexes.

Recurring Architectural Themes

Builders in historic Muslim societies tended to choose from and combine remarkably few spatial ideas and architectural motifs. The enclosed courtyard was the most widely used spatial idea in Islamic architecture, serving purposes that could be commercial, educational, military or religious. While its origins pre-date Islam, it was adopted in both masonry and wood building regions of the expanding Muslim world. Transitions into courtyard enclosures and between adjacent ones were often regulated by using gateways, which could on occasion be monumental in scale.

Large halls were normally built using various combinations of columns and arcades, making the pillared hall a popular form of monumental space. Aside from *masjid*s, audience chambers in palace architecture also used pillared halls to command awe and respect. Pillared halls were covered with flat or gabled roofs, though small domes and barrel vaults were used in regions with more sophisticated masonry building traditions. In such regions, large domed chambers were commonly used in *masjids*, throne halls and luxury apartments in the palace complexes of rulers, as well as the graves of important individuals. While monumental domes became a staple of Islamic architecture in masonry building regions, wood building regions of the Islamic world such as northern parts of South Asia, Southeast Asia and certain areas of China favoured elaborate gabled and sometimes upswept roofs.

From early on, the aesthetic and structural potential of the arch was explored relentlessly in the masonry-building Islamic world. Rounded arches predominated in the west and pointed arches, which could bear more weight, in the east. The arch is also the basis for another popular motif – the arched niche or *iwan* in Persian – inherited from Ancient Persia. *Iwans* were often used with enclosed courts to create the popular four-*iwan* plan, which was especially common in Central Asia, Iran and South Asia. If domes were a favourite monumental device in Islamic masonry architecture, *iwans* would be a close second, often employed for large gateways and chambers opening onto courtyards. Towers of all shapes and sizes, now called minarets, were another recurring feature in Islamic architecture. Typically associated with *masjids*, minarets were landmarks that were also used for ornament and surveillance.

The idea that architectural space should accommodate the separation of unrelated men and women was built upon Byzantine and Middle Eastern cultural precedents, as well as creative inter-pretations of the Quran, and it entrenched itself among elites in much of the Islamic world after the ninth century. Not all Muslim societies embraced this idea, however, and neither did all social segments practise it to the same degree. In palatial and residen-tial design, the practice translated into the development of special zones for women that were forbidden to male outsiders (*haram*). In some regions, the practice led to the outright exclusion of women from mosques; in others they were relegated to separate

Architecture and Community

compartments or balconies, a feature commonly found in *masjid* design today.

Women's rights to own property and amass independent wealth in Muslim societies meant that elite women were often patrons of monumental architecture as a detailed study of Fatimid, Ayyubid, Timurid, Safavid, Mughal and Ottoman architecture would reveal. A study of 12th-century Ayyubid Damascus estimates that women patrons accounted for 14 per cent of the major religious commissions over a period of 85 years.[6]

The ways in which palaces and tombs especially were ornamented also helped foment aesthetic continuities. For the most part, the architectural arts drew from the same visual vocabulary of calligraphic, geometric, organic and occasionally pictorial motifs used by the other forms of art that were popular in the Islamic world. This ornamentation displayed a deep awareness of the portable arts and their visual motifs, which were circulated by traders, travellers, religious figures and soldiers on their journeys.

Glass and stone mosaics, along with wall and ceiling painting, were popular in the Greater Syria region in the seventh century (and wall and ceiling painting in Greater Iran and South Asia after the 15th century). Figural and animal subject matter consistently had no place within prayer spaces, but they could thrive in spaces of authority and luxury.[7] Religious concerns generally wielded more influence over the settings in which such images could appear, and less over their content.

Less costly than mosaic work and more durable than paintings, the humble medium of stucco was by far the most widespread means of embellishing architecture, especially in North Africa, Spain, Iran, Central Asia and India. These typically included moulded and cut displays of complex organic and geometric patterns, as well as Arabic and sometimes Persian calligraphy. Stucco artisans also sculpted *muqarna*s to fill monumental

---

[6] R. Stephen Humphreys, 'Women as Patrons of Religious Architecture in Ayyubid Damascus,' *Muqarnas*, 11 (1994), p. 35.
[7] See Fahmida Suleman's chapter on Islamic art in Sajoo, ed., *A Companion to Muslim Ethics*.

130 · A Companion to Muslim Cultures

archways, squinches and domes. Except for sub-Saharan Africa and parts of China and Southeast Asia, *muqarnas* were used across the Islamic world; they could be made with wood, brick or stone as well.

Although stucco was more pliable than stone, stone-carving was more permanent and commonly employed calligraphic, geometric and organic motifs. Inlaid stonework was cultivated to high standards as in Mughal India, but pierced stonework – commonly used for windows – was perhaps the most eloquent form of stone artistry. Scattered light was also an effect explored with wood, displayed brilliantly in Ottoman Cairo's urban domestic architecture. These city homes had projecting windows made of wood screens known as *mashrebiyyas*, which offered both privacy and quiet spectacles of light on the interior. The growth of ceramic technology after the ninth century sparked interest in using glazed brick, and later of ornamental tile-work, especially in Iran, Central Asia and Turkey. North Africa and Spain developed their own distinctive approaches to tile-work.

Builders in many Muslim societies often coupled the architectural themes noted above with local building traditions in unique ways. These visual ideas, fused with the ritual and symbolic needs of Muslim societies, brought consistency rather than sameness to the architecture of the Islamic world. Wide reliance on this highly adaptable vocabulary helped circulate an ever-evolving group of aesthetic identities. Just as clothing and food helped create senses of communal identity and belonging, architectural aesthetics created their own kind of diffuse sense of community, built around common conventions and tastes.

Colonialism and Modernity

Fresh challenges to Muslim architectural and social identities were provoked with the advent of European (including Russian) imperial power in the 19th century. In addition to confronting the spectre of colonial rule, the cities of the Islamic world wrestled with new ideas of what a 'modern' city should be. Architects and engineers introduced European aesthetics, architectural genres and

Architecture and Community   131

building-methods, as well as forms of public and transportation infrastructure. Out of this prolonged encounter, two overarching yet interwoven approaches emerged: the transplanting of European urban design and architectural forms, and the fusing together of European and Islamic architectural ideas.

These two tendencies are well displayed in French Algiers and in 19th century Ottoman Istanbul. The French colonisation of Algiers led to the making of an entire European quarter, sited on cleared land between the Mediterranean and the historic walled city. The waterfront was transformed by the engineering feat of the Boulevard de l'Impératrice (now Boulevard de Che Guevara), a series of roads and ramps built atop gleaming white arcades, which led to the harbour front and literally cemented French access to the sea. The arcaded boulevard alluded to Islamic architecture, or perhaps to Roman viaducts; but elsewhere, roads and boulevards reminded one of Paris.

In contrast, 19th-century Ottoman Istanbul offers an example of Muslim rulers selectively appropriating European planning and architectural ideas. They favoured the imposition of orthogonal streets onto the existing urban fabric and the building of iron bridges and railways. A wave of building in neo-classical and European-conceived Islamic revival styles occurred, and small-scale residential building shifted away from wood to masonry construction. A potent symbol of Ottoman Europhilia is the Dolmabahce palace, which served as the seat of Ottoman power in the late 19th and early 20th century. Dispensing with the courtyard, the palace was a multi-storied block of buildings whose interiors accommodated Ottoman lifestyles and court structures, but whose facades reflected Renaissance architectural proportions and were ornamented with classical-inspired columns.

When European colonial empires receded from the Islamic world in the mid-20th century, the global influence of the United States grew, as did the reach of the Soviets and the Chinese. Much of the Islamic world was reconfigured with varying success into nation states, and architects trained in Europe and the United States continued to shape the region's urban landscapes. Efforts at transplantation and fusion continued, but the neo-Classical

132 *A Companion to Muslim Cultures*

vocabulary no longer symbolised western progress. It was replaced by the more austere style of the International Modernist movement in architecture, also emanating from Europe and North America. An excellent example is the Istiqlal (Independence) Mosque of Jakarta, Indonesia (Plate 8). Built with reinforced concrete, the mosque is a towering rectangular block crowned with a perfect hemispherical dome, and owes little to the local Javanese tiered-roof *masjids* of the past. The gigantic scale – a symbol of Indonesian independence from Dutch colonial rule and its aspirations at the time to be a leader in the Third World – foreshadowed the subsequent mega-mosque building trend in wealthy Muslim nation-states. This in turn has been overtaken by the construction of massive airports, office skyscrapers, museums, university campuses and medical centres.

As the Modernist architectural model has lost favour internationally, freer experimentation with historical forms using contemporary materials has grown. This neo-traditionalist approach is best exemplified by the elaborate expansions to the Masjid al-Haram or Grand Mosque which surrounds the Kaaba in Mecca. The appearance of a historic building obscures the sophisticated technologies at play, which include retractable roofs and elaborate air conditioning systems.

Affluence among oil-rich Arab states, many without a deep architectural heritage, has spawned extraordinary levels of development in Persian Gulf cities like Dubai, Doha and Riyadh. Mainly Asian migrant labour, and western architectural and engineering companies, have done the building. The lavish Kingdom Centre skyscraper in Riyadh, for example, was designed by architect Scott Berry and built by Bechtel, the largest engineering company in the United States, which attracted much attention when it was awarded numerous Iraqi reconstruction projects after the 2003 US-led Iraq War.

These new catalysts of urban development have also influenced contemporary housing, the two often tied together with roads and cars. As the shift to modern industrial building materials occurs, the construction of modern apartment blocks, high-rise housing, urban and suburban villas, and shanty towns has exploded. The

Architecture and Community   133

influence of local materials, environment and building traditions has given way to a global flow of residential building ideas shaped mainly by the industrialised West, which has established the template for modern living in so much of the Muslim world today.

There is also the phenomenon of diasporic Muslim architecture in the West, with the large migrations of Arabs, Iranians, Africans, South Asians and others into Western Europe and North America. Often, monumental religious buildings have been funded by Saudi Arabia. Using local building industries and technologies, historic forms are often used with varying success to facilitate Muslim ritual practice, as well as to symbolically assert the presence of Muslim communities in the West.

New Perspectives

The direction of contemporary urban development has generally been at odds with the architectural heritage of the Islamic world, in the wake of encounters with colonial cultures. Whether due to cultural ideologies, poverty, economic globalisation, geo-politics, war, pollution, indifference, mismanagement or fundamental shifts in society, the Islamic world's architectural heritage is in crisis. As buildings decay and disappear, so too do historical ways of forming community.

Yet intriguing responses to the challenge have ensued through skilful conservation work and creative attempts to reconcile tradition with modernity the global with the local. The Aga Khan Trust for Culture, for example, was formed in 1988 and supports a trio of agencies concerned with architecture across the Islamic world: the Historic Cities Program dedicated to conserving architectural heritage; the prestigious Aga Khan Award for Architecture for excellence in building; and the Aga Khan Program for Islamic Architecture at Harvard University and MIT in Boston, which focuses on architectural history and education.[8] Two guiding premises of the agencies are that the conservation of cultural heritage

---

[8] The Trust is part of the Aga Khan Development Network, with a presence in over 25 countries: see http://www.akdn.org/aktc.asp

134 *A Companion to Muslim Cultures*

should be integral to economic and social development, and that 'modernity' for the Islamic world should amount to more than mere emulation of the West.

The Historic Cities Program's most stunning accomplishment is the creation of the 30-hectare al-Azhar park in the midst of Old Cairo in 2005, a project that was over two decades in the making (Plate 9). The park takes its name from the historic al-Azhar *masjid*, which was founded by the Fatimids to mark their conquest of Egypt in 969 CE and the establishment of Cairo as their capital; the mosque was subsequently embellished by the Mamluks and the Ottomans. Built over a rubble site, the contours of the park are defined by an excavated city wall that is over 1.5 kilometres long on one side, and a highway on the other. The adjacent Darb al-Ahmar neighbourhood, dense with Mamluk-era tombs, is also among the poorest in all of Cairo. But it has become the locus of various economic revitalisation and heritage conservation initiatives, spurred on by the park and its revenues. The park itself is an unusual mix of serpentine paths, lawns, a manmade pond, Mughal Indian inspired water channels and gardens, and other delights. It would be a mistake to see the al-Azhar project as 'repairing' Cairo's historical ways of forming community, along with its walls and tombs. The resurrected Ayyubid wall no longer secures the populace, and the Mamluk tombs being restored no longer honour the deceased as they once did. The communal relationships that created and sustained these works remain deeply fractured. A radical new space, the park is as modern as a skyscraper, diverging from Cairo's own garden heritage. It engenders a new kind of community built around elevating the importance of architectural heritage and its conservation, the enjoyment of urban green space, and global and local tourism. Clearly a valuable contribution to the quality of Cairo's urban life and identity, it reminds us that the historical relationships between architecture and community have been fundamentally transformed.

In the pre-modern Islamic world, *masjid*s, palace-complexes, tombs, civic buildings and commercial works all helped to produce overlapping layers of different kinds of community, which together played a role in the making of civic cultures. The Muslim world's newer large-scale shopping malls, airports, office towers, conservation efforts and media networks, as with the rest of the world today, foster new and different kinds of community. In this context, conservation and the search for alternate approaches to architecture in the contemporary Islamic world is not just about physical space alone. It is also about how old ways of creating community can be reconciled with the new ones.

Further Reading

Bianca, Stefano. *Urban Form in the Arab World*. Zurich, 2000.

Bishop, Ryan et al, ed. *Postcolonial Urbanism: Southeast Asian Cities and Global Processes*. New York, 2003

Celik, Zeynep. *The Remaking of Istanbul: Portrait of an Ottoman City in the Nineteenth Century*. Seattle, WA, 1986.

Daftary, Farhad, et al, ed. *Living in Historic Cairo: Past and Present in an Islamic City*. London and Washington, DC, 2010.

Hillenbrand, Robert. *Islamic Architecture*. New York, 1994.

Insoll, Timothy. *The Archaeology of Islam in Sub-Saharan Africa*. Cambridge (UK), 2003.

Kultermann, Udo. *Contemporary Architecture in the Arab States: Renaissance of a Region*. New York, 1999.

Raymond, Andre. *The Great Arab Cities in the 16th-18th Centuries: An Introduction*. New York, 1984.

Ruggles, D. Fairchild, ed. *Patronage and Self-Representation in Islamic Societies*. New York, 2000.

al-Sayyad, Nezar, ed. *Forms of Dominance: On the Architecture and Urbanism of the Colonial Enterprise*. Farnham (UK), 1992.

8

Moving Words

Jonathan M. Bloom

Writing is at the heart of Muslim civilisation, witness to the place of the Quran as God's revelation in Arabic to Muhammad. Arabic became the lingua franca of a single linguistic commonwealth from Spain to Central Asia. The Jewish merchants of Egypt and North Africa spoke the same Arabic as their Muslim brethren, although they wrote it in Hebrew characters. Such was the power of the Arabic script that even unrelated languages spoken by those living under the banner of Islam, such as Persian and Turkish, came to be written in modified Arabic scripts.

Few other cultures have elevated the art of writing to the position it occupies in Islam, and medieval Muslims were more likely to be literate than members of contemporary societies elsewhere. Writing was used not only to create documents and books but also to decorate virtually everything from the humblest everyday object to the most sophisticated edifice. Under Muslim rule Arabic, like Greek and Latin before it, quickly became a language of administration, and the bureaucracy that these rulers created needed vast quantities of writing materials – first papyrus or parchment, then paper – for keeping records.

Muslim civilisation became a culture of books, particularly in comparison with Byzantium and western Europe at the time. One estimate is that 600,000 Arabic manuscript (hand-copied) books survive from the period before printing was introduced, and they must represent only a minute fraction of what was originally produced. The significance of writing in Islam coupled with the primacy of the Quran as scripture has fostered the impression

138 *A Companion to Muslim Cultures*

that Islam has always been text-based. The importance of the written word in Islam is undeniable. But since the time of the revelation, Muslims have learned and experienced the Quran primarily as an oral text, not as a written one. Memory and gesture have persisted as equally important means for the transmission of Islamic culture, even if they have not always been recognised as such by Western scholars.

Still, as books, documents and other forms of graphic notation, all of which stood for distinctly new ways of thinking, spread through Muslim society, the growing availability of paper encouraged a transition in medieval Islamic times. A culture based on memory and gesture shifted to one mainly grounded in the written record. Paper, the material that Muslim civilisations carried from China to Europe, was an even greater invention than printing in the history of humankind. Cheaper writing materials not only made old learning more accessible but also encouraged new learning and initiated new ways of thinking and representing thought.

Our impressions of the past are often skewed by later reinterpretations. Early Muslims lived in an intellectually dynamic and fluid milieu, with many different communities of interpretation and schools of thought. The success of the text-focused society that evolved under the patronage of the Abbasid caliphs of Baghdad in the ninth century has encouraged scholars to paint a monolithic picture of early Islam at variance with the evidence gleaned from other sources. Similarly, the text-focused, typographic nature of Middle Eastern culture today may lead us to overemphasise the textual aspects of Islamic culture over its oral and aural ones. And that is where our story begins.

The Quran and Oral Culture

Pre-Islamic culture in Arabia was largely oral, and though writing was known, it was relatively unimportant. Poetry was the highest form of art, and the poet was often likened to a prophet or king. Poetry was the peak of Arabic eloquence, and the *qasida* or ode was the supreme verse form. Pre-Islamic Arabs spoke many dialects

Moving Words 139

of Arabic, but every tribe used and understood the same poetic language, with an extremely refined grammar and vocabulary. The poems celebrated the gods, their own social affairs, their exploits, including raids and battles, and their genealogies. Poems were usually short, especially in comparison to those of Homer or Chaucer, and were composed to be recited in public.

There was no single authentic version of a particular work: poems were constantly reworked and embellished by the transmitters. Professional reciters relied on their prodigious memory, and the great pre-Islamic poems were not written down until several centuries after their composition. Yet Arabs had used writing for centuries before Islam. In Yemen, archaeologists have found inscriptions in South Arabian script dating from long before the Common Era, and in northwest Arabia and Syria they have found Arabic inscriptions in other alphabets. A funerary inscription dated 328 from al-Namara, in Syria, contains Arabic words written in the Nabatean alphabet of Petra (now in Jordan), but the oldest examples of Arabic texts written in Arabic script are three brief historical inscriptions, dating between 512 and 568, found near Damascus and a trilingual one in Greek, Syriac and Arabic found near Aleppo.

For the Meccans, who engaged in long-distance trade before the rise of Islam, writing would have been essential to record debts and credits, control inventories and instruct agents. Merchants would use materials such as palm fronds, wood, bone, pottery and stone for personal notes and jottings, but they would have found papyrus, parchment, or leather more suitable and durable for business correspondence. The Jews and Christians of pre-Islamic Arabia would have copied their scriptures on parchments. Nevertheless, writing did not play a very important role in pre-Islamic Arabia.

God's first revelation to Muhammad (96:1–2) opens with, 'Recite in the name of thy Lord', and reciting the words of this revelation has been a central part of Muslim worship from the beginning. Given the oral nature of pre-Islamic literature in Arabia and the oral nature of the revelation, the primary means of understanding, transmitting and preserving the revelations was, naturally

140 *A Companion to Muslim Cultures*

enough, through hearing and memory. The very word *al-quran* is a verbal noun whose Arabic root basically means 'to recite, read aloud'. Contemporaries therefore conceived the revelations to be oral texts intended to be rehearsed and recited, not read from a book.

The desire to preserve the Quranic text intact eventually developed into a discipline known in Arabic as *ilm al-qiraat*, usually rendered as 'science of readings'. A more accurate rendering would be 'science of recitations', for the discipline has stayed essentially oral and memory-based to the present day. When the Egyptian 'standard edition' of the Quran was prepared in the 1920s, it was the oral tradition that served as the authority for determining the written text.

For modern literates, reading is a silent, wholly mental process, but until quite recently reading in all cultures was a vocal and physical activity. Reading aloud also gave non-literates access to writing, and most literates preferred listening to a statement rather than perusing it in script. Medieval Arabic documents confirm the persistence of orality in medieval Islamic society. Four Egyptian documents dating from the 10th century, more than three centuries after the Quran was revealed, concern the sale of residential property from several villages in the Fayyum. The documents state that the contract had been 'read to the seller in Arabic and explained to him in the "foreign language"' (that is in Coptic, the language of the Egyptian peasantry). Only by reading it aloud was the power of the legal document activated.

The written text was not an end in itself but served as an aid to memory. A modern Western scholar confronted with a page from a medieval copy of the Quran written in the angular 'Kufic' script might puzzle out the individual letters and words to decipher the text (Plate 10). In contrast, a traditionally educated Muslim who had since childhood committed large blocks of the Quran to memory might be unfamiliar with the stylised script but would need to recognise only one group of letters to recognise the entire text. Indeed, the Quran is not read like normal prose. It is chanted or recited in techniques known in Arabic as *tilawa* and *tajwid*, which move between stylised speech and artistic singing. Quranic

Moving Words   141

recital styles have always been transmitted from master to pupil, which has led to the evolution of innumerable personal and regional variations.

The Abbasid caliph Harun al-Rashid made his son al-Mamun recite the Quran for the scholar al-Kisai. While al-Mamun recited, al-Kisai sat with his head bowed until al-Mamun made a mistake, whereupon the scholar raised his head and the young man corrected himself. Eleven centuries later, during the 1940s, the Moroccan sociologist Fatima Mernissi learned the Quran from her *lalla* (aunt) in much the same way:

> For you see, most of the time, Lalla Tam did not bother to explain what the verses of the Quran meant. Instead, we copied them down into our *luha*, or tablet, on Thursdays, and learned them by heart on Saturdays, Sundays, Mondays, and Tuesdays. Each one of us would sit on our cushion, hold our *luha* on our lap, and read out loud, chanting back and forth until the words sank into our heads. Then on Wednesdays Lalla Tam would make us recite what we had learned. You had to put your *luha* on your lap, face down, and recite the verses from memory. If you did not make any mistakes, Lalla Tam would smile. But she rarely smiled when it was my turn.[1]

As a book, the Quran runs about the length of the New Testament, and memorisation of the text has always been an accomplishment of pride and status among Muslims. The *hafiz* (one who 'knows by heart') might be young or old, male or female, layperson or scholar. The 14th-century Persian poet Shams al-Din Muhammad Shirazi, cherished as perhaps the greatest lyric poet of all time, received a thorough classical education, and by an early age had memorised the Quran. This earned him the nickname Hafez (*hafiz*), by which he is universally known. Since memorisation of the Quran was a prerequisite for higher learning, the training of memory was a constant feature of medieval education, involving not only knowledge of the scripture but also on reports

---

[1] Fatima Mernissi, *Dreams of Trespass: Tales of a Harem Girlhood* (Reading, MA, 1995), p. 96.

142 *A Companion to Muslim Cultures*

of Muhammad's words and deeds (the hadith), and the interpretation of the Quran and the sharia.

People with prodigious memories were often the subject of popular anecdotes. The young poet al-Mutanabbi (915–965) won a thirty-folio book written by al-Asmai by memorising its contents after a single reading. The theologian al-Ghazali (1058–1111) is reported to have been robbed of his books while travelling. When he cried out to the robber to take everything but leave him his books, the robber retorted, 'How can you claim to know these books when by taking them, I deprive you of their contents?' Al-Ghazali took the theft as a warning from God and spent the next three years memorising his notes. Such masters of the hadith as Abu Hanifa, Ahmad b. Hanbal, Bukhari and Muslim were said to have memorised hundreds of thousands of them along with their accompanying chains of transmission.

Even though Muslim scholars emphasised stocking and maintaining one's memory, from early times they also believed that writing had an important role to play in transmitting and preserving knowledge. In his *Introduction to the Study of History*, Ibn Khaldun (1332–1382) stressed the value of writing for scholars and bureaucrats in Muslim society.

> Wherever the correctness of a text is not established by a chain of transmitters going back to the person who wrote that particular text, the statement or decision in question cannot properly be ascribed to its (alleged author). This has been the procedure of scholars and experts in (all matters of religious knowledge) in all times, races, and regions, so much so that the usefulness of the craft connected with the transmission of traditions came to be restricted to this aspect (of the process of transmission).[2]

Yet some preferred oral transmission to written texts and invoked prophetic traditions to support their views. Muhammad is reported to have said, 'Do not write anything about me except the Quran,

---

[2] Ibn Khaldun, *The Muqaddimah: An Introduction to History*, tr. Franz Rosenthal (New York, 1967), vol. 2, pp. 393-394.

PL. 10: Page from a Quran in Kufic script; ink and gold on parchment, probably 9th century.

PL. 11: Part of a document recording receipt of payment; black ink on papyrus, Egypt, 723 CE.

PL. 12: Page from a dispersed Quran manuscript, copied on paper by Ali b. Shadan al-Razi, 971–972 CE.

PL. 13: Two pages from a Quran manuscript copied on parchment in broken cursive script, Palermo, 982–983 CE.

PL. 14: Colophon page from a copy of the Quran transcribed by Ahmed b. al-Suhrawardi, Baghdad, 1307.

PL. 15: Authors, scribes and attendants. Frontispiece of a manuscript of the *Epistles of the Brethren of Purity* (Ikhwan al-Safa), Iraq, 1287.

PL. 16: Two students presenting their books to the author for checking. Frontispiece of a manuscript of an Arabic translation of Dioscorides' *De materia medica*, Northern Iraq or Syria, 1229.

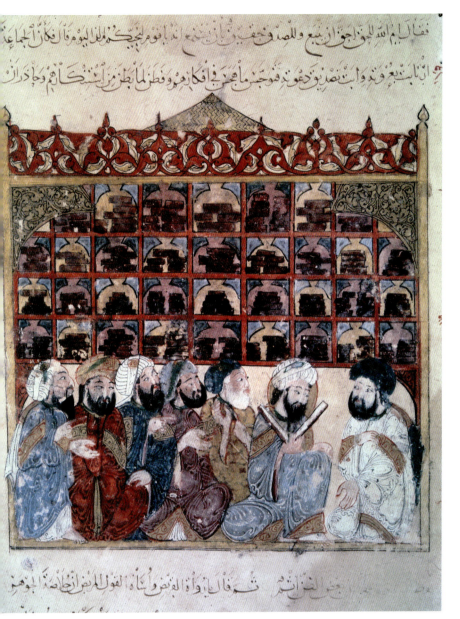

PL. 17: A medieval Arabic library as depicted in a copy of al-Hariri's *Assemblies*, transcribed and illustrated by Yahya al-Wasiti, Baghdad, 1237; ink and opaque pigments on paper.

PL. 18: Blue Chinese paper with gold decoration of 'Landscape with Two Birds in a Flowering Tree', inscribed in Nastaliq script by Sultan-Ali Qaini with Haydar's Chagtai poem 'Makhtam al-asrar', Tabriz, 1478.

Moving Words 143

and if anybody has written anything, he is to erase it.' Mentions in early Arabic literature to *kutub*, the modern word for books, do not refer to books in a literary sense, but to 'writings', notes or collections of sayings recorded for accuracy. In later times books were deemed indispensable for refreshing one's memory, but learning a hadith from a book was less authoritative than hearing it directly, even if it was read aloud from a book.

Two passages in the Quran (2:282 and 24:33) prescribe written documents for particular situations – but legal scholars usually read the verses as recommendations only. By and large, jurists ignored written documents and considered them merely aids to memory or evidence, as long as they were confirmed by the verbal testimony of witnesses. This was mainly because the written word could be manipulated in a way that was impossible with the oral word of trustworthy people; for instance, important clauses in a document could 'accidentally' be torn away. So in law the effective instrument was the verbal agreement in the presence of witnesses who, when necessary, could reiterate and verify what they had seen. Still, the qadi or judge kept written records, and commercial law relied on written documents. They proved extremely valuable in practice, becoming a normal accompaniment of every important transaction and in what flowered into a highly developed branch of law.

Written Arabic

Despite the oral nature of its revelation, the Quran asserts the authoritative nature of the written word. God's revelations to Moses are said to have been copied on sheets (6:91); and Muhammad is assured that even if God sent down sheets of writing for the Prophet's adversaries to hold and feel, they would still reject the revelation (6:7). In several places the Quran refers to itself as *kitab*, 'writing' or 'book'. Just as God's first revelation to Muhammad emphasises the importance of recitation, it also makes explicit the central role of writing, for the text continues:

144   *A Companion to Muslim Cultures*

> Recite in the name of thy Lord,
> Who taught by the pen,
> Taught man what he knew not. (96:3–5)

The pen, which is mentioned several times in the Quran, was according to later commentators either an actual reed or a metaphoric shaft of light. They reasoned that it had to be the first thing God created for a record of events to come. Muslims began to transcribe the revelations in order to avoid the corruption of the sacred text, a perpetual danger with oral transmission. The written text may originally have served as a memory aid, but in all cultures documents tend rapidly to replace rather than to support memory.

It is said that only seventeen Meccans knew how to write in the time of the Prophet. Muslims understand the Quranic phrase *al-nabi al-ummi* to refer to the 'unlettered Prophet'. So Muhammad would have repeated the revelations to his equally unlettered followers, who would have memorised the texts. Later secretaries would have transcribed the texts on materials ranging from palm fronds to potsherds and thin stones. However, some scholars see no reason why Muhammad, who spent his early life as a merchant, would not have known how to write; they take the Quranic phrase to mean the 'Prophet of the common folk'.

The first complete transcriptions of the text may have been made in the time of Muhammad himself, but the third caliph Uthman (r. 644–656) ordered Muhammad's revelations collected and collated to produce a uniform written text. The revelations were transcribed onto sheets (*suhuf*) of equal size, likely made of parchment, which were then gathered in codices (*mushaf*). Copies of this authoritative text were distributed to mosques in the major cities of the realm, where they were preserved as references. Since medieval times people have claimed that a few tattered parchment folios in one mosque or another are fragments of one of Uthman's codices, but none have been authenticated.

For all this, knowledge of the Quran was still more a matter of memory than of reading. At best, a text written in the difficult

Moving Words 145

and often imperfect Arabic script,[3] could serve as little more than an aid for people who had already committed it to memory. No seventh or eighth century manuscripts of the Quran are known to have survived, but within decades of Muhammad's death scribes and calligraphers had regularised and modified the styles of handwriting current in Arabia for transcribing the text. Arabic became the official language of the realm, and inscriptions and coins were produced in the new regularised script.

By the late seventh century the city of Medina was home to a group of professional calligraphers who produced fine copies of the Quran. Al-Nadim, who wrote his *Fihrist* in the late 10th century, records that a certain Khalid b. Abul-Hayyaj – a calligrapher and epigrapher (a designer of inscriptions) for the Umayyad caliph al-Walid in the early eighth century – was the first to calligraph the Quran. Khalid also designed the inscription with a Quranic text that once decorated the *mihrab* (the niche in the Mecca-facing wall) in the mosque of Medina.

Early Arabic handwriting was quite different in style from the well-formed artistic writing used on buildings and coins (and presumably on Quran manuscripts as well), as we can tell from eighth-century papyrus documents found in Egypt (Plate 11). More spontaneous, the writing used on these documents reflects the specific situations in which the documents were produced. Most are private and commercial letters and accounts; only a few are literary or legal works. The few papyrus fragments bearing Quranic verses were personal anthologies of verses rather than copies of the complete text, which was always transcribed on parchment, at least until the 10th century. Nevertheless, whether documents or literary texts, the handwriting on Arabic papyri was a utilitarian cursive script markedly different from the artistic script used for Quran manuscripts and state documents.

The first manuscripts of the Quran that can be dated with some certainty were copied on horizontal-format ('landscape') parchments in one of several angular scripts, commonly called Kufic,

---

[3] See 'Al-Kur'an', in *Shorter Encyclopaedia of Islam*, ed. H.A.R. Gibb and J.H. Kramer (Leiden, 1961), pp. 273-286.

146   *A Companion to Muslim Cultures*

during the mid-ninth century. These early scripts have relatively simple geometric shapes, harmonious proportions and wide spacing between groups of connected letters. Most early manuscripts of the Quran have a horizontal format, where the page is broader than it is tall, though a few are in vertical format. No contemporary source explains the scribal preference for the horizontal format. But modern scholars have often noted that the distinctive shape served visually to differentiate the scriptures of the Muslims from those of the Christians (who used vertical-format codices) and the Jews (who used horizontal rolls).

By the late ninth century, copyists were developing new scripts for different purposes. The earliest of these – known by such names as Qarmatian Kufic, broken Kufic, eastern Kufic, Kufic-*naskhi*, New Style, *warraq* (stationer's) script, or broken cursive – has an accentuated angular character and a deliberate contrast between thick and thin strokes. In some samples the script is quite vertical and elongated. Spaces between the non-connecting letters of a word are differentiated from those between words; and different letters sharing the same shape are distinguished from one another by diacritical points. In contrast to Kufic, which was used only for Quran manuscripts, this new script was used for a wide variety of texts, both secular and religious, Muslim and Christian, over an enormous geographical area from the ninth century to the early 13th.

Most scholars explain the appearance of the new script as a logical outgrowth of earlier Kufic scripts used for copying the Quran. Yet it seems more likely that it was developed by professional secretaries and copyists who regularised the cursive styles of handwriting they used for copying documents onto paper into a new and more legible script appropriate for copying books, now made of paper as well. The emergence of this new script can be linked, therefore, to the secretaries' familiarity with paper as the principal material for writing.

As the Abbasid empire had grown in the ninth century, the bureaucracy had burgeoned, and secretaries, known in Arabic as *kuttab* ('writers'), became important and powerful. Some, as officials and linguists, merely gave written documents the appropriate

Moving Words 147

form; others served as their masters' advisers and confidants and rose to positions of influence. Official documents were increasingly judged not only by their contents but also by the elegance of the wording and the cleverness of hidden allusions in the text. Successful government secretaries had to be thoroughly grounded in Arabic grammar and vocabulary, familiar with proverbs and tales, widely read in all branches of prose and poetry, soundly informed about theories of state and administration, and impeccably versed in the Quran and Muhammad's practical guidance. This knowledge had to be conveyed in an elegant hand, so the art of fine writing moved from the exclusive domain of Quran copyists and became a necessary part of state correspondence and documentation and the growing world of books.

Eventually, calligraphers used the new script to copy the Quran on paper, which now replaced parchment for copies of the holy text. The oldest dated Quran in the new (broken cursive) script is also the oldest dated copy on paper. It was copied in 971–972 by the Persian calligrapher Ali b. Shadan al-Razi, in a four-volume manuscript (Plate 12), now divided among libraries in Iran, Ireland and Turkey.

The advantages of this new script, which was legible and easy to write, made it widely popular among Christians as well as Muslims. They used it to copy the Gospels almost a century before the first existing paper Quran was copied: a manuscript dated 897 preserved in the library of the Monastery of St. Catherine, Mount Sinai. Fragments from a horizontal-format parchment manuscript of the Quran copied at Palermo, Sicily, in 982–83 show how quickly the broken cursive script had reached the Mediterranean lands even in areas where parchment still held sway. The transitional character of this manuscript, however, is evident in the black carbon-based ink with which it was copied (Plate 13).

The new broken cursive script went hand in hand with the adoption of paper and carbon-black ink. These three features encouraged the proliferation of books from the ninth century. Paper would have been cheaper and more widely available than parchment or papyrus. The carbon-based ink was easier to prepare and did not eat away at the underlying surface. Compared to the

148 *A Companion to Muslim Cultures*

earlier Kufic scripts, the broken cursive script was relatively fluent and thus easier and faster to write.

Although broken cursive continued to be used for several centuries, its success paved the way for rounded styles of Arabic handwriting in the 10th century. Normally known as *naskh*, this group of related scripts remains common to the present day, being the type of script most familiar and legible to ordinary readers. Naskh was taken as the exemplar for modern Arabic typography. Tradition has it that the Abbasid secretary (and later vizier) Ibn Muqla (885–940) introduced a new method of writing known as 'proportioned script'. Originally a tax collector in the Iranian province of Fars, Ibn Muqla was made secretary in the central administration and put in charge of opening and dispatching official letters. From the early 10th century he served as vizier to three Abbasid caliphs.

The various styles of handwriting used during the lifetime of Ibn Muqla were eventually codified into six round hands, known as the Six Pens. The master calligrapher Yaqut al-Mustasimi had served the last Abbasid caliph al-Mustasim as secretary and reportedly survived the Mongols' sacking of Baghdad in 1258 by seeking refuge in a minaret. He perfected Ibn Muqla's system of calligraphy by replacing the straight-cut nib of the calligrapher's pen with an obliquely cut one, earning himself such epithets as the 'sultan' and 'qibla' of calligraphers.

Yaqut had six famous pupils, among the most famous of whom was Ahmad b. al-Suhrawardi, calligrapher of the 'Anonymous' Baghdad Quran (Plate 14). Just as the widespread use of paper in the ninth century had encouraged the masters to regularise handwriting in books in the 10th century, so the improved quality of paper in the 13th century, especially in the lands under Mongol rule, encouraged Yaqut and his followers to take the art of Arabic calligraphy to new heights. But the steady refinement of calligraphy and the growth of a more popular style of writing are only part of the story. They accompany a huge leap in the demand for books.

An Explosion of Books

With the rise of the Abbasid caliphate in the middle of the eighth century, books and book knowledge became a general aim of Islamic society. New kinds of literature were encouraged. Scholars wrote about theology, hadith, and *fiqh* (religious law). Early Islamic law had been based on oral transmission, and it combined aspects of Quranic law with pre-Islamic practices. The 'literary period' of Islamic law began in the second half of the eighth century and flowered in the ninth when such scholars as Abu Hanifa, Malik b. Anas, Shafii, and Ahmad b. Hanbal compiled the legal collections that still inform Islamic law today.

Ibadis, Shi'is, Sunnis and other Muslim communities wrote their works of theology and philosophy. A desire to understand the words and linguistic structure of the Quran drove scholars to write on philology, lexicography and grammar. The need to identify the individuals who had transmitted hadith and make sure they had been where they were reported to have been brought an upsurge in biographical writing. Even the conception of history expounded in the Quran, which traced history back to Creation, provided a justification for historians to write about history in a new way; many now began their works with the Creation itself.

Not all learning was religious. Expansion of the government encouraged the writing of administrative texts. General curiosity impelled authors to write works on applied science, astronomy, astrology, mathematics, medicine and alchemy, as well as on poetry, geography and navigation. There was an explosion in collections of stories and other works of fiction in Arabic, including the *Thousand and One Nights* in the early ninth century, as we know from a surviving paper fragment from Syria.

Another unusual genre that enjoyed popularity was the cookbook. Although cookbooks existed in antiquity, they began to be produced in quantity in the ninth and 10th centuries. Al-Hamdani, who died in 945, alludes to a complex culinary literature in his aphorism, 'The food and drink of the Yemen are preferable to [all the] recipes from cookbooks'. Al-Nadim, the 10th-century author of the *Fihrist*, mentions several books about cooked food – and

150   *A Companion to Muslim Cultures*

an equal number about concocting poisons and drugs, amulets and charms. None of these early texts have survived, but they are known to have been written not by cooks but by courtiers, musicians, poets and librarians, which indicates the importance and literary nature of the genre.

One of the earliest surviving cookbooks was written in 1226 by Muhammad b. Hasan b. Muhammad b. al-Karim al-Katib al-Baghdadi, who divides pleasure into six classes: food, drink, clothes, sex, scent and sound. Of these, the noblest and most consequential is food, the discussion of which he divides into ten chapters. The author gives more than 150 recipes, and they are specific enough for a modern cook to follow. Although the cookbooks and other books attest to the social and cultural complexity of medieval life, they should also be seen as the practical result of quite another mentality at work, prompted by the proliferation of paper: that writing something down ensures its survival.

Muslim society fostered such a respect for book learning and scholarship that rulers and the wealthy opened their doors to the learned and lavished large sums of money on them. Caliphs, governors, courtiers, gentlemen-scholars and physicians sponsored new books as well as translations of Christian and Jewish works written in Syriac and Greek. People wrote books simply because they wanted to, or because patrons or rulers suggested they do so. Writers expected to be paid with honours, presents, and often cash. Others, such as secretaries and judges in state chanceries and offices, wrote books in their spare time.

Unlike modern authors, writers in the medieval Islamic lands seldom, if ever, chronicled their personal revelations. Rather, they presented their own selection of a chain of opinions and traditions on a subject handed down from one source to another. When the selected pieces offered diverse points of view, an author might conclude with the phrase '*Wallahu alam*' (And God knows best). Such books still represent the continuous and unbroken oral tradition of knowledge. Since oral transmission was deemed far superior to reading something in a book, people travelled widely to hear eminent scholars speak about or read from their own

Moving Words 151

works. If being in an audience was not possible, reading a book would do instead.

The publication of books was itself an oral procedure. Work was first recited and written down to dictation, usually in a mosque – the centre of most literary activity in medieval society, including matters related to knowledge far beyond the religious sciences. From the early years of Islam, mosques had also been used for public announcements, judicial proceedings and education; so their use as publishing centres was quite appropriate.

Rashid al-Din, the 14th-century Ilkhanid vizier, stipulated in the endowment (*waqf*) deed for his charitable foundation in Tabriz that his collected works were to be copied by scribes 'who possess good, legible hands' and, when finished, brought to a mosque in the complex, where 'each shall be placed on a raised platform between the pulpit and the *mihrab*, and there the following prayer for the donor shall be recited.' The superintendent was to inscribe each book with an attestation and show the copies to the judges of Tabriz, who would record the physical condition of each manuscript.[4] Poets published their works in mosques, and even privately commissioned works had to be published there. The author would sit cross-legged with his auditors seated in a circle before him. His most intimate associate or pupil might sit close by to act as intermediary with the audience. These activities are depicted in the frontispiece to the *Rasail Ikhwan al-Safa* (Epistles of the Brethren of Purity), copied in Baghdad in 1287 (Plate 15).[5] Normally the author himself wrote out his work and followed the draft manuscript in dictating, which was often done from memory. Many anecdotes centre on scholars' prodigious feats of memory. The 10th-century tradition-alist Abu Bakr b. al-Anbari is said to have dictated 45,000 pages by heart; his contemporary, the philologist al-Bawardi, dictated 30,000 pages on linguistics. Authors might stop dictation in the middle of

---

[4] W. M. Thackston, 'Articles of Endowment of the Rab'i-Rashidi, by Rashiduddin Fazulluh', in Sheila Blair, ed. *A Compendium of Chronicles: Rashid al-Din's Illustrated History of the World* (London, 1995), p. 114.

[5] See Nader el-Bizri, ed., *The Ikhwan al-Safa' and their Rasa'il: An Introduction* (London, 2008).

152   *A Companion to Muslim Cultures*

a book for one reason or another, and auditors who were taking dictation had to be content with shortened works.

A copy of a book could not be considered genuine unless it had been authorised by the author. Just as the authenticity of a hadith rested on the chain of its transmitters, so the guarantee of the authenticity of a copy rested on a chain of authorisations going back to the author himself. An author would authorise transcripts of his public readings by having copyists read the transcripts back to him for accuracy. Sometimes the author would assemble an audience for check-reading in the same way he had assembled one for dictation. A famous double-page frontispiece to a 13th-century manuscript of the Arabic translation of Dioscorides' *De materia medica* is usually interpreted as an Islamic rendering of the classic author portrait, with the author instructing and certifying his students (Plate 16). The prevalence of check-reading may explain why medieval Western manuscripts, in contrast to medieval Islamic ones, are so often a tissue of scribal errors by successive generations of copyists.

In medieval Islamic lands, once the necessary materials and scripts were available, the system resulted in an explosion of books. In contrast to the situation in medieval Christendom, where a single scribe made a single parchment copy of the single parchment manuscript on the desk before him, one author in the Muslim world could generate a dozen paper copies from a single reading, and each of these authorised copies could generate another dozen. Within two 'generations' of readings, well over a hundred copies of a single work might be produced. This ingenious and efficient system was extraordinarily effective in increasing the circulation of books. It explains how, in a society without printing, medieval Islamic libraries could have had so many books.

Besides expanding interest in book learning, the explosion of books resulted in new professions. People earned their living copying books commercially in writing rooms, dealing in paper or books, or working as bookbinders. All this led to the creation of public and private collections of books, for books were not confined to schools and learned institutions, but were widely disseminated. A modestly small, but lavishly gilded, thirty-part

Moving Words 153

manuscript of the Quran was made specifically for the library (*khizana*) of Qutb al-Din Muhammad, the Zangid ruler of the small city of Sinjar in northern Mesopotamia from 1198 to 1219. Several surviving illustrated manuscripts made at virtually the same time for the Artuqid court in the nearby city of Diyarbekir argue for the existence of a similar library there. Books and book learning permeated medieval Islamic society.

Collections and Libraries

All sources agree that the libraries of medieval Christendom were uniformly small. In the 14th century, the papal library at Avignon had barely 2,000 volumes. Even after the invention of printing, books remained scarce. The great monastery of Clairvaux had 1,788 manuscripts and only three printed books in 1506. The richest library in Christendom was said to have been the library of the Sorbonne, in Paris; in 1338 it had only 338 books for consultation, chained to reading desks, and 1,728 works for loan in its registers, 300 of which were listed as lost. The collections of other European colleges of the period often included no more than 300 works, among them the basic religious and philosophical texts.

In contrast, there were private and public libraries all over the Islamic lands. Shops in the Suq al-Warraqin (Stationers' Market), the street in Baghdad for paper sellers and booksellers, served rather like private research libraries. The polymath al-Jahiz used to rent shops by the day in order to read the books they kept in stock. Stationers like Ahmad b. Abi Tahir, a teacher, writer and paper dealer, were men of learning. Abul-Faraj Muhammad b. Ishaq, known also as Ibn Abi Yaqub al-Nadim al-Warraq ('the Stationer'), used his extensive professional knowledge to compile the *Fihrist*, his encyclopedia of contemporary books and writers, which remains a mine of information about medieval books and writing.

The lexicographer al-Azhari reports that a predecessor, the Andalusian lexicographer Abu Abd al-Rahman Abdallah b. Muhammad b. Rani al-Andalusi, owned an extensive private library

154   *A Companion to Muslim Cultures*

housed in a structure built for the purpose, where he received all those who came to study with him. He lodged the students and gave them paper with which to copy from his great collection of books. When he died, the collection was sold for 400,000 dirhams, suggesting that he had somewhere between 400 and 4,000 books. At that time an ordinary book cost ten dirhams, and a fine one ten times as much.

The first public collections of books were assembled under the Abbasids, either during the reign of al-Mansur (754–775), the founder of Baghdad, or his successor Harun al-Rashid (786–809). While the earlier Umayyad caliphs had collected writings about principal branches of knowledge, such as hadith and poetry, these were hardly more than collections of notes and single sheets kept under covers or in chests. During the reigns of the early Abbasids and the ascendancy of the Barmakid viziers, translation of Greek, Persian, and Indian works into Arabic became a regular state activity. The Barmakids with their literary and administrative interests had extensive knowledge of what other civilisations could offer. Rich manuscript collections were won as booty in the victories over the Byzantines at Ancyra (806) and at Amorium (838).

Baghdad's caliphal library became a reference centre for physicians and astronomers; Harun appointed al-Fadl b. Nawbakht, the son of the Persian astrologer who had helped al-Mansur found Baghdad, as librarian and Persian translator. The caliphal collection underwent its greatest development when Harun's son, the caliph al-Mamun, created the House of Wisdom (*Bayt al-hikma*), which served as the official translating institution in Baghdad. It and the associated library, the Storehouse of Wisdom (*Khizanat al-hikma*), were created in imitation of the pre-Islamic Iranian academy at Jundishapur, whose director, the Christian Jurjis b. Bakhtishu and his descendants, had served the caliphs as physicians. The caliph sent Salman of Harran, the Sabian curator of the House of Wisdom, a translator of Aristotle who was also conversant with Middle Persian, with a delegation of scholars to purchase philosophical and scientific manuscripts in Constantinople.

In an episode that prefigures the modern academic star system, al-Mamun tried unsuccessfully to hire the brilliant Byzantine

Moving Words 155

polymath, Leo the Mathematician, after one of his former students, who had been captured by the Arabs and set to work in al-Mamun's academy, apprised the caliph of his teacher's knowledge. The caliph's repeated requests only led the emperor Theophilos to offer his mathematician a position in Constantinople; Leo was eventually named director of a philosophical school founded privately around 855. Under al-Mamun's patronage, Greek scientific texts, including Ptolemy's *Syntaxis* (*Almagest*), were translated into Arabic, and the earliest known Arabic treatise concerning astrolabes was written at his court.

Astronomical observatories in Baghdad and near Palmyra were attached to the House of Wisdom, and scholars were charged with devising new astronomical tables to correct those made by Ptolemy. The House of Wisdom was apparently destroyed during the period of orthodox reaction under the caliph al-Mutawakkil (r. 847–61). But Ali b. Yahya al-Munajjim ('the Astronomer'), a man of letters and a friend of al-Mutawakkil and his successor al-Mutamid, built his own private library which was open to scholars of all countries. Similar libraries were established at Mosul, Basra, Hormuz and Rayy.

With the rise of the Buyids in the 10th century, a Shi'i dynasty from northern Iran who became 'protectors' of the Abbasids, the Buyid princes built their own libraries. In Shiraz, their capital in Iran, the geographer al-Muqaddasi saw a huge library that had been built by the Buyid ruler Adud al-Dawla. It was a large free-standing building consisting of a long vaulted hall on three sides of which were a series of rooms. According to the chief official, who took the geographer around, there were 360 rooms, 'one for every day of the year'. The main hall and the side rooms contained carved wooden bookcases with doors; the books lay on shelves, one atop the other. Yahya al-Wasiti's illustration of a library painted some two centuries later, in the copy of al-Hariri's *Maqamat* (Assemblies) that he prepared in Baghdad in 1237, gives some idea of what a medieval Arab library might have looked like (Plate 17).

Libraries not only collected books; they also produced them. Baha al-Dawla, the Buyid ruler of Shiraz in the early 11th century,

156   *A Companion to Muslim Cultures*

appointed the calligrapher Ibn al-Bawwab to be superintendent of his library. The calligrapher found, scattered among the other manuscripts in the library, 29 of the 30 volumes of a manuscript of the Quran penned by the great Ibn Muqla. A prolonged and careful search failed to locate the 30th and last part of the set, and the calligrapher reproached the ruler for treating the precious manuscript so carelessly. The ruler asked Ibn al-Bawwab to make a replacement for the lost volume in Ibn Muqla's handwriting, with the offer that if he failed to detect the forgery, he would give the calligrapher 100 dinars and a robe of honour. So the calligrapher

> went to the library and searched among the old paper for a paper resembling that of the Quran manuscript. There were several sorts of old Samarqand and China paper in the library – very fine and admirable papers. I took what suited me and wrote out the missing volume. Then I illuminated it and gave the gold an antique appearance. Then I removed the binding of one of the [genuine] parts and bound the part which I had written in it. Finally, I made a new binding for the genuine volume and made it appear old.[6]

It was nearly a year before the ruler remembered the incident. He inquired whether Ibn al-Bawwab had fulfilled his promise and was shown the complete Quran manuscript in 30 parts, but was unable to distinguish the replacement from the original. Baha al-Dawla, however, showed no haste in fulfilling his part of the bargain, so the calligrapher finally asked his permission to help himself to sheets of 'China' paper kept in the library. The request was granted, and the calligrapher was kept in paper for years.

Perhaps the most important Abbasid library was the one built in Baghdad in 991 by the Persian Sabur b. Ardashir, Baha al-Dawla's vizier. Known variously as the House of Knowledge (*Dar al-ilm*) or House of Books (*Dar al-kutub*), it contained over 10,000 volumes on a range of scientific subjects. Over the six decades of its existence, several notable scholars were appointed librarian, and many consulted its volumes and added to its collection. It was burned

---

[6] Johannes Pedersen, *The Arabic Book* (Princeton, 1984), pp. 86, 123.

Moving Words 157

during the Saljuq invasion of Baghdad in 1055–56, and only a handful of its books were saved.

The Abbasid libraries were models for those in distant provinces, even when the rulers of these regions did not look to Baghdad for political leadership. In Spain, the second Umayyad caliph, al-Hakam II (r. 961–976), established an enormous library in Cordoba on the model of the great libraries of Baghdad. Al-Hakam seems to have been a greater scholar and bibliophile than he was a leader and ruler. The son of Abd al-Rahman III, whose long reign was marked by the efflorescence of Cordoba as a cultural centre, al-Hakam had been tutored by the best scholars of his time and began to study and collect books in his teens, well before his accession to the throne at the relatively advanced age of 46. Al-Hakam's library served as the focus of a whole set of cultural activities that helped to lay the foundations for the burst in literary production in Andalusia during the century and a quarter after his death.

Al-Hakam's library is said to have contained 400,000 books. The catalogue of titles alone is said to have filled 44 volumes. Even if the actual number of books may be somewhat inflated, at one-tenth the size it would still have been larger than any contemporary library in Christendom by a factor of 50 or more. The Cordoba library lent out books, and outsiders appear to have had some access to them. Librarians, different types of translators and numerous copyists were employed, as well as checkers to verify the accuracy of copies. After al-Hakam's death, his successor, the generalissimo al-Mansur, burned the philosophical and theological works that he and his associates considered heretical, and the rest of library was dispersed.

In Egypt, the Fatimids, who disputed the Abbasids' claim to the caliphate, established several major institutions of learning in Cairo modelled on those in Baghdad. It is said that in 993–994, the caliph-imam al-Aziz was able to produce from his library 30 copies of al-Khalil b. Ahmad's lexicographical masterpiece *Kitab al-ayn*, including one in the hand of the author – as well as 20 copies of al-Tabari's multi-volume *Tarikh al-rusul wal-muluk* (History of Prophets and Kings), including an autograph copy, plus 100 copies of the *Jamhara* of Ibn Durayd. Given how Arabic

158   *A Companion to Muslim Cultures*

manuscripts were normally copied and transmitted, such numbers are not as improbable as they might seem.

The Fatimid caliphs maintained their own House of Knowledge (*Dar al-ilm*, sometimes also known as the House of Wisdom, *Dar al-hikma*) in their palace in Cairo. It contained a library and reading room and served as a meeting place for scholars of hadith, jurists, grammarians, doctors, astronomers, logicians and mathematicians. The historian al-Maqrizi has preserved the annual budget for the library during the reign of al-Hakim (r. 996–1021). The total was 207 dinars, of which the largest single expense, 90 dinars, was on paper for the copyists. (A lower-middle-class family could survive on 24 dinars a year.) The next largest expense, 48 dinars, was for the librarian's salary, with lesser amounts for the attendant's wages (15 dinars), wages for the keeper of paper, ink, and pens and wages for the person who repaired books (12 dinars each); floor mats and drinking water (10 dinars each); felt carpets and blankets for winter (5 and 4 dinars, respectively); and repairing the curtains (1 dinar).

Over the course of the year 1068–69, the Fatimid palace was looted by soldiers who took whatever they thought they could sell. The accounts of the treasures they found are remarkable. One storeroom yielded 18,000 volumes on the 'ancient sciences', another contained 2,400 boxed manuscripts of the Quran written in 'proportioned scripts' (the kind developed by Ibn Muqla). An eyewitness saw 25 camels laden with books valued at 100,000 dinars headed to the house of the vizier Abul-Faraj Muhammad b. Jafar b. al-Muizz al-Maghribi, who had taken them in lieu of the 5,000 dinars in salary he was owed. A month later, the same books were looted from the vizier's house and dispersed.

At his death in 1121, the powerful Fatimid vizier al-Afdal left a library of half a million books; they were then moved to the palace, with many endowed for public circulation. The late Fatimid historian Ibn al-Tuwayr reports that the library contained more than 200,000 bound volumes on such subjects as *fiqh*, hadith, theology, grammar, lexicography, history, biography, astronomy and chemistry. According to the historian Ibn Abi Tayyi, when the Fatimid dynasty fell to Saladin in 1171, the caliph's library contained an estimated 1.6 million other books, many of which Saladin sold.

Moving Words

Ibn Abi Tayyi says that at least 100,000 volumes were transferred to the new Sunni *madrassa* established by al-Qadi al-Fadl, and the rest were sold over the next decade. Just as only one manuscript has survived from al-Hakam's library in Spain, only two manuscripts have survived from the Fatimid royal libraries.

The Power of Paper

What most people have not recognised is that paper was itself an engine of social, intellectual and artistic change between the eighth century and the 16th. Introduced in the Islamic lands to meet the demands of a huge bureaucracy attempting to govern the largest empire the world had ever seen, paper was quickly seized on by writers on all subjects as an ideal medium – strong, flexible, light and cheap – on which to record and transmit their thoughts. This process was encouraged not only by a societal reverence for the written word but also by ingenious and efficient methods of duplicating and disseminating manuscripts.

Writing on an enormous variety of subjects proliferated. Writers also discovered that paper could be used for recording notations other than words, which ranged in these centuries of intellectual curiosity, from mathematical calculations to genealogical charts to battle plans. While much of the appeal of paper arose from its being less costly than parchment and more readily available than papyrus, the two most common writing materials of antiquity, paper was always much more expensive in medieval times than it is today. The invention of papermaking machines and the discovery of virtually infinite sources of fibre have made paper cheaper today than ever before.

Even in the medieval Islamic lands, paper eventually became cheap enough that ordinary people used it for purposes other than transcribing the written word. Once artisans began to use paper, it had a decisive impact on the ways in which the arts began to develop around 1200. Many typical Islamic arts, from Persian miniatures and Oriental carpets to the Taj Mahal, are unthinkable without the direct or indirect use of paper for preliminary sketches, encoded instructions, or measured drawings. Then there

160   *A Companion to Muslim Cultures*

was the sheer aesthetic delight of fine paper, such as the decorative kind from China. One example from Tabriz is the calligrapher Sultan-Ali Qaini's copy of a Chagtai poem in 1478, on blue Chinese paper that bears a typical oriental landscape (Plate 18).

Muslims introduced papermaking in southern Europe in the 11th century, and by about 1500 virtually all of Europe was making paper. The introduction of papermaking in Europe coincided with such European developments as the expanded use of documents, the acceptance of Hindu-Arabic numerals, the refinement of double-entry book-keeping, and a certain freedom in design and drawing. All these paralleled earlier developments in the Islamic lands that came with the use of paper. The degree to which the European developments were due specifically to the introduction of paper is yet to be explored.

In the longer view of history, the tardiness of the Muslim world to adopt printing was just a brief pause in a continuous diffusion of inventions across Eurasia. In this light, the history of printing is not so dissimilar to the history of papermaking. Both were invented in China and spread westward, all the way to the Atlantic. For paper, the route is clear: Europe adopted it from the Islamic lands. For printing, any relation between Gutenberg's invention to earlier uses of movable type in China remains to be established. In any case, printing diffused from Europe to the Islamic lands. The gap between Gutenberg's invention in the 1450s and the beginning of printing in West Asia some three centuries later was not crucial, because Islamic society had already developed practical and effective means of reproducing and disseminating large numbers of texts. The invention of printing did not have a decisive effect on the history of paper in the Islamic lands.

Far more important in distinguishing the histories of these two regions and establishing why the Islamic paper industry withered, was the European development of a 'technicalistic' attitude in the late Middle Ages. Marshall Hodgson, the historian who coined the term, defined technicalism as the expectation of impersonal efficiency through technical precision.[7] From the 16th century, a

---

[7] Marshall Hodgson, *The Venture of Islam,* (Chicago, 1974), vol. 3, p. 200.

Moving Words

technicalistic approach to problems and problem-solving in Europe increasingly differentiated Muslim and European societies.

If later Muslim societies were less receptive to innovation than European ones were, this attitude had not always prevailed. In late eighth-century Baghdad, Muslim bureaucrats had dealt with insufficient quantities of writing material by adopting and producing paper. The early Abbasid period was one of extraordinary cultural curiosity and intellectual ferment, comparable to the European Renaissance. Abbasid scholars were wide open to ideas from all around the world: paper and Hindu-Arabic numerals were among the results. By the late Middle Ages, though, the situation had changed entirely. Muslim societies had become far less enthusiastic about reinvesting capital in technical improvements. It is at this point that Europe took the lead.

Europe's revolution in printing was not just about Gutenberg's invention of movable type. It was part of a much larger capitalist expansion – which included the growth of Germany's economic power, the opening of new mines in the Hartz Mountains (in Bohemia, Hungary and Styria), new techniques of metallurgy, the spread of papermaking and the invention of new oil-based inks, and an intellectual revival that made people eager to have books. A similar technicalistic attitude changed European papermaking from the late 17th century, and differentiated its goods from handmade paper produced elsewhere. The invention of the Hollander beater, which could do in an hour what an old hammer mill took a day to do, was followed at the end of the 18th century by the Fourdrinier papermaking machine; given enough quantities of pulp, it could make an endless strip of paper of virtually any width. Europe's engineers and savants were searching for new raw materials from which to make paper, and new ways to exploit them. Their efforts gave us chemical bleaches, which made previously available stocks of fibre now usable for papermaking, and means to extract nearly limitless quantities of cellulose from trees.

162 A Companion to Muslim Cultures

Conclusion

In the wider history of world civilisation, the shift from oral to scribal culture was as important to the flowering of medieval Islamic civilisation as was the later shift in Europe and elsewhere from a scribal culture to a typographic one. The shift from scribal to typographic culture in Europe, which was marked by the invention of printing with movable type, has received more attention from historians than the earlier shift from oral to scribal culture. Yet the earlier transformation, marked by the introduction of papermaking to the Islamic lands, seems at least as important. The act of remembering is essentially different from the act of referring to a written record, whether copied by hand or printed. As writing penetrated society, systems of memory for preserving traditions gave way to physical texts that could be referred to independently of their human transmitters.

The changes in modes of thinking brought about by dealing with written texts do not result from differences in the mental capacities of oral and literate peoples. Rather, they stem from a basic alteration in the tools available to each. The graphic representation of speech is a tool that encourages reflection on information and the organisation of information. It also changes the nature of how the world is represented, even for those in the culture who cannot write. Just as a text written in book format was easier to access than the same text written on a roll, so information is often far easier to access from writing than from memory, especially when the accuracy of items rather than their general content is essential. To remember a passage of music or the sequence of some lines of poetry, one often has to 'scroll down' from some beginning to the appropriate point. Leafing through a written text, no matter what its format, is far quicker and usually more reliable.

In medieval Islam, the shift from reliance on memory to a comparable reliance on the written record never fully happened. Indeed, in some regions and in some areas of knowledge, such as learning and reciting the Quran, memory systems persist to this day. Still, a watershed seems to have been crossed by the 12th

Moving Words   163

century, when the general availability of paper allowed early patterns of oral transmission of authority and knowledge to be altered. What took their place was greater use of a body of Islamic texts, declared authoritative by professors teaching in new officially-sponsored institutions.

The fateful shift from memory to written word had other consequences, because paper and ink could be used for more than the mere representation of speech. They had vital contributions to make in other fields of human endeavour, such as mathematics, geography, commerce and the arts. Over the course of the seven centuries between 800 and 1500, inhabitants of the Islamic lands – who were largely but not exclusively Muslims – carried their knowledge of paper and papermaking across a vast swath of Eurasia and North Africa. Had they not mediated between the cultures of the Far East and the Far West, Europeans would likely have stayed ignorant of paper, as well as such other Chinese inventions as gunpowder and the compass, until the first European mariners reached Far Eastern ports in the 16th century. Had they not brought paper to Europe, Gutenberg's invention of printing with movable type in the mid-15th century, dependent as it would have been on expensive parchment, probably would not have expanded the reading public in such a revolutionary fashion.

Muslim lands *did* serve, however, as the entrepôt for new ideas from China across the continent to Europe. No firm boundaries divided the Eurasian and African landmass in the way that the Atlantic and Pacific oceans separated the Old World from the New. Over the millennia, virtually any new development or invention, whether the domestication of plants and animals, papermaking, the water-driven hammer mill, the spinning wheel, or the stirrup, was gradually adopted everywhere in Eurasia in the space of four or five centuries, even more rapidly sometimes, as in the case of gunpowder weapons. Following a well-established pattern, then, paper and papermaking, both of Chinese origin, were diffused across Eurasia with the spread of Islam.

The period between the emergence of Islam in the seventh century and the Mongol invasions of West Asia in the 13th, was surely a golden age. During this time the culture evolved from

164 *A Companion to Muslim Cultures*

largely oral to scribal, a momentous change. Writing came to play a crucial and pervasive role in virtually every aspect of life. Although all sorts of reasons have been adduced to explain the change, I believe that the increased availability and use of paper served as a catalyst. As Alfred von Kremer realised more than a century ago, and as we are only now coming to understand, the 'blossoming of mental activity' made possible by paper 'started a new era of civilization'.[8]

Further Reading

Atiyeh, George N., ed. *The Book in the Islamic World: The Written Word and Communication in the Middle East.* Washington, DC, 1995.

Blair, Sheila. *Islamic Calligraphy.* Edinburgh, 2002.

Bloom, Jonathan. *Paper Before Print: The History and Impact of Paper in the Islamic World.* New Haven and London, 2001.

Graham, William A. *Beyond the Written Word: Oral Aspects of Scripture in the History of Religion.* New York, 1993.

Halm, Heinz. *The Fatimids and their Traditions of Learning.* London, 1997.

Makdisi, George. *The Rise of Colleges: Institutions of Learning in Islam and the West.* Edinburgh, 1981.

Martin, Henri-Jean. *The History and Power of Writing,* tr. Lydia G. Cochrane. Chicago, 1994.

Masood, Ehsan. *Science and Islam: A History.* London, 2009.

Schoeler, Gregor. *The Genesis of Literature in Islam: From the Aural to the Read.* Edinburgh, 2002.

Young, M., J. Latham and R. Serjeant, ed. *Religion, Learning and Science in the 'Abbasid Period.* (The Cambridge History of Arabic Literature). Cambridge, 1990.

---

[8] Quoted in Joseph von Karabacek, *Arab Paper,* tr. Don Baker and Suzy Dittmar (London, 1991), p. 72.

9

Moving Sounds

Jonathan Shannon

What are the qualities that make music worthy of appreciation to audiences in the Muslim world? We approach this large question by way of Aleppo – long a cultural oasis not only in Syria but the Near East at large – where the aesthetic values in the performance of classical song revolve around the expression of deep emotion and 'authenticity' in a context of social intimacy. From West Africa and the Middle East to South-Central Asia and beyond, the rich tapestry of musical expression bears witness to the plurality of Muslim cultures. Yet there are shared aspects to those traditions. This chapter explores a typical performance of the Syrian master vocalist Sabah Fakhri as a way of understanding some of those commonalities. We begin with Fakhri's concert in Aleppo, then consider what makes it worthy to a diverse audience performance, focusing on the ways in which musical and cultural authenticity are constituted and evaluated in the course of performance.

An Evening with Sabah Fakhri

It is another hot July day in the northern Syrian city of Aleppo. A colourful sign draped across the light posts at an intersection catches my eye, announcing 'The Great Arab Artist Sabah Fakhri, for One Show Only at The Freedom Club'. Excited at the opportunity, the next day I make my way to the Freedom Club, a premier Aleppo establishment or *nadi*. A *nadi* is a combination social and health club, often with a large swimming pool, gym, meeting hall, lounge, perhaps even a fancy restaurant open to the public in the

166 *A Companion to Muslim Cultures*

evenings. Aleppo's *nadi*s also host concerts, usually accommo-dating both families and unaccompanied youth.

Gates open around 9:30 pm for Sabah Fakhri's concert, and the audience members begin to file in. I sit in the youth section by the pool, surrounded by men with *nargila*s (water pipes), anxious to start in earnest their evening's entertainment. The musicians come on stage a few minutes later and get set up. Their instru-ments consist of a *qanun* (zither), five violins, two cellos, an *oud* (lute), and a variety of drums – including the *riqq* (tambourine), *tabla* (goblet drum) and *daff* (frame drum). Five vocalists appear behind microphones at stage-right, while the instruments are tuned.

Our emcee finally welcomes everyone to the show at 11:20 pm. Yasin al-Ashiq, the composer and Sabah Fakhri's lead violinist, comes before the microphone and with a wave of his bow the orchestra begins to play his piece 'The Dreams of Youth' (*Ahlam al-shabab*). It is an instrumental that traditionally opens Sabah Fakhri's concerts, featuring changes in mode and metre, with several sections of improvisation by the various instrumentalists.

As 'The Dreams of Youth' comes to a close, the family section suddenly bursts into applause. Sabah Fakhri has appeared in the wings. A group of white doves are released and flutter about confus-edly for a moment before scattering to the tops of the club build-ings. The great artist acknowledges the cheer, raising his arms over his head in the fashion of a political leader and bowing, then mounts the stage as the music ends, turning his back to face the musicians. Seeing him on stage, the youth yell and scream too.

The orchestra plays a short introductory piece in the mode *Hijaz kar*, and Fakhri cocks his head to one side as if listening intently. He pays special attention to the percussionists, standing before them and having the volume of their playing adjusted. He then walks over and listens to the violins, says a word or two; several of them retune their instruments. The *qanun* player embell-ishes a descending phrase with quick finger work, and Fakhri nods to him in appreciation. Once the piece ends, Fakhri begins the evening's first song, a *muwashshah*, which is a choral poem with origins in Andalusia. This particular song, *Murru al-tajanni* (Bitter is the Accusation), is one of passionate love, a typical theme for a *muwashshah* and sung in formal Arabic.

Aside from a few youth who are settling in their seats with sandwiches or soft drinks, the audience is quiet and rather subdued, sitting and listening to the great master vocalist and the smooth sounds of the orchestra. This *muwashshah*, while not among the slower ones in the Aleppine repertoire, has a stately metre. Its mode (*Hijaz kar*) hovers in the upper register before finishing in the lower, suggesting a reflective mood, complaint, the bitterness of the accusation resolving in a flood of passion as the orchestra descends to the lower register. As is common in this genre of song, the poetic and musical metres do not precisely coincide; so 'filler' words such as *aman* (peace) and *Ya layl* (O night) are added either at the end or between hemistiches of the poetic verse. These afford the vocalist the opportunity to display his skill and vocal range. The first lines of this *muwashshah* end in *aman*, and when Ustaz Sabah finishes them with a melismatic flourish the audience shouts its approval. A couple of men in the family section jump out of their seats and raise their arms, then sit back down with sheepish grins on their faces. It is only midnight, still early in the evening.

The vocal suite or *wasla* moves on through two more songs. They are recited in the same mode, like the rest of the *wasla*, except for modulations during instrumental improvisations (*taqasim*) or in solo singing. But the latter songs are much faster, and the audience claps along. Some of the youth arise and dance; another group shouts out a traditional wedding chant as an expression of joy and not a little bravado. A couple of men in the family section sing along with the artist, and another mimics the rhythm of the percussionists with his hands. Fakhri waves his arms as he sings, and people shout '*Aywa!*' and '*Ya ayni!*' in approval. A young man to one side of the pool gets up and begins what I have come to term the 'semaphore dance', waving paper tissues with his hands up and down, side to side, as if directing a wayward airplane with vague and confusing signs. He seems a little odd since no one else around him is dancing, though others look on smiling and he is obviously having a good time.

At the conclusion of the last *muwashshah* the orchestra pauses,

168   *A Companion to Muslim Cultures*

and the audience bursts into applause. Fakhri bows and raises his arms, then turns to the orchestra. He has the cellists retune, and says a few words to the *qanun* and *oud* players. Then the orchestra begins the next section of the *wasla*, consisting of the song *Ya nas ana mutt fi hubbi* (O People, I have Died in my Love) by the Egyptian composer Sayyid Darwish (1892–1923). This is followed by the folksy Egyptian song *Ya Mariya* (O Maria), and the formidable *dawr* (multi-part colloquial song) *Ya ma inta wahishni* (O You whom I Miss), by the 19th-century Egyptian composer Muhammad Uthman. These songs are sung in the colloquial Egyptian dialect – which conveys a sense of lightness and modernity, as opposed to the heaviness and antiquity of the *muwashshah*, though such popular songs nonetheless require great skill and mastery. Their metres tend to be simpler and the melodies lighter if still complex, especially the multi-part *dawr*, with its extended vocal improvisations and exchanges between the artist and the chorus. In the section of the *dawr* when the vocalist and chorus exchange operatic 'Ahs' throughout the range of the mode, the audience responses energetically by singing along, clapping, dancing and shouting encouragement. The mood is much more enlivened, though still a little restrained; everyone is having a good time but I have a feeling that we have yet to reach the heart of the matter.

After the conclusion of the *dawr*, the orchestra takes a five-minute break. It is nearly 1 am but the show is only warming up! While Fakhri is off-stage, the orchestra returns and commences the second suite with a prelude in the *maqam rast*, which of all traditional modes is the most popular. The mood is immediately lively and the instrumentalists perform with gusto, adding numerous embellishments. The great master returns to much applause and launches into a *muwashshah*, the slow *Ahinnu shawqan* (I Long with Yearning). It seems to leave the audience a bit distracted; conversations ensue, *nargila*s are refilled, and we are settling in for the rest of the evening. At its close, the *oud* player begins a solo improvisation (*taqsim*). When he gets to the upper range of the mode, a great deal of fast trilling with the plectrum ensues. Unlike many players, he does not make dramatic pauses between sections but plays right on, buzzing like a bee with

Moving Sounds

a display of fancy technique in the highest register. The audience comes alive to his fireworks and shouts '*Aywa!*' and '*Ya ruhi!*' Finally he makes a dramatic ending by coursing through some difficult arpeggios, all the while maintaining a constant bass drone and lightening-fast trilling, then closes on the tonic. The audience erupts into wild applause as the *oud* player settles into a quiet droning, and the *qanun* joins in.

Sabah Fakhri now sings the *qasida* (classical ode) *Salu fuadi* (Ask my Heart), a lover's complaint. In the *qasida*, the artist improvises the melody, usually accompanied by an instrumentalist with whom he engages in a sort of dialogue. Fakhri seems entranced by the mood as he stands almost frozen on the stage listening to the *oud* player's simple phrases in the mode. Musicians refer to this state as *saltana*, when the mood of the mode dominates the artist's emotions. When there is good rapport between the artist and the audience, particularly the more skilled listeners, the artist can enter the state of *saltana* and evoke a corresponding state of *tarab* or musical rapture in listeners.

As he sings the verses of the poem, the master evinces great emotion in his visage and through the movement of his arms and hands. The audience seems enthralled: all eyes are on him. At one point, when Fakhri sings a phrase with considerable feeling, a man from the family section jumps out of his seat with a shout of 'Allah!', hops up on the stage and hugs the great vocalist, then returns to his seat. The audience applauds, some of the youth shout *Ya ayni!*, while a couple of others laugh. Fakhri proceeds into a *layali*, an improvised song, while the *oud* player responds with choice phrases. When they reach a particularly high pitch, well above the range of most singers, the audience is transformed into a cacophony of 'Allah!', '*Ya salam!*', and '*Aywa!*'.

Fakhri then closes with a flourish and descent from the high to the low register of the mode, the audience roars, and the orchestra starts playing a *dawr* immediately, *Asl al-gharam nazra* (The Root of Passion is a Glance). People hop up and start dancing. Up near the stage a handful of men dance together, while over on the side, that same younger man does his 'semaphore dance' again; several of the youth rise and clap, some dance. At one point, Fakhri sings

170 *A Companion to Muslim Cultures*

a phrase with a noticeable cry or *buka* in his voice, and the youth near me cry out, '*Ya habibi!*' (O My Beloved!). This goes on for almost ten full minutes – Ustaz Sabah singing the same line and the audience reacting with various cries and shouts.

Then it happens: Fakhri begins his trademark *saltana* dance, turning his back to the audience, making a few quick steps with arms spread wide, spinning around, first in one direction, then the other, and then more quick steps. It is far from elegant but the audience roars with approval. The great singer is experiencing *saltana* under the influence of the mood and atmosphere of the evening, which reflects well on the audience, for they have contributed with their responsive shouts and cries. A number of listeners sit and rock their heads back and forth to the metre of the stately *dawr*; many gyrate and wave their arms around; semaphore signals are sent; *tarab* is in the air. There is a definite groove about, and I find myself drawn into it.

A few minutes later they are performing the light song *Ibat li jawwab* (Send Me a Reply) by the Aleppine composer Bakri al-Kurdi (1909–1978). Energetic in the modern Egyptian style that was popular among Aleppine composers in the 1950s and 1960s, it is easily the most popular of the traditional songs in Aleppo – and is well-known as far as Morocco. While the orchestra establishes the mood, Fakhri comes out of his *saltana* and adjusts one of the speakers that appears somehow off. A man dancing near the stage offers him a rosary, which he politely refuses by placing his hand over his heart and bowing his head. Things begin to heat up again as the audience sings along with the artist. Now almost everyone is dancing. In the family section, a few women dance with their daughters, husbands and other family members. Two young men on the opposite side of the pool from the semaphore dancer get up and dance in a style reminiscent of women's dance (what we inappropriately term 'belly dancing'); in a parody of feminine grace and motion they gyrate their hips, shake their flat chests, and move their hands and wrists in quick circles. This sort of burlesque inevitably occurs at public concerts, especially during the lighter portions of a *wasla*. The youth laugh at them while their neighbours look on with mirthful grins. The dancers are

Moving Sounds   171

apparently enjoying themselves immensely and this goes on for several minutes. It is now about 2 am.

Sabah Fakhri then launches into a *mawwal,* a colloquial poem sung, like the *qasida,* to an improvised melody with an accompanying instrumentalist. The audience stops dancing but their engagement with the vocalist is still high, for many attempt to sing along with him, sighing 'Ah!' and 'Allah!' after each phrase. Some in the front wave their arms in a peculiar manner, as if unfolding reams of cloth or drawing out something from their chest, each hand alternating with the other in an outward flowing circle. I noticed this as well in Cairo, and it seems to be a trademark motion of the *tarab.* Finishing his *mawwal,* Fakhri seamlessly leads the orchestra into a *wasla* of light Aleppine tunes. These include some of the city's most popular songs: *Ya tira tiri* (O Bird, Fly) and *Ya mal al-sham* (O Treasures of Damascus!), both Arab standards by the famous Damascene composer Abu Khalil al-Qabbani (ca.1832–1904). These quick tunes get everyone up out of their chairs. I have forgotten the evening's chill, and am standing by the poolside clapping and watching the semaphore dancer. Fakhri takes another turn at dancing, people shout, and the atmosphere is mirthful and carefree.

At last, after modulating through a number of folkloric songs, Fakhri brings the concert to a close with an impressive ascent to the note D, two octaves above middle C (*jawwab al-muhayyir,* in Arab musical parlance), well above the range of singers half his age. It is 4 am and he has been singing almost non-stop for over five hours. Fans are quick to point out that this is not unusual for Fakhri; many claim that he holds a Guinness World Record for endurance singing, seventeen hours non-stop at a concert in Venezuela in the 1980s. Putting away his *nargila,* my neighbour exclaims, 'It's still early!' and slaps me on the back as he makes his way toward the exit.

Friends and families pile into cars and taxis, parents hold sleepy children in their arms, some head off to the mosque for the dawn prayer, an anthropologist walks home. Yet there is an air of expectation for the next *wasla* suite; indeed the term *wasla,* which means a connection, a tie, implies continuity between past performances

172   A Companion to Muslim Cultures

and those yet to come. This is an important aspect of the *tarab* culture: ever evolving contexts for experiencing the joy of great music that comes 'from the heart' (*min al-qalb*), and is authentic and honest.

Genres, Venues and Patronage

Fakhri's concert exemplifies the predominant genre of musical performance in contemporary Aleppo, the *sahra*. Literally meaning an evening gathering or soirée, *sahra* refers colloquially to a gathering of friends and family for an event such as a birthday, engagement, wedding or graduation. As a social institution in contemporary Aleppo (as elsewhere in Syria), it is governed by elaborate rules and etiquette: codes of dress, forms of conversation, culinary and other gustatory practices, and a distinct temporality. A *sahra* is a semi-formal, semi-public affair usually held in someone's home; its key ingredient is the idea of closeness or intimacy. Not simply a party, it is an opportunity for members of the middle-class and elite men to engage in forms of polite behaviour that fall under the category of *adab*. Now the poor and working classes may hold *sahras* too, but they tend to be more casual. In addition to *sahras* held for special occasions, some Aleppines host weekly varieties of them. One type is the *sahra bishmariyya*, in which a group of friends take turns hosting a *sahra* every week in one of their homes; alternatively, one will bring food and everyone will split the cost. Another type is the *sahra sahaniyya*, for which everyone brings a dish (*sahn*) of food, like the American potluck dinner. Both varieties feature music and conversation.

   In the 'golden age' of Aleppine music – from approximately the middle of the 19th century through the first half of the 20th – wealthy merchants entertained guests with elegant conversation, music and food. In this period the *sahra* was a domain reserved almost entirely for the men of Aleppo's commercial and religious families. Women hosted analogous women-only *sahras*, such as morning gatherings (*subhiyyat nisa*), the adornment of the bride on her wedding night (*talbisa*) and receptions (*istiqbal*). The musicians would generally not be paid for their services, though they

Moving Sounds

would be served food. Many were not professional in the sense of deriving their primary income from performing. For example, many vocalists have served as imams or muezzins at local mosques; many were also merchants or tradesmen. The famous composer and singer, Umar al-Batsh, was a stone engraver who later earned a modest income from training students in the art of singing and composition. Artists and patrons thereby participated in a system of reciprocity, however unbalanced, which was the context for the production of what some Aleppines consider to be the most beautiful music and song.

As a context for the performance of the *wasla*, the public or commercial *sahra* has come to all but replace those held in private homes. Not surprisingly, admission fees are usually charged. Both men and women attend these medium- to large-scale events, though women are usually found only in the 'families' sections. Many musicians and music lovers in Aleppo attribute the scarcity of the private *sahra* as a context for music-making to Aleppo's commercial-economic and cultural decline, which began with the opening of the Suez Canal in 1869 and continued with the rise of Damascus as a social, economic and cultural hub.

Today, as Aleppo struggles to revive its economic position, mostly through developing agriculture, construction and tourism, the remaining merchant and commercial classes either lack the time or money to host regular gatherings, or no longer reside in the old Arab homes in which they were traditionally hosted. Other members of the upper classes are said no longer to be satisfied with the simpler pleasures of the old days in hosting a *sahra*.

As a result, musical performance has shifted almost entirely to the stage, with recitals and concerts now held in performance halls or public venues. Public venues for the performance of music did not exist in Aleppo or in Syria as a whole until after the first third of the 20th century, and the establishment of cafés and theatres in the major cities. Prior to this, most music was performed in private homes or in the confines of the *zawiya*s (Sufi lodges). Even today, there are relatively few concert or recital halls in Syria devoted exclusively to the performance of music or related arts. For example, Damascus boasts a recital hall in the Asad National Library, the

174   *A Companion to Muslim Cultures*

auditorium of the High Institute for Music, and a newly completed opera house, in addition to multi-purpose halls and conference rooms at hotels and cultural centres, and a handful of theatres.

Aleppo, for its part, has no single performance space devoted exclusively to music. Performances are held in a variety of multipurpose venues, including the dilapidated auditorium of the National Library, the aging Muawiya Hall, the amphitheatre and reception hall of the Citadel,[1] and various 'heritage' buildings that are being renovated to serve as performance spaces. The numerous clubs, hotel lounges and cabarets provide another set of venues, though they can hardly be considered designed for the performance of music.

Nonetheless, a concert held at a hotel lounge, night-club or cabaret might also be called a *sahra*, in order to suggest the more intimate setting of a private gathering. In fact, restaurants that feature music often present it as a *sahra* as well. A large concert is generally called a *hafla*, since the degree of intimacy implied by a *sahra* is not expected there, nor the many social rules of a *sahra*. Women may attend these events freely, though often they do so in the company of male relatives in 'family' sections. A concert in a large venue such as a sports arena in which the singer is separated from the audience by a great distance with little or no probability of interaction will be a *hafla*. In contrast, the Sabah Fakhri concert, at which there was continuous interaction between artist and audience, was a *sahra*. The difference may also be a matter of repertoire and orchestra; the *wasla* is performed primarily at *sahra*s, whereas modern songs and larger orchestras appear in *hafla*s.

Authenticity in Performance

Why do so many Aleppines flock to concerts to hear the songs of the *wasla*? Why, especially, was the youth section full when critics have pronounced the death of traditional music, and the domi-

---

[1] This medieval palace in the old city has recently benefitted from major restorative work by the Aga Khan Trust for Culture, in collaboration with the Aleppo Archaeological Society.

Moving Sounds 175

nance of modern pop songs in the hearts and minds of Syria's youth? Why are these genres considered by many to be exemplars of authenticity and musical taste?

What makes a song both 'good' and 'authentic' depends on the context of its performance as much as on its specific musical qualities. Despite the well-established tradition of discourse on modes, rhythms and performance practices in Arab music, what matters the most for today's musicians and audiences is the engendering of culturally valued emotional states in performers and listeners. This is vital to the '*tarab* culture' of the Arab East, in which participants engage in a rich tapestry of dialogue of the emotions and the self.[2] Through music, performers enact and present culturally specific cues that are understood by listeners as evidence of internal emotional states, such as the *saltana*. For their part, listeners present certain culturally understood cues of internal emotional states, which are read as the prime index of a successful – and authentic – performance.

Like their counterparts in Cairo and elsewhere in the Middle East, Aleppine musicians and music lovers evaluate music through the use of an aesthetic language. In Aleppo, this comprises a set of terms that I call the 'Three Keys' to a good song: melody (*lahn*), words or song lyrics (*kalimat*) and voice (*sawt*). They articulate in musical terms the performative qualities of engagement: emotional honesty (*sidq*), rapture (*tarab*) and what many Syrians refer to as 'oriental spirit' (*ruh sharqiyya*). A close examination of what is said and written about performances reveals that the musical elements are often not the decisive factors in judgements of value or authenticity. Nor are they always important in producing the experience of *tarab*. Rather, it is the overall social context of a performance that counts, in which the music may be incidental to the experience of highly charged emotional states in the course of performance. Music lovers may not even understand the lyrics, or know much about Arab music tonality, yet have a deep appreciation of the performance.

---

[2] See A.J. Racy, *Making Music in the Arab World: The Culture and Artistry of Tarab* (Cambridge, 2003).

Melody (*lahn*)

A wealth of treatises in the Arab tradition discusses music theory, and especially the melodic and rhythmic modes that are the basis of classical compositions. Numerous efforts have been made in the modern period to systematise and classify the modes and metres, especially after the landmark Cairo Congress of 1932. Yet Aleppine musicians and music lovers still argue about the exact number of modes and their interrelationships – as well as their given emotional connotations. The rhythmic modes engender less debate. There are many treatises that specify their arrangement of accents, metre components, and occasionally their origin in certain natural phenomena and cultural practices, like the rhythm of the camel's gait, the weaver's loom, or the rocking of a crib.

But mode and rhythm alone do not make a good melody. What matters is how these and other features are wielded to express musical ideas. The art of composition (*talhin*) requires mastery of the modes and rhythms, to be sure; yet it also requires imagination (*khayal*) and the ability to create new musical ideas. Many Syrian composers remark that mastery of the technical language of the music is a first step toward creating good songs, but that the art of composition depends more importantly on a strong sense of oriental spirit and having a good musical ear. These capacities develop only through intensive listening and as a result of God-given talent. Formal study may, of course, nurture those capacities and many contemporary composers have pursued lessons in music theory and composition not only in Syria and Egypt, but also in western academies.

Lyrics (*kalimat*)

The most important function of the melody is to convey the meaning of the words. In fact, most people with whom I spoke argued that the words are the most important component of a good song. Without meaningful words, even the best melody will not be genuinely good. But what are meaningful words – and how does a melody express their meaning?

The lyrics of Arab songs often derive from classical poetry, or from contemporary poetry that follows the classical conventions of metre and rhyme. The link between the classical poetic tradition and such genres as the *muwashshah* and *qasida* gives these songs special authority as 'authentic', and provides a model for contemporary musicians and composers who aspire to emulate this standard. The esteem granted to classical poetry and poets in Arab culture helps us understand why the lyrics might be so important to these artists and listeners. For they may relate to deeply-held notions of identity: eloquence (*fasaha*), imagination (*khayal*) and sincerity (*sidq*) are the most valued features here. But other genres of the *wasla* are sung in colloquial Arabic, such as the different varieties of *mawwal* and *dawr*, as well as light songs that close the performance of the *wasla*. There, authenticity lies not in the eloquence of the language but in the meaning and meaningful rendering of the colloquial words themselves.

Musical Expression (*tabir musiqi*)

Aleppo's musicians and music lovers commonly say that a melody should express the meaning of the words it accompanies. Some critics have argued that Arab music, unlike European music, is not capable of expressing emotional states. Others have argued that, on the contrary, Arab music is highly expressive, using many compositional techniques to suggest emotional states such as sorrow and passion, natural conditions such as the wind and rain, and so forth. Syrian musicians and listeners engage in dialogue about musical expression, and expect that there should be a relationship between a song's melody and its words. Classical writings argued for a correspondence between the melodic modes and moods; today, some artists say that certain *maqamat* are directly associated with the experience of specific moods. For example, I was told that the mode *saba* evokes sadness, while *rast* instils bravery and courage. Similar associations have been noted between melodic modes (*ragas*) and emotional states in South Asian music; jazz and blues musicians also speak about 'blue' notes and the ways melodic structures produce different moods in performers and listeners.

178   *A Companion to Muslim Cultures*

However, these kinds of associations may not always occur in practice. I asked a well-known Syrian composer about the association of the melodic modes with certain moods, and how this may influence his choice of mode when fitting music to words. He picked up an *oud* and played a melody in the mode *zinkulah* (also called *zinjiran*); in medieval theory, this should conjure 'the distant desert'. Indeed, the melody sounded sad, mournful even. But it turned out to be the melody of a song by the Egyptian composer Sayyid Darwish, called *Ya halawat al-dunya* (O the Sweetness of the World), whose words are decidedly upbeat and cheerful! Barring the deliberate and ironic use of a 'sad' mode to sing about the sweetness of life, there is no link between mode and mood in this instance. A good composer, according to this artist, can create any type of song in any mode. The cosmological models, he suggested, are myths. Echoing a common modernist sensibility, he asserted that musical expression relies on the genius of the composer and the poet-lyricist, and ultimately on the skill and sensitivity of the artist to convey it. Certainly audience expectations play a large role in the making of affective associations between lyrics and melody; yet the modal system offers much room for negotiation and interpretation among performers and listeners.

Voice (*sawt*)

The interpretation of lyrics and the apt expression of what they mean in the melody is the responsibility of the composer. But the meaning of the lyrics and the beauty of the melody are apparent only through the voice of the artist. Not surprisingly, there is a wide and precise vocabulary for describing the human voice. Most commonly used are terms from various domains of cultural life, such as the ubiquitous *hilu* (sweet), which captures anything considered good or beautiful: a voice, person, house, car, song, dog, painting, dress, food, the moon. Other terms include *daif* (weak), *naim* (delicate, tender or smooth), *hassas* (sensitive), *rakhim* (mellow, melodious), *safi* (clear), *qawi* (strong, loud), *ali* (high or loud), *hadd* (high and sharp), *ghaliz*

Moving Sounds 179

(low, bass, or coarse), and *nashaz* or *nashiz* (discordant, out of tune).

From the Shaykhs: *min al-mashayikh*

In *The Voice of Egypt*, Virginia Danielson discusses the common Egyptian belief that their greatest artists are '*min al-mashayikh*' or 'from the sheikhs'.[3] In a similar vein, many Aleppines argued that their best vocalists are those who have had religious training in such Islamic practices as *adhan* (call to prayer), *tajwid* (Quranic recitation), *inshad* (religious song) and *dhikr* (meditative recital). Outstanding examples are the artists Sabri Moudallal and Hassan al-Haffar, muezzins at the Great Mosque in Aleppo and well-known *munshid*s (reciters of religious songs). Other great vocalists have also served at one point or another as muezzins, including Bakri al-Kurdi, Sabah Fakhri, Muhammad Khairi, and others. The late Adib al-Dayikh was famous both for his pre-dawn supplication recitals and his rendering of *qasida*.

Many younger vocalists in Aleppo have followed in this tradition. Some well-known vocalists actually made the reverse progression, becoming muezzins later in life when they could not find work as singers in clubs. This shows the fluidity of the boundaries between sacred and spiritual domains, as well as the value placed on the human voice for rendering the word of God and in praising Him.

Reference to the religious background of a singer is exceedingly important in Aleppine discourses of musical authenticity. Often when a young singer begins to make a name for himself as an artist, his religious background will be cited as the decisive early conditioning factor. For example, in a biographical entry on the young singer Nihad Najjar, the first few paragraphs describe the religious school he attended, which has produced numerous other well-known singers in its time. Even though Najjar no longer performs what Aleppines would regard as primarily spiritual

---

[3] '*The Voice of Egypt*': *Umm Kulthum, Arabic Song, and Egyptian Society in the Twentieth Century* (Chicago, 1997).

180   *A Companion to Muslim Cultures*

genres of song, his roots in the religious tradition are emphasised as the most important factor in his success and authenticity as an artist.

This is true for non-Muslim artists as well, among the region's many and venerable Christian communities. For example, Shadi Jamil (né George Jubran) is described in a musical biographical entry as having developed his 'heavenly throat' in the choir of the Orthodox Church in Aleppo. The biography does not hesitate to announce that Jamil, who like so many other young singers today performs in the style of Sabah Fakhri, also studied Quranic recitation and other genres of spiritual song with some of Aleppo's great Muslim teachers. By emphasising his links to the Islamic tradition, the biographical entry grants him an added degree of authenticity.

Religious training is thought to inculcate proper pronunciation, skill in the interpretation of the lyrics, and a proper moral stance in order to interpret the words and convey their meaning sincerely to an audience. Nur Mahanna's biographical entry states that his father would allow him to pursue a career as a singer only if he abided by the strict moral standards to which a 'great artist' must adhere: honesty, dedication and morally upright behaviour. Danielson notes that Umm Kulthum – who had a strong background in Islamic song – was known for the clarity of her pronunciation. A musician friend with whom I attended a Nihad Najjar concert commented extensively on how properly and clearly he pronounced the lyrics. Like many critics of the modern pop song, he argued that few contemporary pop stars have the culture or the background (that is, a religious one) that would prepare them for singing properly. The great Amr Diab, he claimed, commenting on one of the giants of contemporary Arab pop music, not only had a 'weak and discordant' voice that was fixed in the studio, but also lacked a connection to the *mashayikh*.

Emotions and Musical Performance

An essential ingredient 'makes or breaks' the Arabic song, even if everything else is present: emotional sincerity or *sidq*. The best of lyrics sung to complex and expressive melodies by a strong yet

Moving Sounds 181

feeling-less and insincere vocalist will fail to inspire listeners. Time and again, when I asked people at concerts or music conferences what they found most appealing about a certain artist or song, they mentioned this quality of *sidq*. Sharing linguistic roots with the word *sadiq* for 'friend' and also for 'honest', *sidq* implies genuine feeling, a lack of artifice, and surrender by the vocalist to the true meaning of the song. It reflects the artist's appreciation of the words and his capacity to express their meaning through his own feelings. To be authentic, then, an artist must be *sadiq*, endowed with *sidq*. This is how a mere singer-performer stands apart from a true artist who can evoke *tarab*, in the eyes of critical Aleppines. All great vocalists are felt to possess a high degree of *sidq*, whereas most contemporary singers are thought to lack this quality. A journalist despaired at the majority of the performers and their songs as 'empty speech', both in studios and on stage. Another critic insisted that singers at best mimic the experience of love; others lamented that modern vocalists 'are really only interested in sex'. The composer and performer Abd al-Fattah Sukkar also noted the importance of *sidq* in our long conversations. For him, what distinguishes good from bad in any art form – whether a composition, a poem or a painting – is this quality of sincerity. Why aren't a lot of the newer songs and singers sincere? 'Before a singer can be sincere with the audience', he argued, 'he must be sincere with himself. These days it is getting harder for people to be honest with themselves, so how can they produce good art?'

Bakri al-Kurdi is often cited as the foremost example of a 'sincere' artist. Known for having a weak and delicate voice, Sheikh Bakri, as he is called, could evoke *tarab* in listeners nonetheless because they felt that he was singing 'from the heart'. Some musicians criticised Sabah Fakhri as insincere because in their view his voice is strong (*qawi*) but devoid of feeling. Others (the majority) react more positively to his singing, such as the man who jumped on stage to hug him after Fakhri sang a particularly moving phrase. Some Syrian artists and music fans even described the legendary Umm Kulthum as 'insincere'. One prominent artist claimed that he cannot listen to her for more than five minutes because she is overly emotional; her feelings are exaggerated and artificial.

182   *A Companion to Muslim Cultures*

Interestingly, for the same reason he claimed that he cannot read Naguib Mahfouz for more than a few pages – the Egyptian novelist is just too maudlin for his tastes.

According to many Aleppine musicians and music lovers, *sidq* is intimately related to a performer's 'oriental spirit' (*ruh shar-qiyya*). Such a person is thought to be properly sensitive, with an intuitive grasp of the nuances of melodic modes. The Westerner, on the other hand, is described as direct and rationalistic, barely capable of understanding the modes at all. If these descriptions strike the reader as Orientalist in nature, for many Aleppines and other Arab musicians I have known elsewhere they are matters of both fact and pride. Who wouldn't want to be emotional, sensitive and intuitive? There are Syrians who criticise such characterisation; but for many Aleppine musicians, emotionality is basic to the complexity and beauty of their music.

The longer I stayed in Syria and the more I studied the music, the more I was asked by friends and acquaintances to play something on the *oud* or sing, in order for them to assess my knowledge and oriental spirit. Initially it seemed that one possesses this spirit rather than develops or acquires it – or is possessed by it, as in the idea of *duende* in Flamenco deep song.[4] At best my interlocutors would politely encourage me in my efforts; I usually failed the test, and they would note my lack of oriental spirit. Saddened, I asked my teacher what it meant not to have this spirit. 'If you're playing and someone says to you, "There isn't any spirit", he said, 'this means that you still haven't entered the music or represented it fully, so that your personality and presence can come through in it.' Having oriental spirit amounts to having *sidq* as a performer; indeed, the latter presumes the former. It is this that induces *tarab* in listeners, the true measure of quality.

Conclusion

The aesthetic elements of performance are, in essence, a language for the emotions in music. Harmonious combinations of strong

---

[4] See Federico García Lorca, *In Search of Duende* (New York, 1998).

Moving Sounds

melody, sensitive lyrics and good voice capture the fluid process of musical creation and reception in performance. It is here that a musician becomes 'good', 'authentic', or otherwise: performance makes aesthetic merit, not the reverse. For it is here that the vital qualities of emotional sincerity (*sidq*) and the elusive oriental spirit (*ruh sharqiyya*) are put to the test.

These qualities link the domain of the public concert or *hafla* to that of the *dhikr* and other Muslim, notably Sufi, liturgical practices. The genres and songs, and to a large extent the lyrics, are similar if not identical in secular and sacred contexts. These are but vehicles for the expression of emotional sincerity, itself a prerequisite for the pursuit of spiritual goals. Hence, a masterful performance on a concert stage can index the same values performed and recreated in a much more intimate religious setting. The close relationships of these domains should come as no surprise to listeners in the West, not only because of the prominent role of sacred music in European art music, but because of the strong presence of artists from the Muslim world in popular and 'World Music' circuits today – from *qawwali* artists to Gnawa masters and troupes of 'whirling dervishes'. In this regard, Aleppo's *wasla* is tied to traditions far beyond its Syrian roots.

Further Reading

Danielson, Virginia. *'The Voice of Egypt': Umm Kulthum, Arabic Song, and Egyptian Society in the Twentieth Century*. Chicago, 1997.

Frishkopf, Michael. 'Music', in Andrew Rippin, ed. *The Islamic World*. London and New York, 2008, pp. 510–526.

Hyder, Syed Akbar and Carla Petievich. 'Qawwali Songs of Praise', in Barbara Metcalf, ed. *Islam in South Asia in Practice*. Princeton, 2009, pp. 93–100.

Levin, Theodore and Fairouz Nishanova, 'Civil Sounds: The Aga Khan Music Initiative in Central Asia', in Amyn B. Sajoo, ed. *Muslim Modernities: Expressions of the Civil Imagination*. London, 2008, pp. 93–117.

184 A Companion to Muslim Cultures

Lohman, Laura. *Umm Kulthum: Artistic Agency and the Shaping of an Arab Legend, 1967–2007*. Middletown, CT, 2010.

Racy, A. J. *Making Music in the Arab World: The Culture and Artistry of Tarab*. Cambridge, 2003.

Sawa, George. *Music Performance Practice in the Early Abbasid Era*. Toronto, 1989.

Shannon, Jonathan. *Among the Jasmine Trees: Music and Modernity in Contemporary Syria*. Middletown, CT, 2006.

Shelemay, Kay. *Let Jasmine Rain Down: Song and Remembrance among Syrian Jews*. Chicago, 1998.

Shiloah, Amnon. *Music in the World of Islam: A Socio-cultural Study*. Detroit, 1995.

Stokes, Martin. 'Abd al-Halim's Microphone', in L. Nooshin, ed., *Music and the Play of Power: Music, Politics and Ideology in the Middle East, North Africa and Central Asia*. London, 2009.

Touma, Habib Hassan. *The Music of the Arabs*. Cambridge, 1996.

10

A Taste of Mecca

Mai Yamani

Mecca has attracted pilgrims from across the Muslim world and beyond since the seventh century – and earlier still as a site of pre-Islamic gatherings. Some of these pilgrims have, for various reasons, settled and intermarried in the city after the performance of the hajj, one of the five 'pillars' of Islam. These multi-racial settlers have obviously brought with them a host of customs and traditions, including culinary ones. With time, these have adapted to the local taste, adding to the body of what is termed 'Meccan' food. Dishes are no longer labelled Afghani, Bosnian, Indian, Indonesian, Egyptian, Moroccan, Syrian or Turkish; all are now proudly 'Meccan'. Some names of dishes remained unchanged from the original language, for example, *laddu*, a sweet of Indian origin. Others were modified in order to sound Meccan-Arabic, such as *zurbiyan* from *biryani*, an Indian rice dish. Yet others are known by the name of their country of origin, like *ruz Bukhari* (Bukhara rice). Meccan culture, like its food, is distinctly hetero-geneous. The variety of ethnic groups who settled in the city retain family names indicative of their countries of origin. Typically, the families of Masri, Damanhouri, Mansouri and Domiati are from Egypt. Prominent Indian family names include Baksh, Delhi, Kashmiri and Sindhi, while the Kabli family is from Afghanistan, and Lari and Krohaji are from Iran. Not surprisingly, the Bukhari family hails from Uzbekistan, the Yamani from Yemen, and the Turki and Istanbuli from Turkey. Then there are the Basnawi from Bosnia, the Filinban from the Philippines, the Fatani from Thailand, and the Nakshabandi from Mauritania. A number of core families

186   *A Companion to Muslim Cultures*

identify with the Arab tribe of Quraysh, to which the Prophet Muhammad belonged.

These multiethnic Meccans represent a pan-Islamic cultural and religious pluralism. Both Sunni and Shia are an integral part of this milieu, in addition to various Sufi traditions. Until the beginning of the 20th century, the Great Mosque in Mecca hosted the 'circles of knowledge', which provided a unique opportunity for dialogue among Muslims from all of the diverse branches of Islam. Central Asians, Indonesians, Malaysians, Indians, Persians, Egyptians, Turks – indeed, all those who represent the *umma*, the worldwide community of Muslims – came not only to perform the pilgrimage, but also to seek knowledge. The Great Mosque was like a university, and Mecca a place where Islam renewed and enriched itself.

In today's Saudi Arabia, that famed Meccan inclusiveness is visible during the hajj when the city once again becomes a cultural hub. But it is also found in its architecture, patterns of dress, music … and its cuisine. This latter is distinguished by Mecca's intricate recipes, in contrast with the spare desert tastes elsewhere. Indeed, the variety and versatility of Meccan cuisine can be sampled far beyond the city, from Bosnia to Tunisia and also in the Central Asian, Indian and Turkish restaurants of London and New York.

This chapter is a journey into the world of Meccan food, in its larger cultural setting. As with architecture, dress and music, the choice of what and where to eat is closely tied to the social and economic locus of individuals and families. Food choices also have much to do with the particulars of heritage – what one's family and community has preferred over time, and successfully passed on. Yet there are shared aspects, of course, to the cuisine which one associates with certain cultures and places. So while some of what we encounter in our journey here may be specific to certain groups, like those who belong to the business or clerical (*ulama*) class, these variations are part of the picture of Mecca's remarkably plural culture of food today.

The Setting

History has made Mecca a quite extraordinary place. For centuries, the background and outlook of its people has been urban in character, their way of life constantly shaped by exposure to other cultures. Not only has the pilgrimage brought waves of Muslims from across the world, but Meccans themselves have travelled widely since the 19th century, and sent their children to study in various Muslim countries. Contact with non-Muslim cultures is more recent, stemming from the discovery of oil which opened the Saudi economy to an influx of western as well as other expatriates. But direct contact happens outside Mecca, since the city retains the unique quality of being a sacred site reserved for Muslims.

Along with its neighbouring cities of Jeddah and Medina, Mecca has been a centre of regional trade – as well as international commerce linked to the Red Sea ports. In addition, the city's status as a pilgrimage site yielded tax and other revenues. All this made it more prosperous through much of history than the other regions of the Arabian Peninsula, until the discovery of oil in the eastern region in the 1930s. From the beginning of the 20th century to the 1930s, trade with India was vital, while other imports came from Singapore, Indonesia, Ethiopia (coffee), and neighbouring Middle Eastern lands. After the 1930s, specifically after the Second World War, most imports originated in the West. Even those commodities previously bought from the East and still available there (such as rice) began to come from the West, notably Holland and the United States.

Yet beyond its place in this commercial network, Mecca has been viewed by Muslims as being 'otherworldly', not quite of this earth. It is referred to as *Makka al-mukarrama*, 'the honourable Mecca'. Everything that happens there is somehow felt to be special. Good deeds and prayers are felt to magnify in value when performed there. Muslims from elsewhere, according to this belief, come to receive its unique blessing and hence to settle if they can. All in all, Mecca has a central place in the Islamic imaginary – one that is echoed in western secular parlance, as in 'the Mecca of' a particular social activity.

188 *A Companion to Muslim Cultures*

After the conquest of the Kingdom of the Hijaz where Mecca is located, and its incorporation in 1932 into the Kingdom of Saudi Arabia, the barriers between the Hijaz and other regions were eliminated. But as in much of the world, people continue to be distinguished according to their place of origin.[1] And being Meccan today symbolises the identity of a people who view themselves as distinct from others. Meccans are Hijazis. Yet they also exist in the context of their country, Saudi Arabia, within which they see themselves and are seen by others. Meccan culture, and in particular Meccan food, generally merges with their national identity, especially in encounters with outsiders.

In this context, Meccan food may be cast as Saudi food. Indeed, it is Saudis generally who like to identify Meccan food as theirs, for this gives them a distinctiveness in relation to all others, within and outside the Middle East. Since the 1980s, with rise of the oil economy, food has acquired a nationalistic flavour, alongside the usual regional consciousness that goes with it. Yet in both national and regional identities, the attachment to Mecca also means belonging to the wider Islamic world, in which the city enjoys its unique symbolic identity.

Food and Social Change

The manner in which food is cooked, presented and eaten tells us much about the people involved, in relation to ourselves and all others. There are specific rules for serving the guest, in which formal invitational expressions and compliments are exchanged between host and guest – ending with the appropriate giving of thanks for the meal. Again, in refined and elegant Meccan ways of presenting food, meat and vegetables are cut into very small pieces. Nothing is presented in large chunks, except when a whole lamb is used for special occasions. This is again a contrast between the urban and the bedouin cuisine where larger morsels are served.

Rules and language in this regard are often the preserve of elite

---

[1] Mai Yamani, *Cradle of Islam: The Hijaz and the Quest for Identity in Saudi Arabia* (London, 2009).

groups, whom others seek to emulate. Abiding by the standards of 'good taste' is closely linked to upholding the value and demonstration of generosity, in the context of time and place.

But there is also the matter of social status. Meccans who are associated with 'important' families are referred to as 'the face of the people' (*wujaha*), or 'the example of the people' (*ayan*). For these families, the kind of food and its presentation is a matter of great significance. The minutest details serve to distinguish their status in public, notably at formal events. Status is also closely tied to 'seemliness' or *tajammul*, which gives honour or added credit and 'brightens the face' of the family. Food is a way of showing *tajammul*: it allows for the display of a well-defined code of behaviour or *adab*, known and shared by the society, to which it imparts a sense of togetherness.

At the cultural level, as noted earlier, food has become ever more of an indicator of distinctiveness since the 1980s. This is an outcome of the rapid increase in social and geographical mobility with the advent and steady rise of the oil boom in the mid-1970s. Additional changes have come about as a result of contact with western cultures. In the midst of all the social and economic upheaval of the 1980s, people became relatively more conservative with regard to their identities and sense of belonging. Social change was often feared. Sectarian consciousness and practices tied to one's 'traditional' identity were heightened, often as a means of defending what were seen as core cultural or national values from the corruption of modernity.

Hence, traditions were revived, modified and often simply invented. The goal for Meccans and others in the nation was continuity and legitimacy, in order to garner the cohesion of the group. And the rituals of food became part and parcel of this preoccupation. Specific dishes, a special combination of spices, the manner of presentation and of consumption, even the timing of a meal – all acquired greater weight. Given the place of Mecca in the wider imaginary, its food becomes all the more vital – as a test both of tradition and of the willingness to accommodate creativity and change.

Ceremonies have been recreated from the past, distinguished

190 *A Companion to Muslim Cultures*

through traditional objects and food. Consider, for example, the *ghumra* henna ceremony during a marriage ceremony, the party held for the naming of a child on the seventh day (*al-sabu*), or the annual commemoration of a death (*hawl*). Food is a central object here. In the henna ceremony, special silver trays called *al-maashir* carry the traditional Meccan sweets, namely *laddu*, *labaniyya*, and *mahjamiyya* which are milk-based, *halawa tahiniyya* (sesame-based), *harissa* (puréed meat and wheat served with sugar), as well as the traditional Meccan breads *shurayk* and *kak*, and Meccan goat cheese and olives. These are served at room temperature and displayed in a prominent place. The combination of sweets, bread and cheese is ordinary food in everyday life, but during the henna ceremony it acquires symbolic significance in standing for the past, when such foods were luxuries.

The re-emphasis on tradition is nowadays closely linked to both Islamic heritage and to conspicuous consumption. A well-presented meal is expressive of Meccan cosmopolitan culinary tradition, but it is also very large and costly. With wealth, people are able to organise social occasions at which they display grand meals and demonstrate the rules of generosity and propriety. But wealth does not, on its own, determine identity or establish status; traditional criteria of belonging and status also matter. Perhaps at the beginning of the oil boom, freely available wealth became something of a social leveller. Now, however, people are returning to traditional themes in order to distinguish themselves.

In the 1980s, people began to move from abundance to quality in matters of food. For example, a plate consisting of fava beans, *ful midammas*, prepared with a sauce of clarified butter, cumin and lemon juice, stands out. This traditional Meccan dish and others are special because of their perceived link to the past, and hence convey a sense of continuity to Meccans. The revival of traditional Meccan food that had almost disappeared during the previous two decades also legitimised new activities. For social change had brought new ways of living for these Meccans, and this experience needed structure and definition if it was to be tolerable; the rituals of food played a role in making change digestible.

Food and Faith

Since religion is such a large part of the life of Mecca, it is no surprise that food is routinely tied to the observance of numerous festivities and rituals in the daily lives of Muslims. Indeed, there is a traditional Meccan dish or a combination of dishes for every event. Shared by Meccans both within the city and in Meccan communities outside of it, these special foods become a robust symbol of unity. Here, not only are the consumers distinguished from others, but the events are also defined in relation to the people who observe them. With the general re-emphasis and strengthening of religious practices, many events or gatherings are in fact given their distinction by the choice both of food and prayers.

To mark the *mawlid*, the end of the celebration of the Prophet's birthday, the traditional meal of a whole roast lamb on rice, with side dishes, is served. The sweet dish *ashuriyaa*, made from ten different kinds of grains, is offered to commemorate the 10th of Muharram or *ashur*. Then there are the special foods prepared only during Ramadan, the month of fasting. They include a dish of barley soup, *ful midammas*, cheese and meat pastries (*sambusak*), along with meat on a bed of bread immersed in stock flavoured with cardamom and covered with yoghurt (*fatta*). Also at this time are served sweet dishes such as filo pastries filled with almonds and immersed in honey (*gatayyif*). For the Muslim New Year, milk, fruit and a particular local goat cheese are considered most auspicious, because they represent purity. Of course, today these products are plentiful all over the country, where if not available locally, they are readily imported; but they still remain vital to proper celebration of the event.

The feast of Eid al-Fitr at the end of Ramadan is marked with a sweet dish, *dubyaza*, made from whole, dried and cooked dates as well as dried apricots, dried figs, sultanas and almonds. A roast lamb is also cooked (*al-minazzala*) for this occasion; it is cut into pieces before cooking, rather than presented whole. A different choice marks the feast of Eid al-Hajj, which follows the pilgrimage: local pastries filled either with dates or almonds (*ma'mul*), and

192   *A Companion to Muslim Cultures*

shortbread flavoured with cardamom (*ghurayyiba*).[2] On the 15th of Shaban, the month preceding Ramadan, Meccans prepare yet another pastry dish (*mishabbak*). At Mina, the final place to visit during the performance of the pilgrimage, a very fine layer of pastry covered with powdered sugar (*zallabiyya*) is prepared. Meccans who are not performing the hajj during that year still prepare this sweet to mark the event.

For the event of death, a specific meal is cooked and served to mark the end of formal condolence (*gataza*) on the third day. The main dish for this occasion is rice with chickpeas and meat (*ruz bi-hummus*), an aromatic dish of finely chopped tripe and liver (*sagat*), and sometimes squash stew with meat and split peas; squash is considered to have been the favourite of Prophet Muhammad. A meal consisting of whole lamb on rice (*mandi*), with accompanying dishes such as sesame-seed paste with cucumber salad (*salatat tahina*), is served at the ceremony to commemorate a death anniversary (*hawl*). Likewise, special food is cooked for the events of birth or marriage. Then there is the serving of 'the sugary clouds' (*al-ghaym al-sukkari*) on an overcast day. This meal consists of rice with lentils (*ruz bi-adas*), salad of tamarind (*salatat huma*) and fried fish, fresh from the Red Sea. On Fridays before prayers in the mosque, Meccans prepare a dish consisting of thinly sliced camel liver infused with cumin and pepper.

It is further noteworthy that during such ceremonies as the celebration of the birth of the Prophet or a death anniversary, the meal is always served on a white plastic tablecloth placed on the floor. Plastic has been used since it became available in the country to prevent staining of the carpets underneath. Before the introduction of plastic, people used a circular mat made of palm leaves (*misaffa*), about one metre in diameter. For everyday meals, as well as at other less traditional events such as a wedding party at a hotel, food is now served at western-style dining tables, with dishes from various nations, eastern and western. At more tradi-

---

[2] Dates grow in Medina and almonds in Taif, the mountainous town to the south of Mecca.

tional religious events, the right hand or spoons are used rather than forks and knives.

Hospitality, Bonding ... and Status

Meccan families, wherever they happen to be, also hold 'Meccan nights' with familiar themes, objects and food, some of which are recreated from the past. Combinations of typically Meccan dishes, such as small grilled meatballs heavily spiked with garlic (*mabshur*), wonton-like steamed pastry filled with minced meat (*mantu*), and (*mittabbag*), a fine layer of pastry filled with eggs, minced meat and chives, and sweet *mittabbag* made with honey and bananas or with local cheese and honey, are served by men dressed in old-style Meccan dress and consumed by guests seated on high-backed Meccan benches. Since this item of furniture has come back into fashion, a brisk trade has developed in reproducing benches, the originals having practically disappeared amongst these Meccans. Rosewater and water with flavours such as that of the *kadi* plant are drunk from special Meccan water containers and bowls.

The return or revival of 'tradition' is apparent in the conduct of both men and women. Gender segregation is minimal at family gatherings, but is observed at most formal celebrations. Food at women's parties is almost always more elaborate than at the men's. At the men's observance of a wedding ceremony, the dinner always follows the same menu, a simple and traditional choice of 'Meccan' food: several whole roast lambs, rice, salad made of sesame sauce and cucumber, and *turumba*, little fingers of pastry soaked in honey. At the women's ceremony, however, the food is much more varied and colourful. Not only Hijazi food (from Mecca, Jeddah or Medina), but also Lebanese, Egyptian, Moroccan and other Arab dishes and even western delicacies such as avocados and smoked salmon are presented. The whole lamb remains a central part of the meal, but for the women it is pre-carved off the bone. No woman would consider carving the lamb on such an occasion, for it would be considered indelicate. Several men explained to me that the difference between men's and women's food, dress, and the elaborate manners of formal greeting and speech, is that

194   *A Companion to Muslim Cultures*

women are more concerned than men about 'appearances' (*mazahir*), and that they prefer variety, which is not in the nature of men.

Extending hospitality and showing generosity to the guest is one way of establishing or maintaining status and respectability. Indeed, generosity and hospitality require that from the beginning of a party until the last guest leaves, the host or hostess should stay on their feet to show courtesy (*mujamala*) and recognition (*tagdir*) for their guests. Serving the guests (*al-mubashara*) is described by Meccans as a matter of honour as well as generosity (*muruwa*). In Muslim tradition, even a host who enjoys higher status than the guest must serve first and eat later. Meccans repeat the hadith, 'He who loves Allah and His Messenger should be generous to his guest.'

Even with a large number of domestic staff, it is the 'people of the house' (*ahl al-bayt*) who actually serve the guests. While the servants bring the food from the kitchen, the host or hostess and their extended family offer it in the appropriate manner to the guests. The guest is not left for a moment without being offered food: juices, nuts, dates, coffees (Turkish or Meccan almond), mint tea (or the Lipton brand), then dinner which is delayed for as long as possible since the rule is that the guest leaves immediately after; thereafter, more teas, coffees and a peculiarly Meccan mix of 'digestive' spices, betel-nut, cardamom, cloves and peppermints. Incense (*ud*) is burned and passed around before and especially after food as another sign of hospitality, along with oil-based sandalwood, amber or rose perfumes. Throughout the party, the host or hostess and their extended family implore the guest, by Allah, to eat. No matter how much the guest is actually eating, the host or hostess repeats, 'You have not eaten! . . . By Allah you have not eaten!' The guest replies with one of the many set compliments in acknowledgement of this generosity, such as 'May Allah make your house always prosperous!', to which the host replies, 'With your presence only', or 'May Allah make you more generous!', to which the host replies, 'We only follow your generosity'.

Hospitality in the past meant feeding the guest directly, from the host's hand to the guest's mouth. A very honoured guest could

A Taste of Mecca

not be allowed to eat with their own hand, but would be properly fed from the moment of seating. 'If the members of the house number eight, each would offer her at least one morsel', was the custom. That practice has died out. Nowadays, the host only helps the guest eat by perhaps shelling pistachios, cutting meat or chicken into smaller pieces for them, or adding food to their plates – even if these are already full. The rules for serving the guest (*al-mubarasha*) express social status, as they do in all traditional cultures and places. Thus at a dinner party, the more honoured guests are seated at 'the head of the table' and served by the more senior members of the family; junior guests are seated at the opposite end and are still served, but only by relatively junior family members.

Although food is a central preoccupation at every social gathering, the word 'food' is not directly mentioned. To do this in public is considered ill-mannered. Even if the hostess and her family have gone to the trouble of preparing an assemblage of three dozen dishes to cover their entire serving space, the guests are never asked to the table to partake of the 'food' or to 'eat'. 'Please oblige us, honour us!' is the plea of the hostess.

Excess, Generosity and the Evil Eye

The sheer amount of food served is still a measure of generosity. Presenting a whole lamb, for example, is a gesture of honouring the guest. At formal events, there is always at the table considerably more food than can possibly be consumed by the guests and household. What happens to the leftovers from such lavish banquets? They are usually distributed to friends and relatives, and to poorer families by way of alms or *sadaqa*. Every family of high status has several poor families to whom they regularly offer charity – in food as well as clothes, money and so forth. Thus, the same evening or the morning after a big meal or religious event, the food is distributed from house to house. Most relatives get their share of the leftovers. The type of food keeps well; indeed, it improves in flavour overnight. The explanation is that by the following day, the spices and flavours mingle well in the dish and

196 *A Companion to Muslim Cultures*

become more flavourful. Meat is a traditional form of alms *sadaqa*.

Meccans regularly slaughter lamb in their own courtyards; they keep part of the meat for their own household's consumption and send the rest to those in need. Sometimes the lamb is slaughtered with a specific intention (*niyya*), such as a sacrifice for the recovery of a family member who has been ill. But the slaughter is usually in order to protect the family and maintain prosperity. Meccans eat *harri* (lamb) meat only from a region south of Mecca; they do not like imported lamb, and they consider beef to be inferior. Chicken and varieties of fish from the Red Sea are also everyday food. Pork is simply un-Islamic and never eaten.

Food is traditionally offered to people as a gift. One form that this takes is *tuma*; mealtimes often feature at least one plate on the table that is *tuma*, sent by a relative or friend. One should never return this plate empty; it is returned filled with food, or failing this, with sugar. But food should be sent to the house, never brought by the guest as an immediate appreciation of a dinner. This can only be done by a close relative, because between family members there is no formality or embarrassment. The *dakhla* is another gift of food, but is often in the form of a feast given in honour of a person who has returned from a trip. Sometimes the *dakhla* is sent to the home. Food is commonly offered to extended family afflicted with a death. Distant relatives and close friends send cooked food, especially during the first three days of formal condolence, a practice that is based on a hadith.

Despite all the conspicuous consumption that relates to food, there is a constant fear of the evil eye attached to it. Food being connected with basic beliefs and values, a sense of identity and belonging, and with social status, but primarily food being essential to life, makes it appear especially susceptible to the evil eye or *hassad*. Anyone, whether consciously or not, may cast the evil eye. The fear is more for certain types of food, and particularly if the person who is to consume the food is either vulnerable or in a position to be envied. For example, the special chicken broth (*masluga*) consumed by the new mother is especially prone to the evil eye, as is the milk for an infant. These vulnerable foods are always covered by a cloth or opaque paper for protection. Fruits

A Taste of Mecca

197

are also susceptible; baskets of fruit are always covered until the moment they are to be eaten. All food that was formerly a rarity or considered a delicacy is considered more prone to the evil eye.

Polite guests always use the expression *Mashallah*, 'By the grace of Allah', in a stage whisper on seeing a banquet. This expresses both their goodwill and also their admiration. It is customary for women to eat a light meal (*talbiba* or *tasbira*) at home to appease their hunger prior to attending a formal dinner party. This is partly to look elegant and refined since appearing hungry in front of others is not considered dignified, and partly because of the evil eye, since eating heartily in front of a large group risks exposure to this.

Guests in Mecca are seated at a meal at the same time. But when a guest finishes eating, he or she should leave the table and not wait for others who are still eating. This is felt to accord with the Quranic verse, 'And if you have eaten, disperse, even if you are enjoying conversation.' People explain that it is ill-mannered for those who have finished eating to sit 'counting the morsels'. This could cause the evil eye. Although people do exchange a few words at mealtimes, there is no tradition of formal conversation at table as in other societies. Furthermore, all dishes are presented together to be consumed at the same time; there is no sequence of courses to be waited for. Hence, the time spent at a meal depends on how much and how quickly an individual eats.

There are various preventative measures against the evil eye, other than covering the food. One should not mention the actual name of a particular dish, such as meat (*lahma*), but instead call it something else (such as *kuku* or *hayla*). Children are taught this for they are most vulnerable. When a person is suspected of having got the evil eye while eating, a condition people describe as 'receiving a morsel' (*jatu lugma*), a *sayyid* (religious man) is sought to remove the morsel by the power of his prayers. The antidote universally acknowledged for this purpose is the invocation of the sura *al-Falaq*, the 113th verse of the Quran, seeking protection from all evils.

198   *A Companion to Muslim Cultures*

New Ways, Old Proprieties

Home is where food is properly cooked and served. Both innovation and tradition occur here – the home as preserver and generator of the local or national identity of cuisine. Until quite recently, there were no restaurants in Mecca, except for popular public eating places called *gahawi* (cafés), where men eat outdoors seated on high benches, rounding off their meals with tea and a water-pipe (*shisha*). No woman would ever eat in a public place; it was considered shameful to do so in commercial spaces (*souks* and the like). Today western-style restaurants have opened, most being part of international hotel chains that offer American, Asian, European and Middle Eastern food. They cater mainly to expatriates living in Saudi Arabia, though some locals have started to patronise them.

Food in the home has always been cooked by women; Meccan men rarely cook. Recipes are visually and orally transmitted from mother to daughter. Formerly female slaves who lived as part of the family helped in cooking the family recipes. Today, some Meccan women do not cook the food themselves. Meccan food is cooked by male foreign cooks. The latter are usually Filipino, Lebanese, Sudanese, Egyptian or Moroccan. The male cook is never Meccan. The professional cook is taught the recipes of Meccan food by a knowledgeable female member of the maternal or paternal family. Although a woman may not cook herself, she still takes pride in knowing traditional Meccan cuisine.

The first national Saudi cookbook was published in 1984 – written jointly by six Saudi women from high status groups in various parts of the country, with recipes from assorted cities and regions which are not identified in the text.[3] Likewise, when Meccan food in its regional and international variety is savoured in restaurants in London or New York, there is a lack of awareness of its origins. This, of course, is fully in the tradition of the

---

[3] See Pater Heine, 'The Revival of Traditional Cooking in Modern Arab Cookbooks', in Sami Zubaida and Richard Tapper, ed. *A Taste of Thyme* (London, 2000), pp. 143–152.

city as a place where cultures and peoples converge into a 'melting pot'.

Amid rapid change in a globalising world, perhaps the final bastion of individual expression is food, which can speak to people's beliefs, identity and consciousness. 'Eat what you like and dress as others would like you to', as the Arab proverb goes. Then again, one might see in Mecca's cosmopolitan cuisine a call to renew the open and inclusive traditions that lie at the heart of Islam itself.

Further Reading

Heine, Peter. *Food Culture in the Near East, Middle East and North Africa*. Westport, CT, 2004.

Khare, Ravindra and M. Rao. *Food, Society and Culture: Aspects in South Asian Food Systems*. Durham, NC, 1986.

Pilcher, Jeffrey. *Food in World History*. New York, 2006.

Ramazani, Nesta. *Persian Cooking: A Table of Exotic Delights*. Bethesda, MD, 2000.

Roden, Claudia. *The New Book of Middle Eastern Food*. Rev. ed., New York, 2000.

Salloum, Habeeb and James Peters. *From the Lands of Figs and Olives*. London, 1997.

Waines, David. *In a Caliph's Kitchen: Mediaeval Arab Cooking for the Modern Gourmet*. London, 1995.

Watson, James and Melissa Caldwell, ed. *The Cultural Politics of Food and Eating*. Oxford, 2005.

Yamani, Mai. *The Cradle of Islam: The Hijaz and the Quest for Identity in Saudi Arabia*. London, 2009.

Zubaida, Sami and Richard Tapper, ed. *A Taste of Thyme: Culinary Cultures of the Middle East*. London, 2000 (reprinted 2010).

11

Cosmopolitanism:
Ways of Being Muslim

Karim H. Karim

Cosmopolitanism is a much-debated idea. At its basis, the concept refers to openness toward other cultures. The ancient Greek origin of cosmopolitan suggests the idea of 'a citizen of the world'. A popular contemporary image of cosmopolitans is that of wealthy jet-setters who travel to exotic locations, speak many languages effortlessly and are at ease in engaging with people from different parts of the world. In the past, only a few individuals in society were privileged enough to travel or to come into contact with other cultures.

> However, in the contemporary world, cultural and linguistic diversity is omnipresent, and the capacity to communicate with others and to understand their cultures is available, at least potentially, to many ... Travel and immigration have led to the necessity of cheek-by-jowl relationships between diverse peoples at work or at street corners, and in markets, neighbourhoods, schools and recreational areas.[1]

We can therefore now speak of 'everyday' or 'ordinary' cosmopolitanism.[2] Muslims are part of the contemporary

---

[1] Steven Vertovec and Robin Cohen, 'Introduction: Conceiving Cosmopolitanism', in Steven Vertovec and Robin Cohen, ed., *Conceiving Cosmopolitanism: Theory, Context and Practice* (Oxford, 2002), p. 5.

[2] Daniel Hiebert, 'Cosmopolitanism at the Local Level: The Development of Transnational Neighbourhoods', in Vertovec and Cohen, ed., *Conceiving Cosmopolitanism*, p. 212.

202   *A Companion to Muslim Cultures*

experience of cosmopolitanism. They participate in the mass migrations of our age as well as in business and tourist travel. Adherents of the Islamic faith are also members of the multicultural populations of western countries and many of their homelands have diverse populations. But this is not a novel occurrence. History provides evidence of cosmopolitanism among Muslim societies that were composed of people of several ethnic and religious backgrounds. A pluralist outlook fostered the engagement of multiple viewpoints. There was also a strong tradition of travel – for trade, pilgrimage and learning. Land and sea routes were well-established and well-serviced. Providing assistance to the traveller was integral to the Islamic ethic. Indeed, Muslim cosmopolitanism arose in large part out of religious sensibility. The Quran encourages the believer to embrace humanity.

Indeed, the roots of Islam itself are pluralist. Certain of its key elements cannot be separated from the influences of other traditions. Islam's message is positioned within the Abrahamic tradition of which Judaism and Christianity are older members. Openness to other civilisations was vital to the religious, cultural and intellectual growth of Muslim societies. The development of Islamic law, theology and philosophy drew from the knowledge of older cultures. Muslims borrowed from the heritage of the lands in which they settled and, in turn, made substantial contributions to the store of human learning. The unfolding of the European Renaissance was indebted to Muslims, not only for the preservation of ancient knowledge but in substantially expanding the worlds of philosophy, science and technology.

On the other hand, religious arguments have been used – to this day – to support an anti-cosmopolitan stance by some Muslims who oppose interaction with people of other backgrounds. Opposition to cosmopolitanism has emerged several times with significant force in the history of the faith. Anti-cosmopolitanism has gained ground among Muslims in contemporary times. These tendencies are also taking hold in some parts of the West, which prides itself on adopting liberal philosophical approaches. The 'clash of civilisations' thesis and strong anti-immigrant positions are contributing to such tendencies. It is noteworthy that the

Cosmopolitanism: Ways of Being Muslim

contesting sides in both civilisations respectively refer to common bases in stating their claims – cosmopolitans as well anti-cosmopolitans among Muslims cite traditional Islamic sources and their counterparts in the West look for justifications of their particular claims in the Enlightenment.

Din and *Dunya*

Faith or *din* and one's interaction with the material world, *dunya*, are interlinked in Islamic worldviews.

> One of the central elements of the Islamic faith is the inseparable nature of faith and world. The two are so deeply intertwined that one cannot imagine their separation. They constitute a 'way of life'.[3]

The practice of faith, the Quran repeatedly asserts, is not limited to the performance of rituals. Apart from active membership in the religious community, Muslims are expected also to participate fully in the material world. Islamic beliefs do not permit withdrawal into a monastery or convent. Engagement with the world enables believers to test their beliefs and strengthen their faith. Ethics, drawn from religion, can guide one's behaviour in various aspects of existence, including family life, business and politics.

Muslim behaviour toward people of other cultures and religions may similarly be shaped by faith. A strong sense of humanism appears in the Quran and the hadith (the sayings of the Prophet). Islamic scripture promotes the recognition of a common origin of humanity, that it comes from a single universal soul, as well as of its diversity. Several verses in the Quran speak of the dignity of human beings, who in Muslim discourses are 'the crown of creation' (*ashraf al-makhlukat*). Muhammad encouraged his followers to be kind and gentle to all, particularly to the weak and the vulnerable. His own behaviour was characterised by the respect

---

[3] His Highness the Aga Khan, *Where Hope Takes Root: Democracy and Pluralism in an Interdependent World* (Vancouver, 2008), p. 125.

204   *A Companion to Muslim Cultures*

that he showed to others. These teachings form the ethical foundation of the Muslim's engagement with the world.

The word '*dunya*' refers in the literal sense to the expanse of the earth. The Prophet Muhammad reportedly counselled his followers to 'seek knowledge even as far as China'. For early Muslims this metaphorically meant the end of the known world. The Prophet's advice appears to have strongly encouraged the emergence of a travelling culture driven by trade and a search for knowledge. Faith and world remained interlinked in the Muslim spirit of journeying to the Far East as well as to the far west.

Engagement with Other Cultures

Following the Prophet's death, the momentum of events within Arabia propelled Muslims to continue moving and venture outside the peninsula as a conquering force. They went into neighbouring lands of Syria, Palestine, Iraq and Egypt – where they were frequently welcomed as a replacement to the rule of the Byzantines who were not always sympathetic to local peoples. Muslim leaders signed agreements to protect the inhabitants. Christians and Jews were seen as the 'People of the Book' (*Ahl al-Kitab*), in the belief that there was a common source of inspiration underlying the Bible and the Quran. They were given the rights to run their own systems of family law. Whereas in the long course of history some individual Muslim rulers mistreated non-Muslim subjects, these were exceptions to the prevailing practice of a pluralism in which Jews and Christians attained high offices of the state. It is notable that whereas many Christian communities were to be found in lands under Muslim rule, the opposite was not true in the European domains of Christian rulers. When the Jewish community in Muslim Spain was threatened by the rise of the Almohad dynasty, Maimonides, one of the greatest medieval Jewish scholars, travelled not to Christian Europe but to North Africa. He later rose to the prestigious position of a physician in the court of the Sultan Salahuddin (Saladin) in Cairo.

The rapid expansion of the Muslim empire in the seventh and eighth centuries CE brought the followers of the new faith into contact with many religions, cultures and ethnicities. They encountered multiple forms of Christianity and Judaism as well as Zoroastrianism and other religions that existed then in the Middle East. Among the peoples that the Arab Muslims came across were the Assyrians, Philistines, Arameans, Chaldeans, Mesopotamians, Egyptians, Kurds and Persians. The Arabs themselves formed a small part of the populations of the various lands in which they settled. They engaged with the cultures of the local inhabitants and, even though they formed the ruling class, their own culture and language were modified over time by the contact with other peoples. In the course of many centuries, a large part of the local populations converted to Islam. Their cultures further enriched the Muslim community. A number of great Muslim figures who are often referred to as being 'Arab' actually had Persian, Kurdish, Central Asian or other origins.

Muslims ruled in Spain for some 800 years (early-eighth to late-15th centuries). There developed a very distinct Spanish Muslim culture due to close engagement with the local people. The artefacts and architecture produced in that land during this time resulted from a coming together of different cultures and the flowering of a civilisation. The palace of Alhambra and the particular designs of Andalusian mosques are indications of both the sophisticated nature of the civilisation as well as its distinctiveness in relation to Muslim architecture in the East. Even though certain periods in the history of Muslim Spain were marked by intolerance, there was a high degree of harmony among Muslims, Christians and Jews for most of the eight centuries. This period has come to be recognised as an exemplary case of pluralism by contemporary agencies such as UNESCO.[4]

Later in history, the large westward migrations of Turkic and Mongol tribes – which initially caused severe conflict and devastation in Muslim lands – eventually added to the cultural diversity of Islam. As Muslim domains expanded into India and what is now Turkey, the various peoples – immigrant and indigenous

---

[4] UNESCO, 'Historic City of Toledo', World Heritage, http://whc. unesco.org/en/list/379.

206   *A Companion to Muslim Cultures*

– helped to build the civilisations like those of the Mughals and the Ottomans.

The Cosmopolitan Pursuit of Knowledge

Muslims took to heart the Prophet's guidance to seek knowledge wherever it existed in the world. The region which is now called the Middle East was a meeting point of streams of knowledge originating from places like India, China and Greece. It had been part of the vibrant Hellenic world where people studied the works of philosophy, science, religion, literature, music and art. Manuscripts in many languages were to be found in places of learning. During the Middle Ages, the Church authorities in Europe prohibited the examination of the works of ancient scholars which were thought to be contradictory to officially approved Christian teachings. This caused the narrowing of scholarship and eventually led to the decline of learning. However, even as Europe sank into its Dark Ages, the study of the writings from ancient Greece and elsewhere continued in the East.

Muslims encountered learned Christian scholars who were well versed in the knowledge of the day. They also came upon a renowned academy of learning in the city of Jondishapur, which was the intellectual centre of the Iranian Sassanid empire. It had been for centuries a centre for study and training for Persian, Greek, Indian, and Roman scholars in medicine, philosophy, theology and science. The followers of the Prophet were keen to obtain these and other forms of knowledge. They were encouraged in their reading of the Quran to observe the objects in the heavens and earth in order to understand the creation better. There appears to have been a genuine intellectual curiosity that was prompted by religious faith. Muslims became the students of the teachers at places like Jondishapur in order to fulfil their Islamic obligations with regards to acquiring knowledge.

They studied the writings of European and Eastern civilisations. A translation movement ensued. Numerous manuscripts were translated by Muslims from various languages into Arabic. This increased access to the most advanced knowledge of the day

Cosmopolitanism: Ways of Being Muslim

and promoted intellectual growth, fostering what is today referred to as a 'knowledge society'. Muslim scholars in various fields contributed to the treasury of human learning. They provided original philosophical insights into old problems and introduced new modes of thought; discoveries were made in mathematics and various sciences; innovative techniques in engineering and other technical fields were developed. Substantial advances were made in the study of medicine, including ophthalmology, anatomy as well as surgical procedures. The Canon of Medicine, a 14-volume medical encyclopaedia completed by Ibn Sina (Avicenna) in 1025, was used in the centres of learning around the world. Based on a combination of his own medical practice, medieval medicine in the Muslim world, the writings of the ancient Roman physician Galen, the Indian physicians Sushruta and Charaka, and ancient Persian and Chinese scientists, it became a standard medical text in European universities for many centuries. The engagement with non-Islamic thought produced some heated debates among Muslim philosophers, as when Zakariya al-Razi (Rhazes), drawing upon Platonic-Pythagorean influence, argued against prophecy.

A key Muslim contribution was to the scientific method itself. Much of the knowledge of the ancient world was theoretical. The Quran encouraged the practice of direct observation of worldly phenomena as a means to understanding *din* and *dunya*. The practice of this method led to the growth of empirical study as an important basis of scientific discovery. Among the earliest practitioners was the Fatimid optical scientist Ibn al-Haytham (Alhazen), who used the empirical method two hundred years before European scholars. Additionally, religious requirements, such as knowing the proper times for ritual prayer and fasts as well as the direction of Mecca for the physical orientation of worship, prompted research into astronomy and geography. Highly accurate calculations were made in these fields. These were some of the ways in which the linkage of faith and the material world in Muslim existence fostered dynamism and creativity.

The openness of Muslims to other cultures provided for the intellectual flowering of their own religion. It comes as a surprise to contemporary Muslims that certain key aspects of the Islamic

208 *A Companion to Muslim Cultures*

faith which have become integral to its structures of belief owe their development to scholarly methods derived from other civilisations. The only textual sources that emerged from Prophet Muhammad's time were the Quran and the hadith. In the next few centuries, Muslims developed the basis of Islamic law (*fiqh*), theology (*kalam*) and philosophy (*falsafa*). However, the production of these bodies of work required the intellectual tools of analysis and philosophical reasoning. The inhabitants of seventh century Arabia had not been learned in the sciences or in what are now called the humanities. Muslims who went out into neighbouring lands acquired rational modes of analysis, categorisation and philosophical thought, with which they gave shape to Muslim intellectual discourse.

The intellectual culture of the lands under Muslim rule continued to foster exchange between the learned individuals of various origins. Scholars of Jewish, Christian, Hindu and other backgrounds thrived variously in Baghdad, Cairo, Cordoba, Samarkand, Agra and Istanbul. It was not uncommon for learned persons to be able not only to speak several languages but even to be able to compose poetry in them. The courts of caliphs and sultans became places of high culture; indeed, newly established rulers felt the need to ensure that they had scholars in their retinue. It is reported that Mahmud of Ghazna went as far as to kidnap the great scientist and geographer al-Biruni and keep him as a virtual prisoner in his court.

Al-Biruni's writings about India provide one of the most detailed pre-modern accounts by a person of one culture about another. He wrote thorough descriptions of the Indus valley and surrounding regions as well as of the beliefs and practices of their inhabitants. Al-Biruni's lifetime pre-dated the establishment of Muslim rule in India. Whereas, his 'patron' treated the land of the Hindus primarily as a place for plunder, the scholar demonstrated great respect for the people of India and wrote about them in a manner comparable to the social scientific approaches of modern scholarship.

Travelling Culture

A key element in Muslim cosmopolitanism is the ideal of the global Islamic community, the *umma*. It provides for the acceptance of a brotherhood and sisterhood that is inclusive of all cultures and ethnic groups. The concept of the *umma* can be traced back to the beginnings of the small Muslim community in Medina, where the Prophet and his followers had settled to escape persecution from the Meccans. As the religion expanded in the following centuries far beyond Arabia, Muslims took with them a strong sense of communal self. The sense of belonging to a global community became a primary feature of Islamic identity.

The annual pilgrimage to Mecca (hajj) which was also practised before the Prophet and brought within the fold of Islam by him, has become the occasion of a communal gathering that brings together Muslims from many regions of the world. Gathering at the Kaaba from many points on the planet signifies in physical and spiritual terms the assembling of the members of a human community at a single place. The languages and practices of people from various locations become visible to those who attend. Individuals who have been living their lives only among their respective ethnic groups are made aware of the broad diversity of Muslims. The hajj enables interaction and familiarisation of the cultures that make up the *umma*. This experience has had a significant impact on the lives of people who have participated in the pilgrimage. For example, Malcolm X, an African-American Muslim leader who had initially been drawn to Islam as an expression of racial opposition to dominant American society, became more accepting of other peoples following his hajj in 1964.

Other types of pilgrimage also draw Muslims together. Gatherings take place at the tombs of Sufi shaykhs or *pirs*, especially during their birth anniversaries. It is noteworthy that many Hindus, Sikhs and followers of other faiths also frequently offer prayers at such Muslim shrines in India. And, correspondingly, it is the tendency among some Muslims in South Asia to seek spiritual grace at the holy places of other faiths, even though this practice is severely frowned upon by those who are more orthodox.

210 *A Companion to Muslim Cultures*

Shia Muslims from various parts of the world visit the shrines of their Imams, particularly on the significant days of their religious calendar.

Vigorous trade among Muslim societies and between them and others gave rise to regular forms of journeying. Indeed, Muhammad had travelled to Syria as a merchant before the call to prophethood. Transportation systems for long-distance commerce provided the backbone for other kinds of travel. It encouraged investment in infrastructure and services including caravans, ships, ports, roads, bridges, rest houses, security, communications and food provision, as well as in developing specialised skills on the part of the labour force involved in maintaining and monitoring the various networks. State bureaucracies were involved in ensuring the regulation, proper functioning of travel and collection of customs duties.

Land and water routes flourished in Asia and Africa as well as across the seas and oceans. Despite occasional conflicts between European and Muslim powers along the Mediterranean, there was a steady exchange of goods from north to south and east to west along the long sea. Places along the extensive rim of the Indian Ocean as well as the Red Sea and the Persian Gulf were engaged in trade of materials that brought in objects from as far away as China. Dhows plied the high seas in the directions dictated by the trade winds during particular times of the year. The fabled 'Silk Route' was actually a network of carefully maintained roads and caravanserais that ran from the Far East to the outskirts of Europe.[5] Regular caravans had marked out courses of travel through harsh terrain that included scorching deserts and snow-clad mountain regions. Several of these routes had pre-existed the advent of Islam; however, Muslims considerably extended the transportation systems that connected various parts of the *umma* to themselves and to others. Geographers like al-Idrisi produced a series of maps of the world known to them, and the improvement of navigational instruments like the astrolabe aided the journeying of travellers.

---

[1] Frances Wood, *The Silk Road: Two Thousand Years in the Heart of Asia* (Berkeley, CA, 2002), p. 36.

Cosmopolitanism: Ways of Being Muslim 211

Numerous biographies from the medieval period tell of the treks that notable individuals undertook in their lives. Some like the eminent philosopher-mystic Ibn Arabi travelled for many years, seeking knowledge and religious enlightenment. Travelogues provide extensive details of the cities and countryside of Muslim lands as well as the modes of journeying. The *Safarnama* of the Persian traveller Nasir-i Khusraw narrates carefully the observations that he carried out in his sojourns in Mecca and Cairo, where he witnessed the ceremonies of the Fatimid capital. One of the most famous medieval Muslim travel-writers was Ibn Batuta. Leaving his home in Tangier in north-western Africa as a young man, he performed the hajj and then journeyed extensively in various parts of Asia and Africa.

The popularity of fabulous fictional travel stories like those in the *One Thousand and One Nights* ('The Arabian Nights') point to the manner in which the imagination of Muslims was captured by the prospect of journeying to faraway lands and meeting people with customs that seemed amazing and marvellous. Scientific, biographical and literary accounts all enriched a cosmopolitan culture that welcomed engagement with other civilisations. This attitude co-existed with the anti-cosmopolitanism among those Muslims who were suspicious of alien cultures, as will be discussed later in the chapter.

Modern Western Encounters

The contemporary world in which mass travel and instant global communication are the norm affect Muslims as much as other people. Globalisation has provided a set of conditions for life that have not occurred before in history. Whereas the factors which have facilitated worldwide travel and communication are technological, they have enabled new ways of thinking about the relationships between human communities. One needs to recognise, however, that although the pace of globalisation has accelerated in recent decades, this trend did not emerge full-blown but had particular historical developments that led up to it.

The European voyages of discovery that occurred four to five

212   *A Companion to Muslim Cultures*

hundred years ago laid the foundations for linking the world through colonialism. Lands and peoples in Africa, Asia, the Americas and Australasia were brought under European control. Colonies were connected to the imperial capitals such as London, Paris, Lisbon, Madrid, the Hague, Rome, Berlin and Moscow. Transportation and communication links were developed to ensure that raw materials flowed from the rest of the world to be processed in the 'mother' countries and then sold to the colonies to increase the wealth of the imperial powers.

New transportation networks were established to serve the interests of colonial trading systems and economies. In many cases, this led to the disruption and destruction of older transportation and communication networks that had been built over many centuries. The primary orientation of the new structures was toward the European powers that had gained political control over most of the world. As the former settler colonies, particularly the USA, gained worldwide prominence, this dominance became more broadly western.

The new power of the West drew the attention of the rest of the world. Of particular interest to political and military leaders elsewhere, including Muslims, were the West's technological and military advancements. The acquisition of these instruments seemed to them to be the means by which they could regain power in their societies. For some other Muslims, the philosophies that had emerged in the Enlightenment period held more interest. They saw these developments as being at the basis of progress in the scientific outlook which had led to the dominance of the West over other parts of the world.

Muslims had been journeying to Europe long before the advent of colonialism. Places along the Mediterranean had seen the exchange of merchants and artisans for many centuries. But some Muslim traders, diplomats and scholars had also visited cities as far as London and Moscow. Following Napoleon Bonaparte's use of superior arms to conquer Egypt and Syria, missions were sent to Europe with the purpose of understanding its technical advancements. Among the members of such missions was Rifaa al-Tahtawi, an imam in the new Egyptian army who was a member of his

Cosmopolitanism: Ways of Being Muslim 213

country's mission to Paris from 1826 to 1831. He acquired an excellent command of French and studied the philosophy and literature of France. Upon returning to Cairo, al-Tahtawi translated numerous European books into Arabic, bringing to his compatriots the knowledge of political and social thought of liberal philosophy. In this, he was among the earlier individuals who helped to initiate a process of westernisation in Muslim countries that continues to this day.

These developments of recent centuries have produced a global culture in which all things western have acquired high value. The technological, economic and political supremacy of the West was extended to its way of life – western manners of behaviour increasingly came to be seen as exhibiting the height of civilisation and modernity. For many of the peoples who had been colonised, the acquisition of European languages, traditions, customs and clothing was a way to become 'modern' and to move closer to the centres of power. Cosmopolitanism for many of those in the East came to be seen primarily as an expression of elite western lifestyles rather than a broader engagement with various cultures of the world. Travel to the metropolitan centres of the West increasingly became the mark of entry into this exclusive status. Indeed, it began with participation in western colonial lifestyles and in gaining access to places of privilege frequented by settlers.

But much more than fashion, mannerisms and accent, it is westernisation in the form of thought that had much greater influence. Contemporary scientific and technical achievements of the West coloured the perception that European culture was superior to all others. The civilisational history of other cultures came to be seen as being of less consequence. This positioning was also echoed in the presentation of religions, where adherence to Christianity held greater cultural value than being a follower of Islam or any other faith.

Viewing world history through European lenses in colonial schools and the acceptance of ideas in which other cultures and religions, including one's own, are devalued began to raise serious questions. Critics in the colonies began to examine the very nature of liberal philosophy which had among its core values the respect

214   *A Companion to Muslim Cultures*

for human individuals. It became clear that despite the intellectual achievements of the Enlightenment and its worldview that promoted human freedom, the West's actions in the world had produced colonial empires whose societies were based on racial structures. With the emergence of a strong critique of colonialism, apartheid and racism since the latter part of the 20th century, there have developed less Euro-centric approaches to modernity and cosmopolitanism. This has also led to the separation of the concept of modernisation from Westernisation – one does not have to adopt western worldviews and behaviour to be modern. There are multiple pathways to modernity and they can draw from the contexts of the various societies and civilisations around the world. Nevertheless, the dominance of the West continues in the contemporary world and many societies continue to adopt Western lifestyles.

There have been attempts by Muslim scholars since the late 19th century to develop philosophical frameworks that seek to develop Islamic approaches to modernity by drawing from traditional sources. Thinkers like Muhammad Abduh, Jamal al-Din al-Afghani and Muhammad Iqbal sought to suggest ways in which Muslim leaders would embrace modern-day Islamic forms of governance. However, as majority-Muslim countries gained independence, most of their governments tended to view *din* and *dunya* as separate in terms of the predominant western model. Worldly affairs of the state were therefore largely removed from the religious values of the majority.

The lack of economic progress led to the frustration of expectations among Muslim populations. Preachers with narrow and dogmatic views of Islam took advantage of these situations by presenting narrow 'Islamic' solutions that disregarded the broad intellectual and cultural scope of Muslim heritage. Several governments, fearful of their hold on power, adopted the rhetoric of 'Islamisation', and in some cases, parts of the most punitive features of Muslim legal codes. This has not proved satisfactory for groups like the Taliban who promote even more rigid views of an 'Islamic' society. Here, narrowly conceived interpretations of faith triumph over the ethics of engaging in a sincere and pragmatic manner with *dunya*. In some Muslim countries, cosmopolitan engagements are also put aside in favour of political modes of control that restrict communication among Muslims and with the world at large.

Anti-cosmopolitanism

The lack of openness to other cultures that has appeared in some Muslim circles goes against the long history of engagement with various other societies and traditions. However, the tendencies of anti-cosmopolitanism can be traced to earlier times. There had appeared in the medieval period notions that divided the world into 'the territory of Islam' (*dar al-Islam*) and 'the territory of war' (*dar al-harb*), which was defined as the place where Muslims did not have security of life and property. Such a polarisation of political geography has occurred in other contexts of history. For example, the 17th-century Calvinist theorist Hugo Grotius, whose work is said to have formed the foundation of contemporary international law, split the world between European Christians and other peoples (including eastern Christians) whom he regarded as uncivilised. In the 20th century, Cold War propagandists saw the world as divided between the supporters of capitalism and communism.

Present-day Muslims who oppose interaction with others often find inspiration in the writings of the 14th-century theologian Ibn Taymiyya. He expressed fierce hostility to the forms of thought among Muslim scholars that had been derived from non-Muslim sources – or from those he regarded as not authentically Islamic, such as Sufis, Shia Muslims and Sunnis deemed to be non-conformists. In doing this, Ibn Taymiyya sought to reverse generations of engagement with other communities of interpretation within and outside Islam, which had led to the flourishing of Muslim civilisations. His puritanical stance gave rise to the Salafi movement that rejected Muslim thought developed after the first three generations following Muhammad, a longing that has revived in some quarters today. Whereas the steady decline of Muslim achievements in science, philosophy, art and architecture has many

216 *A Companion to Muslim Cultures*

explanations, the narrowing of intellectual and societal outlook that Ibn Taymiyya stood for certainly played its part.

The arrival of European powers in the Middle East in the 19th century brought the realisation of the extent to which Muslims had fallen behind scientifically. Although advancements in military armaments had paralleled those in other forms of technology when Muslim civilisations flourished, their weaponry could no longer match that of the Europeans who were embarking on colonisation. Most Muslim-majority lands came under European control within a matter of decades. Whereas some adherents of Islam have sought to understand the cultural and philosophical bases of Western power, others have been wary of what they view as contamination of their way of life. This perception is, of course, not limited to Muslims but is shared by many in other societies which have complained of western cultural imperialism. However, the growing military presence of the West in Muslim-majority countries in recent times has increased the fear among a significant number of Muslims of the threat posed to their cultural and religious integrity. This has led to a militant anti-Western posture and to acts of political violence by groups like al-Qaeda. Ironically, these militants have an affinity for things Western even as they attack the West. It is noteworthy that most of the hijackers of the attacks on September 11, 2001 had technical training, with several of them having studied in Western institutions of higher learning. Yet there was a separation of *din* and *dunya* in their worldview, which sought a purity of religious piety that was removed from their own daily experience and sources of their material knowledge. They found justification for their actions in the same primary sources of Islam where others find the fostering of a compassionate and caring stance towards all of humanity.

Anti-cosmopolitanism is not found only among Muslims. Some proponents and beneficiaries of globalisation in the West fiercely oppose aspects of it. They may favour the free flow of goods, but not that of people. The protection of national interests is cited for raising barriers, especially against people from certain Muslim-majority countries. Paradoxically, arguments for anti-cosmopolitanism of this sort as well as for cosmopolitanism are made based on ideas from the Enlightenment. Even though philosophers like Immanuel Kant saw the potential for the achievement of worldwide peace through cosmopolitanism, the time of the Enlightenment was also the period during which major nation states like France and the USA took shape. It is interesting that just as Muslims on both sides of the issue draw from their own particular interpretations of the fundamental sources of Islam, secular thinkers on both sides of the fence tend to trace their intellectual genealogy to the Enlightenment. There are also similarities taking shape among people who otherwise see each other as having opposing interests. Cosmopolitan Muslims will tend to agree in broad terms with those secular thinkers who have a humanist approach. On the other hand, anti-cosmopolitans like the leaders of al-Qaeda are likely to share the idea of 'the clash of civilisations' with those non-Muslims who present Western and Muslim societies being essentially opposed to each other.

Contemporary Muslim Cosmopolitanism

'Everyday cosmopolitanism' is increasingly the norm in many societies around the world. It is a result of the particular aspects of contemporary times like mass transportation, the ability of communication technologies to connect people around the world, the desire of individuals of different backgrounds to interact with each other, and policies of multiculturalism and pluralism. Significant numbers of Muslims, like other people, travel around the world and remain in touch with each other across the seas by using the Internet and international telephone services. They are increasingly familiar with media from different cultures around the planet. Muslim migrants have settled in different parts of the world in large numbers and are coming in direct contact with various peoples.

Whereas exposure to such experiences has fostered a contemporary cosmopolitan outlook on the part of some, others have tended to turn inwards. It is not uncommon to find concentrations of various ethnicities and cultures in particular areas of large

218 *A Companion to Muslim Cultures*

cities. People may choose to engage only with their own kind – often out of fear of losing their own identity. However, it is frequently the youth who seek new ways of expressing themselves through forms of art and music that borrow from multiple traditions. Cultural hybridity is not new to human history; but the vastly increased interaction between peoples of different backgrounds is producing an unprecedented level of intermingling. Muslims have adopted aspects of local cultures since they emerged from Arabia 14 centuries ago. It is not surprising that some young Muslims in our times should use contemporary western styles of popular music to express their multi-layered identities. What is new is that the global interconnectivity made possible by the Internet and other means enables these cultural forms to travel quickly around the world to produce new transnational cultural languages of music and art.

The Somali-Canadian singer K'naan Warsam, who has achieved worldwide fame, combines influences from his homeland, Bob Marley's reggae style, American hip-hop and protest poetry to call for an end to bloodshed in Somalia. Encouraged by this success, other Somali youth around the world like Waayaha Cusub, based in Kenya, use rap music to encourage their compatriots to speak out against those who have terrorised their homeland. Similarly other music groups like the Pakistani Sufi-inspired rock band Junoon, who have also attracted a transnational following, sing against the use of violence of terrorists.

Muslim artists in many locations are engaging with global influences and reinterpreting them in local forms. And there is the engagement with creative excellence in the built environment by the Aga Khan Award for Architecture, drawing on a wide array of cultural influences (as discussed in Hussein Keshani's chapter in this volume). Its goal of encouraging building concepts that address the practical needs and aspirations of societies in which Muslims have a significant presence is part of the larger appeal to social conscience and action on the part of the Aga Khan Development Network, not only in Africa and Asia but also in Europe and North America. The Aga Khan, who is the hereditary Imam of the Shia Ismaili Muslims, has spoken with deep passion

Cosmopolitanism: Ways of Being Muslim 219

about the value of embracing a cosmopolitan ethic to foster partnerships among different peoples to advance every citizen's quality of life.[6] Governments in various Muslim-majority countries have also seen, in their own particular ways, the value of enabling greater interaction between their Muslim citizens and people of other backgrounds. However, they often express concerns that influences from abroad will lead to the loss of the Islamic character of their societies. There generally is a tendency to view tradition and modernity as being in opposition to each other. This often stems from a perception that Muslim tradition is static and unchanging. However, there is a growing recognition that Islamic theology has allowed for change in accordance with evolving circumstances.

Early in the 21st century, humanity finds itself standing at an historic crossroads. On the one hand, globalising tendencies are bringing people of many backgrounds to live close to each other and, on the other, the anti-cosmopolitanism of some is promoting the belief that individuals belonging to different civilisations will never be able to get along. The voices of those who speak out against openness to other cultures receive more attention in the mass media. This is particularly the case when they are Muslims, since the tendency among careless journalists is often to highlight the actions of persons according to the stereotypes of the group to which they belong. Those Muslims who seek to support a future in which the global community confidently engages with other peoples are promoting a rediscovery of the cosmopolitanism which has been central to the development of the Islamic civilisation. Indeed, it is more rooted than the cosmopolitanism of the Enlightenment, which is of more recent origin. In the humanistic message of the Quran and the Prophet's teachings, there is already a beckoning to the fundamental openness of *din* toward *dunya*.

---

[6] Aga Khan, *Where Hope Takes Root*, pp. 124-131.

Further Reading

Appiah, Kwame Anthony. *Cosmopolitanism: Ethics in a World of Strangers*. New York, 2006.

Beck, Ulrich. 'The Cosmopolitan Society and Its Enemies'. *Theory, Culture and Society*, 19 (2002), pp. 17–44.

Benhabib, Seyla. *Another Cosmopolitanism: Hospitality, Sovereignty and Democratic Iterations*. New York, 2006.

Euben, Roxanne. *Journey to the Other Shore: Muslim and Western Travelers in Search of Knowledge*. Princeton, 2006.

Hamdun, Said and Noel King. *Ibn Batuta in Black Africa*. Princeton, NJ, 2003.

Matar, Nabil, ed. and tr. *In the Lands of the Christians: Arabic Travel Writing in the Seventeenth Century*. New York, 2003.

Simpson, Edward and Kresse, Kai, ed. *Struggling with History: Islam and Cosmopolitanism in the Western Indian Ocean*. New York, 2008.

Vertovec, Steven and Robin Cohen, ed. *Conceiving Cosmopolitanism: Theory, Context and Practice*. Oxford, 2002.

Index

Abbasids, 119, 124, 154–155, 157
  House of Wisdom (academic institution), 154–155, 158
Abraham (Ibrahim), 26
  Abrahamic traditions, 2, 21, 202
Abduh, Muhammad, 214
Abu Bakr (caliph), 64, 151
adab (code of behaviour), 172, 189
adat (custom), 12
al-Afghani, Jamal al-Din, 214
Afghanistan, xii, 16, 53, 74, 78, 80, 90–102, 185
Aga Khan, Prince Karim, 17, 20, 60, 133, 174, 183, 203, 218–219
Aga Khan Development Network (AKDN), 133, 218
Aga Khan Trust for Culture (AKTC), 17, 133, 174
Ahmed, Leila, 31, 79,

Akbar (Mughal ruler), ix, 3, 47, 49, 183
Alameddine, Rabih, 2
Aleppo, 2, 18, 118–119, 124–125, 139, 165–166, 170, 172–175, 177, 179–180, 183
Alevis, 50–51, 61
Alexander ('the Great'), 10–11
Algeria, 65
Alhambra, 70, 120, 205
Ali (Caliph-Imam), 8
Amanullah Khan (Afghan king), 91
anti-cosmopolitanism, 202, 211, 215–216, 219
'Arab Spring', 13
Arabic, xii–xiii, 1, 3, 7, 12, 38, 57, 63, 67–69, 71, 110, 119, 129, 137–140, 143, 145–149, 152, 154–157, 160–161, 164, 167, 177, 179–180, 183, 185, 206, 213, 220
arches, 17, 128
architecture, xi, xiii, 17, 19–20,

67–68, 117–120, 123–124, 126–135, 186, 205, 215, 218
Aga Khan Award for Architecture, 20, 133, 218
civic, 8, 10, 12, 15, 17, 37, 42–47, 49, 52, 117, 123, 125, 134
commercial, 41, 117, 125–127, 134, 143, 145, 172–173, 187, 198
conservation, 133–135
and heritage, 134
art, xiii, 13–15, 19, 25, 27, 35, 67–70, 73–74, 129, 137–138, 147–148, 173, 176, 181, 183, 206, 215, 218
'Islamic art', xi, xiii, 19, 67–69, 74, 129
asabiyya (communal attachments), 11
Asharites, 9
Atatürk, Kemal, 50, 66
Authenticity, 18–19, 97, 152, 165, 174–175, 177, 179–180
Ayodhya, 49
Al-Azhar Park, 17, 134
Al-Azhar University, 107
al-Aziz (Caliph-Imam), 157

Babri Masjid, 49
al-Baghdadi, Junayd, 59
Bahai, 50
Bamiyan (Buddha statues), 74, 91, 94

baraka (blessing), 29
Barelwi, Sayyid Ahmad, 47
al-Basri, Hasan, 58
bazaars, 17, 125–126
bimaristan (hospital, also *maristan*), 123
bioethics, 114
al-Bistami, Abu Yazid, 59
Bosnia, 51, 185–186
Buddhists, 48, 80
Burhanuddin, Syedna Mohammed, 60

calligraphy, 18, 69–70, 129, 148, 164
caravanserai, 125–126, 210
chahar bagh (four-quartered design), 120
charity, 6, 195
Chihil Sutun complex (Isfahan, Iran), 120
China, xii, 12, 16, 65, 78, 80, 85–87, 90, 101, 128, 130, 138, 156, 160, 163, 204, 206, 210
Christians, 1–2, 7–8, 12, 22, 46, 48, 50, 57, 61, 67, 71–72, 80, 111, 126, 139, 146–147, 204–205, 215, 220
cinema, 15, 19, 73
citizenship, 12, 15, 43, 45, 47–49, 52–53
'civic reason', 44
civility, 42, 51
'clash of civilisations', 5, 202, 217

Index

colonialism, 45, 52, 72, 130, 212, 214

consensus (in legal reasoning), xi, 38–40, 107, 109, 112

Constitution of Medina, 5, 8, 12

cosmopolitanism, xiii, 2, 8, 14, 19–20, 201–202, 209, 213–214, 216–217, 219–220

courtyards, 17, 128, 196

Damascus, 22, 69, 123, 129, 139, 171, 173

dance, 18–19, 63, 66, 94, 97, 167, 169–171

Danish cartoons controversy, 4

dastango (South Asian storyteller), 3

Dawoodi Bohras, 29, 60

dhikr (remembrance of God), 28, 64, 179, 183

dhimma (protected minorities), 46

diaspora, xiii, 12, 54

din (faith), 19, 203, 207, 214, 216, 219

Dome of the Rock, 70

domes, 6, 68, 123, 128, 130

donor sperm and eggs, 16, 106

Druze, 61, 113

dunya (material world), 19, 203–204, 207, 214–216, 219

Egypt, xi, 14, 29, 31–33, 35, 41, 44, 65–67, 72, 103, 107, 115, 134, 137, 145, 157, 176, 179, 183, 185, 204, 212

Eliot, T.S., 14

Enlightenment, 13, 35, 203, 211–212, 214, 217, 219

ethics, ii, xii–xiii, 2, 7, 9, 12, 25, 32, 37, 39, 55, 69, 114–115, 129, 203, 214, 220

etiquette, 7, 18, 172

'evil eye', 33, 195–197,

Fadlallah, Ayatollah Muhammad Husayn, 109

Fakhri, Sabah, 18, 165–166, 169, 171, 174, 179–181

Fatimids, 134, 157, 164

female circumcision, 32

feminists, 80, 83

Ferghana Valley, 81

Fez, 17, 117

fiqh (legal tradition), 5–6, 15, 39–40, 46, 107, 109, 149, 158, 208

food, 18–19, 96, 130, 149–150, 172–173, 178, 185–186, 188–199, 210
   and religion, 23, 38, 45, 47–48, 89, 203, 213
   and social change, 52–54, 80, 89, 101, 103, 188–190
   and status, 141, 190, 193

fortifications, 17, 117–118, 120

224   *A Companion to Muslim Cultures*

gardens, 14, 17, 117, 120–121,
134
gender, xi–xiii, 14, 31–32, 46,
50, 77–80, 82, 85, 87, 89,
92, 95, 99, 101, 114–115,
193
al-Ghazali, 9, 142
*ginan*s (devotional hymns),
28
globalisation, 5, 10, 17, 86, 90,
100, 103, 133, 211, 216
Golmohammadi, Feeroozeh,
73
Granada, kingdom of, 70

hadd (serious crimes), 40
Hagar (Abraham's wife), 26
hajj (pilgrimage to Mecca), 29,
45, 75, 185–186, 192,
209, 211
and *Eid al-Hajj*, 191
hakawati (storyteller), 1–2,
19
*hammam*s (public
bathhouses), 123, 127
Hamzanama, 3–4, 20
Hanafi (school of law), 39–41,
80
Hanbali (school of law), 39
Hebrew Bible, 69
hijab (head-covering), 9, 31,
43, 51
Hindu, 2, 19, 28, 47–49, 51,
70, 160–161, 208
hospitality, 18, 193–194, 220
hudud (sharia punishments),
7, 96

Hugo of St. Victor, 10
human rights, xi, xiii, 13, 15,
37–38, 42, 47, 50, 53–54,
77, 87, 99
Husayn (Muhammad's
grandson, Imam), 27–28,
62, 73, 109
Husuni Kubwa complex
(Kilwa, Tanzania), 119

ibadat (duties toward God), 5
Ibn Arabi, 66, 70, 211
Ibn Khaldun, 11, 20, 59, 142
Ibn Sina, 59, 207
Ibn Taymiyya, 215–216
idda (woman's post-divorce
waiting period), 49
ijtihad (independent
reasoning), 39
in-vitro fertilisation (IVF), 16,
103
India, xiii, 3, 10, 27, 30,
47–49, 51, 60, 63, 65–67,
70, 120, 129–130, 187,
205–206, 208–209
Indonesia, 12, 44, 51, 53–54,
132, 187
inheritance, 111
Iqbal, Muhammad, 214
Isfahan, 17, 117, 120, 125–126
Ismail (son of Abraham and
Hagar), 26
Istanbul, 124–126, 131, 135,
208
Istiqlal Mosque (Jakarta,
Indonesia), 132
iwan (arched niche), 128

Index

Jad al-Haqq, Shaykh Jad
al-Haqq Ali, 107–108
Jafari (Shia school of law), 39
jahiliyya (pre-Islamic period),
21, 32
Jain, 10
Jamat-i Islami (India), 66
Jerusalem, 70
Jesus, 60, 70, 72
Jews, 1–2, 7–8, 12, 22, 46, 50,
67, 126, 139, 146, 184,
204–205
jihadi (militant religionist), 1–2
jizya (poll tax), 8, 46, 50

Kaaba, 6, 121, 132, 209
Kadeer, Rebiya, 87
Karakhanids, 81
karamat (saintly gifts), 30
Karbala, 28, 31, 35, 62
Karzai, Hamid, 96
Kashgar, 81, 86
Khamenei, Ayatollah Ali, 109,
113
Khan, Nusrat Fateh Ali, 66
Khan, Sayyid Ahmad, 47
Khomeini, Ayatollah
Ruhollah, 73
K'naan, 218

laïcité (secularism in France),
43
Lebanon, xii, 16, 27, 61, 104,
109, 112–114
libraries, 17, 147, 152–153,
155, 157, 159
localism, 10

Madjid, Nurcolish, 53
madrassa (traditional school),
93, 121, 123–124,
126–127, 159
Maimonides, 127, 204
Majallah (Ottoman law of the
land), 40
Majidi, Majid, 73
majlis (assembly), 27
Makhmalbaf, Mohsen, 73
Maliki (school of law), 39, 41
al-Mamun (Abbasid caliph),
141, 154
Mao, 82, 85
mashrebiyya (screen feature in
buildings), 17, 130
masjid (site of prayer), 6, 49,
117, 121, 123–125,
127–129, 132, 134
mawlid (remembrance of
saintly figures), 29, 63,
191
Medina, 5, 8, 12, 46, 58, 62,
121, 145, 187, 192–193,
209
memory, xiv, 7, 20, 52, 84,
138–145, 151, 162–163
memorisation, 141
Mernissi, Fatima, 78–79, 83,
102, 141
Mevlevi ('whirling dervishes'),
63, 66
mihrab (prayer niche), 122,
145, 151
*millet*s (autonomous Ottoman
communities), 49
modernity, ii, v, xiv, 12–15,17,

226 *A Companion to Muslim Cultures*

19, 34, 37–38, 41, 48, 50,
52–53, 57, 60, 74, 77,
100, 130, 133–134, 168,
184, 189, 213–214, 219
modernisation, 40, 86, 214
muamalat (social relations), 5
mudejar (Moorish culture in
Spain), 71
Muhsin, Hajji, 47
mullaya (leader in Shia
women's devotional
gathering), 32
music, xiv, 13–14, 18, 34, 63,
66, 74, 94, 96–97, 124,
162, 165–166, 172–178,
180–184, 186, 206, 218
instruments, 19, 97, 166,
210, 212
muezzin (caller to prayer), 27,
173, 179
Muhammad (the Prophet),
2, 4–5, 25, 38, 58, 64,
78, 121, 186, 192, 204,
208
Muharram, 27–28, 191
Mulla Sadra, 59
muqarnas (honeycomb feature
in architecture), 68, 123,
129–130
Muslim Brotherhood (in
Egypt), 66
Mutazilites, 9
muwashshah (choral poem),
166–168, 177

Nahj al-balagha (*Peak of
Eloquence*), 8, 61

'names of God', 32, 64
nasab (legal kinship), 109
N'Dour, Youssou, 63
Nigeria, 44, 118
niqab (face-covering), 6
Nizari Ismailis, 60

Orientalism, xiii, 20, 71, 73

pagan practices, 21
Pahlavi, Reza Shah, 99
Pakistan, 27, 30, 44, 48, 63,
65, 90, 93, 96, 98, 102
palaces, 69, 119, 127, 129
Palestine, 20, 204
pancasila (Indonesian
secularist doctrine), 53
paper (as cultural medium),
xi, 17–18, 52, 86, 95, 99,
101, 137–138, 146–150,
152–154, 156, 158–161,
163–164, 167, 196
papyrus, 137, 139, 145, 147,
159
parchment, 137, 139, 144–145,
147, 152, 159, 163
parochialism, 11
Pashtun, 16, 91, 93–95, 97,
99–100
pashtunwali (cultural code),
16, 95
patriarchy, 7, 39, 100
'People of the Book', 7, 22,
204
'people of the house', 18, 194
Persian, ix, xii, 3, 7, 18–19, 47,
57, 63, 70, 80, 120,

Index

128–129, 132, 137, 141, 147, 154, 156, 159, 199, 205–207, 210–211

piety, xiv, 2, 14, 21, 23–28, 30–34, 51, 58, 60, 216

pilgrimage, 5–6, 14, 21, 26–27, 29, 45, 62–63, 65–66, 121–122, 186–187, 191–192, 202, 209

pillared halls, 17, 128

pirs (saintly figures), 62, 209

pluralism, xiii, 11, 15, 23, 37, 42–44, 49–50, 52–53, 55, 186, 203–205, 217

poetry, xiii, 1, 19, 26, 57, 63, 66, 69, 70, 83, 122, 138, 147, 149, 154, 162, 177, 208, 218

polygamy, 108

printing, 18, 71, 137–138, 152–153, 160–163

puritanism, 15

al-Qaeda, 19, 216

qasida (classical ode), 6, 169, 171, 177, 179

Qatar, 52

qawwali (musical recital in South Asia), 63, 183

Quran, xiii, 1–2, 5–7, 11–12, 14–16, 21–29, 31–33, 37–40, 54, 58, 69–70, 74, 78, 82–83, 107, 121, 123–124, 137–138, 140–149, 153, 156, 158, 162, 197, 202–204, 206–208, 219

and diversity, v–vi, 7–8, 10–11, 23, 37, 51, 53–54, 67, 78, 113, 117, 201, 203, 205, 209

and individual responsibility, 38–39, 54

and motherhood, 106, 110

and 'Night of Power', 58

and recitation, 27–28, 33, 64, 74, 140, 143, 179–180

and visual arts, 63, 69

and women, 4, 16, 29–32, 35, 39, 42, 46, 49, 51, 53, 62, 66, 73, 77–92, 94–102, 104–106, 111, 119, 125, 128–129, 170, 172–174, 193–194, 197–198

and writing, 17, 26, 32, 72, 137–140, 142–143, 145–150, 152–153, 159, 161–162, 164, 220

Quranic script, 5–6, 11, 49, 58, 70, 91, 110, 140, 144–145, 149, 179–180, 197

Ramadan (fast), 7, 24–25, 191–192

and Eid al-Fitr, 191

al-Rashid, Harun (Abbasid caliph), 3, 141, 154

al-Razi, Ali ibn Shadan (calligrapher), 147

Registan Square (Samarkand, Uzbekistan), 124

228   *A Companion to Muslim Cultures*

Revolutionary Association for the Women of Afghanistan (RAWA), 98
rida (milk kinship), 111
rosary, 32, 170
Rumi, Jalal al-Din, 57, 66, 74

Sachar report (in India), 48–49
Şahin, Leyla vs. Turkey, 50
sahra (evening social gathering), 172–174
Said, Edward, 10, 73
saltana (ecstatic dance), 18–19, 169–170, 175
Samarkand, 17, 117, 124, 208
al-Sanhuri, Abd al-Razzaq, 41
Saudi Arabia, 31, 45, 103, 133, 186, 188, 198–199
science, xii, 17, 20, 24, 33, 92, 103–104, 113, 115, 124, 140, 149, 164, 202, 206, 215
secularism, 38, 43, 45, 48, 50–54
Seddiqi, Suhaila, 98–99
September 11, 2001, 19, 216
Shafii (school of law), 39, 41, 149
Shah Bano case, 49
sharia, xii, 5–7, 15, 19, 23, 34, 37–42, 46–47, 49, 52, 54, 93, 108, 142
Shariat Allah, Hajji, 47
Shehrazade, 2
'Shia Personal Status Law' (Afghanistan), 96

Sikander, Shahzia, 19
Sikhs, 48, 209
Silk Road, 74, 80, 90, 210
Sistani, Ayatollah Ali, 113
stories, 1–3, 13, 19, 24, 26, 30, 68, 83, 124, 149, 211
Sufi, xiii, 15, 27–29, 32, 38, 50, 57–59, 62–66, 70, 74, 81, 122, 173, 183, 186, 209
'People of the Bench', 58
Suhrawardi, 59, 65
Sunna (the Prophet's practice), 22, 26, 38–40, 49
surrogacy, 105, 109–110

al-Tahtawi, Rifaa, 212
Taj Mahal, 70, 122, 159
tajwid (science of Quranic recital), 24, 140, 179
Taliban, 19, 53, 74, 90–91, 93–94, 96, 98–99, 214
tarab (rapture in music), 169–172, 175, 181–182, 184
tariqa (spiritual path), 64
tawhid (unity of God), 38
'test-tube babies', 104, 107
'Thousand and One Nights', 3, 149, 211
tombs, 14, 61–63, 66, 121–124, 127, 129, 134, 209
triumphalism, 11
Turkey, 26, 31, 43–45, 47, 49–51, 53, 61, 90, 99, 130, 147, 185, 205
Twelver Shia, 27, 60, 64, 113

Index

Uthman (caliph), 44, 168
Umar (caliph), 8
Umayyads, 119
Umayyad Mosque, 69
urbanisation, 79
Urdu, 3, 70
urs (South Asian anniversaries of saintly figures), 30, 63
Urumqi, 81, 86
Uyghur, xii, 16, 80–90, 100–101
Uzbekistan, 90, 185

veiling, 6, 31, 79, 111
Virgin Mary, 61

al-Wahhab, Abd, 62
Wahid, Abdurrahman, 54
Wali Allah, Shah, 47

waqf (charitable endowment), 6, 50, 52, 151
wudu (ablutions), 23

Xinjiang, xii, 16, 78, 80–83, 85–90, 100–102

Yezidis, 50

Zahir Shah (Afghan king), 91–92
zakat (alms-giving), 8, 52
zakir (reciter of Shia martyrdom narrative), 28
Zanzibar, 17, 117
zar (healing rite in Egypt, sub-Saharan Africa), 32
Zaynab (granddaughter of the Prophet), 31
Zengin vs. Turkey, 50
zina (adultery), 108–111